Rebels & Chicks

A History of the Hollywood
Teen Movie

Rebels

&

Chicks

A

HISTORY

OF THE

HOLLYWOOD

TEEN

MOVIE

STEPHEN TROPIANO

Back Stage Books

Senior Editor: Mark Glubke
Project Editor: Ross Plotkin
Cover Design: Eric Olson
Interior Design: Leah Lococo, Ltd.
Production Manager: Ellen Greene

First published in 2006 by Back Stage Books, an imprint of Watson-Guptill
Publications, a division of VNU Business Media, Inc.
770 Broadway, New York, NY 10003
www.wgpub.com

Library of Congress Cataloging-in-Publication Data
The CIP data for this title is on file with the Library of Congress
Library of Congress Control Number: 2005937229
ISBN: 0-8230-9701-3

Manufactured in the United States of America

First printing 2006

1 2 3 4 5 6 7 8 9 / 11 10 09 08 07 06

This book is dedicated in loving

memory of my friend,

Denis L. Keenan

(1961–2005)

Contents

A Genre of Their Own

*T*he history of the Hollywood teen movie begins in the 1950s, the same decade in which American teenagers came into their own, complete with their own way of talking, dressing, dancing, and having a good time. Hollywood's contribution to a thriving teen culture was films about teenagers, mostly low-budget horror and science-fiction films, and socially conscious dramas about an "epidemic" sweeping the country better known as juvenile delinquency. The success of early teen flicks like *I Was a Teenage Werewolf* (1957), and bigger budget studio movies about JDs like MGM's *The Blackboard Jungle* (1955) and Warner Brothers' *Rebel Without a Cause* (1955), proved that teenagers were a viable market. Consequently, both the major studios, and smaller, independent companies, started to churn out films made specifically for teenage moviegoers on a more regular basis.

Movie magazines also did their part in helping to launch the careers of Hollywood's new crop of screen idols. The covers of fan magazines like *Modern Screen*, *Photoplay*, and *Picturegoer* featured the fresh, young faces of newcomers like James Dean, Sandra Dee, Troy Donahue, Sal Mineo, and Natalie Wood. The pages inside were filled with half-truth, "tell-all" stories and intimate details about their private lives. As the first true teenagers of the American cinema, they played a significant role in shaping the archetypal image of the American teenager.

Of course young actors did work in Hollywood prior to the 1950s, though most did not succeed in making the transition from child to adult performers. The careers of some of the screen's most famous child actors, like Margaret O'Brien and box-office champ Shirley Temple, who both received special Academy Awards, peaked before they even reached their twelfth birthday. Those who successfully made the transition were often typecast in certain roles, only to find themselves trapped in a perpetual state of adolescence. For example, the teenage actors who re-created their stage roles as juvenile delinquents in the screen version of the hit Broadway play, *Dead End* (1937), remained in the same roles (or some variation thereof) in a series of low-budget films as the "Dead End Kids" in the 1930s, the "East Side Kids" in the 1940s, and the "Bowery Boys" in the 1950s. Huntz Hall was eighteen when he made his film debut in the role of "Dip" in *Dead End*. Seventeen years later, he appeared in his last Bowery Boys film, *In the Money* (1958), at the age of thirty-nine. Fellow *Dead End* cast members Gabriel Dell (T.B.) and Leo Gorcey (Spit) were also both in their thirties when they made their last Bowery Boys film.

Some of Hollywood's young, A-list stars had the same problem. Mickey Rooney started as a child actor in the late 1920s in a series of silent comic shorts. As a seventeen-year-old under contract at MGM, he originated the role of Andy Hardy in *A Family Affair* (1937) and continued to play him for the next ten years in fifteen more films (and once again in 1957). Judy Garland, who played Betsy Booth in three *Andy Hardy* films, was another MGM star often cast in younger roles. The studio's first choice for her most famous role, Dorothy in *The Wizard of Oz* (1939), was ten-year-old Temple, but she was under contract with Twentieth Century–Fox and they refused to loan her out. So the role was given to Garland, who was forced to bind her bosom to hide the fact that she was a sixteen-year-old playing a younger girl.

This wasn't the case for all young stars. Another MGM contract player, Elizabeth Taylor, was allowed to grow up faster onscreen. In 1948, sixteen-year-old Taylor played a twenty-one-year-old bride in *Julia Misbehaves*. Two years later, she walked down the aisle again in *Father of the Bride* (1950).

The MGM films starring Rooney, Garland, and Taylor would not qualify, by today's standards, as "teen films"—that is, films made *about* teens *for* teens. However, there were films produced in the 1930s and the 1940s by independent companies on the margins of the Hollywood film industry for an adult audience that focused specifically on troubled youth. Heralded today for their camp value, exploitation films like *Narcotic* (1933), *Cocaine Fiends* (1936), *Marihuana* (1936), *Reefer Madness* (1936), and *Assassin of Youth* (1937) demonstrated how booze and dope leads kids down the wrong path to a life of crime and illicit sex. Parents needed to hear their message because according to these films, bad parenting was the number one reason why kids go astray. The advertising tagline for *Mad Youth* (1939) posed the question "Are modern mothers to be blamed for the wild escapades of their sons and daughters?" Apparently they are according to this cult classic in which Marian Morgan (Mary Ainslee), the product of a broken home, is ignored by her party-animal mother (Betty Compson). Marian starts hanging out with a bad crowd and eventually falls in love with a gigolo—who is also wooing her mom.

There's no question that Jimmy Wilson's mother and father are at fault in the aptly titled *I Accuse My Parents* (1944). Before Jimmy (Robert Lowell) is sentenced for manslaughter, he tells the judge that his neglectful parents should have never had children. "I don't believe they were ever unkind to me," he explains. "They gave me everything I wanted except time and attention." Cue the violins as Jimmy describes how as a result of his mom's boozing, Dad's gambling, and their constant fighting, he gets mixed up with the Mob and starts seeing a gangster's girlfriend, a nightclub singer named Kitty (Mary-Beth Hughes). While exploitation films concerning teens and their problems continued well into the 1950s and the 1960s, the majority of bona fide teen films produced in the postwar era did not, fortunately, resort to such obvious theatrics.

As the following pages will reveal, there is a difference between films like *I Accuse My Parents* and films about teens that are made for as well as marketed to a teenage audience. *Rebels & Chicks* chronicles the history of the American teen film from the 1950s to the current day. I am by no means a purist when it comes to deciding what constitutes a teen film. Although the majority of the films discussed in this book are about and made for teens, I also discuss films about young people in their early twenties, such as the counterculture films of the late 1960s, the R-rated nostalgic teen movies of the 1970s, and the Generation-X films of the 1990s.

As you are reading this book, there are two important points that you should keep in mind.

1. Teen movies are made by adults, not teenagers. Although the filmmakers were teenagers once themselves, teen films depict the world of a teenager from an adult's point of view.

2. Hollywood operates within a capitalist system, so the primary reason any film is made in Hollywood is $$$$. While many teen films certainly have artistic merit and effectively convey a social message, they are still produced for the primary purpose of making a profit.

Rebels & Chicks is not intended to be a definitive history of the teen genre. As you are reading this book, you will no doubt notice that certain films receive very little attention, while others (perhaps some of your favorites) are not mentioned at all. I'm sorry about that. Picking and choosing which films to discuss is difficult and, unfortunately, some films were left "on the cutting-room floor."

A brief word about language: I repeatedly make reference to the "filmmakers." As film is a collaborative art form, "filmmakers" in this case refers to everyone involved in the making of the film, from the director to the production assistant. I try to be more specific when referring to the contribution of certain individuals (like the producer, director, writer, et al.).

The word "Hollywood" refers to the Hollywood film industry as a whole. However, I often distinguish between films produced by one of the Hollywood studios as opposed to one of the independent (also known as "indie") companies.

Another word that will appear frequently is "genre." I consider the teen movies as a whole a genre and will often refer to specific types of teen films (beach-party movies, slasher films) as "subgenres."

This book would not have been possible without the support,

assistance, and patience of Mark Glubke at Back Stage Books, my copyeditor extraordinaire (and fellow IC alum) Ross Plotkin, and designer Leah Lococo. In addition, special thanks to my students Matthew Beck, June Clark, Timothy Shary, Gary Jones, Dianne Lynch, Ray Morton, Neil Spisak; as well as my colleagues at the Ithaca College LA Program, particularly David Kelley, Marc Klein, Robert Meunier, and Susan Reiner.

As always, thanks to Steven Ginsberg.

Funding for this project was made possible in part by a James B. Pendleton Grant from the Roy H. Park School of Communications at Ithaca College.

—STEPHEN TROPIANO
Los Angeles, California
February 2006

Rebels & Chicks

A History of the Hollywood Teen Movie

Before settling down at *Bonanza's* Ponderosa Ranch and a *Little House on the Prairie*, Michael Landon starred as teenage werewolf Tony Rivers in the horror classic *I Was a Teenage Werewolf* (1957). © Corbis

PUB-9
#201-178

The Teen Movie is Born (1955–1965)

Sex-Crazed, Rock 'n' Roll–loving,
Juvenile Delinquents

"The correct information at the correct
time in the correct way"

"I was a teenage . . ."

"You never dream it could happen to your kids"

"A safe and sane dance for all young people"

"Should a girl 'play house'
before marriage?"

"The perfect summer when the
urge meets the surge!"

Teenagers have been roaming the Earth since prehistoric times; nevertheless, it took thousands of years before anyone seemed to notice.

In the late 1940s, immediately after the Second World War, Americans started to take an interest in these newly discovered creatures, who by now had distinguished themselves by the way they dressed, spoke, drove, and danced.

In one way, it's ironic that what we now think of as the "modern American teenager" was born in the postwar period. At the time, teens counted for a relatively small percentage (around 8.5%) of the U.S. population due to a sharp, temporary drop in the birthrate during the Great Depression.

But the teen population was on the rise again in the early 1950s, and by mid-decade the U.S. was home to over sixteen million teenagers. They were soon joined by the 14.4 million babies born at the start of the postwar boom (1946–1949), who reached "teenhood" en masse in the early 1960s, raising the total to twenty-two million by 1964.[1]

Still, the numbers alone don't explain how and why the youth of America had suddenly made their presence known and became a major cultural force to be reckoned with in the postwar era.

Sex-Crazed, Rock 'n' Roll–loving, Juvenile Delinquents

The economic boom in the United States following the Second World War created what economist John Kenneth Galbraith characterized as an "affluent society."[2] The size of the middle class grew (and the economic gap between the middle and the working classes widened) because more Americans were taking home a bigger paycheck. Consequently, many people had extra cash in their pockets, which they were quick to start spending on everything from automobiles to furniture to a whole lot of other "stuff" Madison Avenue convinced them they couldn't live without.

Low-interest G.I. loans and affordable housing made it possible for the 1950s mom, dad, and their 2.5 children to make the big move out to the suburbs and into a house of their very own. And of course what new home isn't complete without such labor-saving appliances as a Westinghouse 100% frost-free refrigerator (retail price $149.99), a Maytag automatic washer/dryer combo ($179.99), and, to keep Mom's floors shiny, a Regina Twin-Brush polisher and scrubber ($64.50)? As for the family room—how about a brand-new, state-of-the-art, RCA Victor twenty-one-inch "Big Color" TV ($695)?[3] Like their parents, teenagers also had extra money in their pockets to spend on *really* important "stuff" like Elvis's latest single, dungarees, poodle skirts, makeup, jewelry, *Vault of Horror* comics, and, of course, the movies.

At first, many advertisers were skeptical about the youth market—they didn't believe teenagers were as reliable and consistent as their parents when it came to spending money. But that all changed when a young marketing specialist named Eugene Gilbert started researching the spending habits of high-school and college students. His ongoing study proved that the youth market was indeed worth exploiting because teenagers, on the whole, were serious consumers who established a preference for certain brand names at an early age and had a say in their family's purchasing decisions.[4]

Many big-name companies, including Pepsi-Cola, Philip Morris, and Johnson & Johnson, took Gilbert's advice and hired his marketing firm, the Gilbert Youth Research Company, to help them go after a piece of the $9 billion he estimated boys and girls under the age of twenty had at their disposal each year.[5] As a result, products were now being made specifically for the youth market and then sold through advertising campaigns designed to maximize their appeal to America's next generation of consumers.

The exploitation of the teen market also contributed to the rapid growth of youth culture in postwar America. The advertising industry, the mass media (television, radio, publishing, etc.), and the movies, all kept teenagers, along with the rest of the American public, up to date on all the latest fads and trends. Magazines like *Seventeen*, *Modern Teen*, *Teen Parade*, and *Teen World* offered teenage girls fashion tips and dating advice. Teenagers bought 45s, listened to rhythm-and-blues on the radio, and did the Mashed Potato in front of their TV sets after school to the musical sounds of their favorite dance-party show. On weekends, they flocked to the local drive-in to see *Blackboard Jungle* (1955), *Rock, Rock, Rock* (1956), *I Was a Teenage Werewolf* (1957), and a host of other movies, which, in time, would belong to a genre bearing their name—"the teen film."

Although advertising and the media fueled the postwar boom in youth culture, it wasn't a purely economic phenomenon. The American teenager's role in society was also redefined by the many social changes that occurred during and after the war. Postwar teens reaped the benefits of the independence young adults gained during wartime when Dad was busy fighting overseas and Mom was doing her part working in the local factory. Consequently, parents were less involved in the lives of their teenagers, who had the freedom to pursue and enjoy an active social life consisting of after-school activities, hanging out with friends, attending parties and dances, and enjoying young America's new favorite pasttime—dating.

Just as their parents were concerned with "keeping up with the Joneses," teenagers also became increasingly more preoccupied with maintaining their social status among their peers, which was measured by their ability to fit in, make friends, and achieve a certain level of popularity. Having the extra money to buy the latest styles or the #1 LP on this week's music chart aided a teenager's "quest for popularity," which, in turn, became "the driving force" behind the teenage market.[6]

Teenagers had more opportunities to have an active social life because they had become more mobile. The automobile became an important status symbol in the postwar era for both teenagers and their parents. Between 1945 and 1955, car sales went through the roof as the number of registered autos on the road doubled.[7] If he earned enough money after school or his parents had the dough, a guy might be able to afford his own machine to cruise around in (complete with its own backseat to fool around in). As for teens without their own wheels—they had no choice but to borrow Dad's keys and conduct their "quest for popularity" behind the wheel of the family's Pontiac station wagon.

Teenagers' consumer power, independence, and mobility all contributed to the American public's growing perception of teens as a homogenous group—a generation defined by their age and bound by their presumably common interests, tastes, and attitudes. As film historian Thomas Doherty explains, teenagers had a sense of community, a public identity as a group, which, unlike past generations, was "carefully nurtured and vigorously reinforced by the adult institutions around them, such as the marketplace, the media, the education system, and parents."[8]

Still, there were some adults who yearned for the good old days when children were seen, but not heard, and the word "teen-ager" simply meant someone over twelve and under twenty years of age. They believed some parents were giving their kids way too much freedom and, as a result, teenagers, along with their loud music and crazy fads, were taking over. As the paranoid authors of a 1951 study entitled *Sexual Conduct of Teen-Agers* warned:

> Adolescent influence has made itself felt in every sphere of society—so much so that a great many grown-ups feel the pendulum has swung too far in the opposite direction. . . . What has happened is teen-agers, recognizing the strength and bargaining power of numbers, have banded together in many different ways to command public attention and consideration.[9]

The older generation feared that its diminishing influence and lack of control over young people was making it possible for a youth culture, which many believed promoted immorality and anarchy, to thrive. Unless the pendulum started swinging back the other way, the youth of America were in danger of becoming nothing more than a generation of sex-crazed, rock 'n' roll-loving, juvenile delinquents.

As a result, keeping teenagers under control became a national priority in the 1950s, and naturally the burden fell on their parents, who received some support from community leaders and both local and national law-enforcement agencies. Public-school teachers also did their part to keep kids in line with the help of an innovative new teaching tool that combined a popular form of entertainment with a little military know-how.

"The correct information at the correct time in the correct way"

The first films about teenagers made specifically for teenagers never played at the local movie house or drive-in. There was no admission fee, no concession stand, and you were required to sit through the *entire* film.

Motion pictures were first shown in public schools in the 1930s when teachers started to incorporate short, educational films into their daily lesson plans. At the time, this teaching method was still considered experimental, although a 1938 study commissioned by the New York Board of Regents was generally optimistic about its future. In fact, the study recognized the profound effect motion pictures could potentially have on "the present techniques and sequence of instruction and the very content of education," provided they were used to "impart the correct information at the correct time in the correct way."[10]

By the late 1940s, educational films were being screened on a regular basis in classrooms throughout the country. They were used in history, geography, civics, mathematics, and science classes to supplement textbook readings, explain complex concepts (like atomic energy in *A is for Atom* [1953]), and expound upon a specific theme or topic (like Native Americans in *Navajo Canyon Country* [1954]). They were also popular among progressive teachers who believed the public education system was not only responsible for their students' intellectual development, but their social development as well. To help shape and mold young people into healthy, normal, American citizens, teachers turned to the producers of educational films, who responded with a whole new "subgenre" of classroom films known as "the social-guidance film."

From the 1940s through the 1960s, the three leading makers of educational films—Coronet, Encyclopedia Britannica, and Centron—produced hundreds of social-guidance films in their own pint-size motion-picture studios, located far from the glitz and glamour of Hollywood in places like Illinois and Kansas. The typical film was ten to thirteen minutes in length, and shot in a couple of days on a shoestring budget. The actors were non-professionals, whose performances gave a whole new meaning to the word "amateur." To add some credibility to the proceedings, the name of an "expert" who served as the film's consultant—a physician, registered nurse, psychologist, counselor—appeared in the opening credits.

In his book *Mental Hygiene: Classroom Films (1945–1970)*, historian Ken Smith describes social-guidance films as "preachy and melodramatic"—a product of a time "when concepts of right and wrong were rigidly defined."[11] Their basic aim was to teach their young audience the difference between socially acceptable and unacceptable behavior or, in simpler terms, to show kids how adults wanted them to behave. Consequently, many of the early films addressed the issues that mattered most to parents, like good manners (*Johnny Learns His Manners* [1946], *Mind Your Manners!* [1953]); good habits (*Good Eating Habits* [1954], *Habit Patterns* [1954]); and good hygiene (*Body Care and Grooming* [1947], *Care of the Hair and Nails* [1951]). In addition, social-guidance films responded to the pressure teenagers were under to maintain an active social life by explaining—from an adult's perspective of course—how to make friends, fit in with the crowd, attain popularity, and ask a girl out on a date.

The typical "plot" (for want of a better word) revolved around a teenager with a personal problem or issue. Over the course of the film, he or she solves the problem by changing his/her behavior and/or adjusting his/her attitude. According to Smith, the filmmakers and the teachers believed that through watching this "uniquely American blend of ivory tower psychology and Madison Avenue marketing," the young audience "would unconsciously adopt 'correct' behavior patterns by seeing themselves as the characters on the screen."[12] To ensure they would have the same effect on schoolchildren around the country, social-guidance films were designed to appeal to a wide, mainstream audience. Consequently, they were all set in the same white, middle-class, suburban wonderland that dominated the media's representation of American family life in the 1950s, as seen on such popular TV shows as *The Adventures of Ozzie & Harriet* (1952–1966), *Father Knows Best* (1954–1960), and *Leave It to Beaver* (1957–1963).

Surprisingly, educators borrowed this method of programming America's young minds from Uncle Sam. During World War II, training films proved to be an effective and cost-efficient way for the U.S. military to educate troops about the war, prepare them for battle, and boost their morale. The information conveyed in *Dating: Do's and Don'ts* (1949) may seem trivial compared to a World War II film like *Our Enemy: The Japanese* (1943). Yet, as propaganda, classroom and military films shared a common purpose: *to influence the thoughts and actions of their intended audience*. This sounds an awful lot like mind control, but as Smith points out, social-guidance films were not made by evil-minded or even socially conservative people, but liberal, progressive thinkers who were offering young people what they believed to be proper direction and guidance so they will grow up to be "well-adjusted, happy, and independent (within limits)."[13]

In addition to addressing issues like manners, popularity, and dating, social-guidance films also tackled some of life's more serious problems, like venereal disease, alcohol/drug abuse and addiction, juvenile delinquency, and driver safety. The information they conveyed was not necessarily accurate, but truth was not a priority when the main objective was to scare a young audience into submission. Consequently, these films generally approached their subject matter in a highly sensationalistic fashion, beginning with the title, which in some instances posed the "big question" the film was presumably going to answer, like, *What Made Sammy Speed?* (1947), *What About Juvenile Delinquency?* (1955), and *Why Vandalism?* (1955). Some names doubled as a warning, as in the case of *Don't Talk to Strangers* (circa 1950s), *Boys Beware* (of homosexual child molesters) (1961), and *Girls Beware* (of anyone with a penis) (1961). The scenario usually focused on a teenager whose lack of good judgment endangered his/her own life and/or the safety and welfare of others. The filmmakers believed that if young people witnessed a marijuana "addict" going out of his mind (*Drug Addiction* [1951]), or the charred bodies of car accident victims (*Terrible Truth* [1951]), they were more likely to think twice before taking that first hit off of a marijuana cigarette or putting the pedal to the metal when out "joyriding" with their friends.

While the filmmaker behind the camera and the teacher running the projector may have had their students' best interests at heart, the subject matter and themes of social-guidance films were not chosen at random. As teenagers were developing their own identity as a generation and gaining more independence from their families, parental involvement and influence over children's daily lives started to diminish. Although it may not have been the filmmakers' intentions, these kinds of films provided a means for adults to reclaim and exercise some of their parental control, but in a way that was considered at the time less threatening and potentially entertaining.

Family-themed shorts like *You and Your Family* (1946), *Your Family* (1948), *Friendship Begins at Home* (1949), *A Date with Your Family* (1950), and *You and Your Parents* (1950) reminded teenagers with an active social life that their families must always come first. Their aim was to convince a young audience, who presumably don't appreciate their families enough, that spending time with their parents and siblings can be just as much fun as being with friends.

That's the lesson a surly teenager named Barry learns in *Friendship Begins at Home*. Feeling unappreciated by his family, he decides to stay at home and hang out with his friends instead of going on his family's annual camping trip. But once his family is gone, he discovers who his real friends are when all of his pals are suddenly (and suspiciously) busy. So poor Barry spends the next two weeks sitting at home feeling like a pathetic loser. And then it dawns on him—he's been taking his family and all the thoughtful things they do for him for granted. When they return, he pledges his allegiance to them and starts to make up for lost time by being a better son and brother. He even makes the ultimate sacrifice and volunteers to escort his kid sister to her school dance, which, no doubt, cemented his "loser" standing for the remainder of his high-school career.

A Date with Your Family is another promotional film for the nuclear family, though it could be mistaken for an episode of *The Twilight Zone*. Once again, the film tries to sell its young audience on the idea that spending time with your family is something you should look forward to and not take for granted. So when two teenagers, identified by the disembodied voice of the male narrator (who is the only voice we hear) as "Daughter" and "Brother," come home from school, they start getting ready for a "special occasion" or as it's known to the rest of us on the planet Earth, "dinner." Actually, while Brother is upstairs doing his homework, Daughter, no doubt rehearsing for her future career as wife and homemaker, is in the kitchen slaving away. Fortunately, she also managed to find the time to put on something more "festive" to wear, because as the narrator points out, "the women of this family seem to feel they owe it to the men of the family to look relaxed, rested, and attractive at dinnertime."

But how could anyone relax in this house? Once Dad comes home ("The boys greet their dad *as though they are genuinely glad to*

Coming Soon to a Classroom Near You

Appreciating Our Parents (1951): Little Tommy appreciates his folks once he figures out who picks up after him.

As Boys Grow (1957): Coach holds a Q & A session with the track team about puberty, the penis, and the joys of masturbation.

Boys Beware (1961): Be afraid. Be very afraid. There's a killer homosexual in our midst.

Dating: Do's and Don'ts (1949): Woody asks Ann to the Hi-Teen carnival and the hijinks ensue . . .

Going Steady (1951): Not a good idea because it can lead to heavy petting (or worse).

Habit Patterns (1954): Barbara is sent over the edge when her bad grooming habits almost destroy her social life.

How to Say No: Moral Maturity (1951): Pre–Nancy Reagan film telling you to just say "no" to alcohol, cigarettes, and heavy petting.

How To Be Well Groomed (1948): Don and Sue teach teens how to look neat and pretty.

Last Date (1950): *Bewitched's* Darrin #1 Dick York is a speed demon who commits "teenacide" in this award-winning driver safety film.

The Terrible Truth (1951): A few puffs off a marijuana cigarette turns poor Phyllis into a heroin addict.

All of the social-guidance films referred to in this chapter can be viewed online in the Rick Prelinger Archives, which you can access at www.archive.org.

see him," observes the narrator) and the family is seated, we are told that they engage in "pleasant, *unemotional* conversation," because it "helps digestion." But just to make sure the three "Stepford" children will continue to suppress any sudden urge to express an opinion, thought, or feeling, the narrator then runs down a laundry list of what children must *not* do at the dinner table. The directives include:

- Don't monopolize the conversation . . . [it] destroys the charm of the meal.
- Don't discuss unpleasant topics such as gruesome sights or sounds or unpleasant occurrences.
- Don't insult your brother and sister.
- Don't make unkind comparisons about your standard of living . . . it makes Dad and Mother uncomfortable and unhappy.

When it all comes down to it, *A Date with Your Family* and other social-guidance films are not really about keeping kids happy, but about keeping adults with kids happy. As the narrator advises in his closing remarks to teenagers, "Be yourself. Just make sure it's your *best* self." What the filmmakers are really saying by "*best* self" is your "best self *as defined by your parents.*"

Ironically, when social-guidance films weren't jamming the joys of the American nuclear family down their young audience's throats, they were teaching them the social skills they needed to develop strong friendships outside of their family circle, gain the acceptance of their peers, and if all goes well, attain a certain level of popularity. The amount of attention this subject received from films and self-help books written for teens indicates the value that was placed on a teenager's social success and how it had become the barometer for measuring the modern teenager's personal success. As Ellis Weitzman, Ph.D., explains to young readers in his essay, "How to Grow Up Socially," which appears in the 1954 anthology, *How to Be a Successful Teenager*, social development is "more important that any other phase of your growth . . . because it influences how well you get along with others now, but also because it later will influence how successfully you can get and keep a job, and how far you can go in this social world of ours."[14]

A good example of what Smith calls a "fitting in" film is *Shy Guy* (1949), which, as the title suggests, tells the story of the new geek in town, Phil Norton (played by a young Dick York, best known as the original Darrin on the TV series, *Bewitched*), who is having trouble making friends at his new school. As the voice of the ever-present narrator (future *60 Minutes* host Mike Wallace) explains, "You're sitting on the outside looking in . . . there's a barrier and you don't know how to break it down." As usual, it's an adult, in this case Phil's dad, who has the answer: "Pick out the most popular boys and girls at school and keep an eye on them. Try to figure out why people like them."

The following day, Phil trades in his suit for a sweater and slacks (to look like the other guys) and begins stalking the in-crowd to see what makes them tick. By the end of the day, he concludes that in addition to dressing for the part, to be accepted—to be one of *them*— he needs to be polite, a good listener, speak up when he can contribute to a conversation, and offer to help other people because, as Phil exclaims to himself, "It pays off in friends!"

In the end, Phil (and the viewers) realize that the key to fitting in and being accepted by them is to conform—*to look, think, and act like everyone else*. Phil is what sociologist David Riesman described in his influential indictment of postwar America, *The Lonely Crowd*, as an "other-directed person"—someone who "wants to be loved rather than esteemed" and is willing to adjust their desires, ambitions, and beliefs in accordance with the larger community in order to belong.[15] That certainly seems to be the case with shy guy Phil. Yet, it's hard to deny that he looks a whole lot happier in the final scene, standing there with a smile on his face, surrounded by his new best friends. Giving up his individuality certainly seems to agree with him.

The issue of "fitting in" is taken a step further in the 1947 film *Are You Popular?* It begins with a question: "What makes people like some people more than others?" We get our answer in the form of a comparison between two teenagers: Carolyn Ames, the new girl who everyone seems drawn to, and Ginny, the school slut with no last name. As the narrator explains, "Ginny thinks she has the key to popularity—parking in cars with boys at night . . . Does that make her really popular?" Apparently not, because when she enters the cafeteria she is dissed by the guys who are part of the popular crowd, including the ones who spent some one-on-one time with her in the backseat of their car. "No, girls who park in cars are not really popular," the narrator explains, "even with the boys they park with—not even when they meet at school or elsewhere."

Of course there's the old double standard when it comes to the guys, who are not criticized for making out with Ginny. But there is also a downside. When one fellow brags about being with her, only to discover all the other guys have too, the narrator informs us that this makes him feel "less important."

The focus then shifts to Carolyn Ames. "Why is she so popular?" the narrator asks. We discover it's because of the way she looks, because she is interested in what both girls and boys have to say, and, perhaps most importantly, there's "no scandal about her." The boys obviously want to do something about that last part because they suddenly all want to ask her out on a date.

The remainder of the film is devoted to the dos and don'ts of dating, a popular subject addressed by magazine and newspaper articles, self-help books for teens and their parents, and social-guidance films. They all offered teenagers strict guidelines for dating and designated specific roles for the boy and the girl. In *Are You Popular?*, the narrator guides the audience through the first half of the date, from Wally's phone call inviting Carolyn to a skating party to his arrival at her house on the big night to pick her up. Of course her parents invite him in, no doubt to check him out and remind him that their daughter, the ever popular Carolyn Ames, has "no scandal about her"—and it better stay that way.

Fortunately, by the late 1950s, social-guidance films were no longer the only show in town for teenagers. Hollywood finally woke up and recognized that there was an untapped audience of young filmgoers who were more than willing to spend their parents' hard-earned change on a movie. As a result, three cycles of teen genre films emerged simultaneously between the years 1955–1960: teen horror/sci-fi flicks, juvenile delinquent dramas, and rock 'n' roll musicals.

Contemporary teen life and culture served as the backdrop for all three cycles, so they shared certain elements in terms of characters (the misunderstood teen, the good girl, the frustrated father), settings (high school, the malt shop), and plots (teenagers vs. monsters or parents or authority figures). They also made a conscious effort to appeal to teenagers by telling stories from a teenager's perspective and by tackling themes that presumably mattered to young people, such as alienation, rebellion, and the generation gap. In the process, these early teen films were highly critical of parents and other authority figures, whose ne-glect and lack of understanding were at the root of most teenagers' problems.

Still, it's important to remember that although these films were conceived and marketed to teenagers, they were written, directed, and produced by adults. So while they were generally sympathetic toward the plight of their teenage characters, in the end they also conveyed, from an adult perspective, in a manner perhaps more subtle (and entertaining) than social-guidance films, proper behavior for the modern American teenager.

"I was a teenage . . ."

The first official cycle of films for and about teenagers was comprised of updated versions of the great horror movies produced by Universal Studios in the 1930s through the early 1940s. These films put a 1950s spin on such classics as *Dracula* (1931), *Frankenstein* (1931), and *The Wolfman* (1941) by turning them into modern-day horror tales of angst-ridden teens who fall victim to sinister scientists and supernatural forces. The kids in the audience were no doubt expected to sympathize with the teenage protagonists of *Blood of Dracula*, *I Was a Teenage Frankenstein*, and *I Was a Teenage Werewolf* (all 1957). They are not only victimized by adults, but criticized as well for what is perceived as antisocial and improper behavior. Consequently, the teen characters are treated by the adults (and the filmmakers) as if they are juvenile delinquents, but instead of wearing a leather jacket and carrying a switchblade, they (literally) become monsters.

The monster-teenage combo was the brainchild of two producers, Samuel Z. Arkoff and James Nicholson, cofounders of the independent production and distribution company, American International Pictures (A.I.P.). In 1957, the company released a horror/science fiction double feature, *I Was a Teenage Werewolf* and *Invasion of the Saucer-Men*. As the title of the first and the advertising tagline for the second ("SEE Teenagers vs. the Saucer-Men") suggest, young ticket buyers were the target audience for this pair of low-budget flicks.

Arkoff and Nicholson made a conscious decision to make movies that would appeal specifically to the younger crowd because teenagers were the ones going out on Saturday night while their parents stayed at home to watch Jackie Gleason and *Perry Mason*. "The teenager was the most valued force coming to the theatres," Arkoff told an interviewer, "so what did we do? We decided to make pictures for teenagers, about teenage objectives, with teenagers."[16]

Arkoff's instincts paid off. *I Was a Teenage Werewolf*, which was shot in five days for $82,000, raked in a whopping $2 million at the box office and became the tenth highest-grossing film of 1957. A.I.P. tried to duplicate *Werewolf*'s success with *Blood of Dracula* and *I Was a Teenage Frankenstein*, which were immediately rushed into production and then released in late 1957 during Thanksgiving week.

The success of all three films is certainly due in part to their sensationalistic ad campaigns, which would become A.I.P.'s signature. In a 1958 interview with *Cosmopolitan* magazine, Arkoff admitted to giving more attention to a film's advertising campaign than the writing and development of the script. Most A.I.P. films began with a title idea, which Arkoff then ran by one of his distributors. "If he likes it— and if it's gory enough, of course—we give it to a writer and tell him to write a script for it," Arkoff explained, "and then we get on to more important things, like the promotion campaign."[17] Consequently, A.I.P.'s decision to "greenlight" a film was based primarily on the amount of hype a film's title and subject matter could potentially generate through newspaper advertisements, theatrical trailers, and other promotional material. The advertising tagline for an A.I.P. film was never understated (or short on exclamation points):

"The Most Amazing Motion Picture of Our Time!"
—*I Was a Teenage Werewolf*

"Body of a Boy! Mind of a Monster! Soul of an Unearthly
Thing!"   —*I Was a Teenage Frankenstein*

"In Her Eyes . . . Desire! In Her Veins . . . the Blood of a
MONSTER!"   —*Blood of Dracula*

The tongue-in-cheek humor of both the ads and the films was apparently lost on some of the older folks, who were concerned about the
negative effects of A.I.P.'s horror movies on young, impressionable
minds. In a 1958 interview with the *New York Times*, Nicholson
defended A.I.P.'s films as fantasies that should not be taken seriously.
"Our stories are pure fantasy, with no attempt at realism," he explained.
"Teen-agers, who comprise our largest audience, recognize this and laugh
at the caricatures we represent. . . . Adults, more serious-minded perhaps, often miss this joke."[18]

The first and the best of the films, *I Was a Teenage Werewolf*,
established the formula for the subsequent films. The teen in the
title is high-school student Tony Rivers, who is played by future
Bonanza and *Little House on the Prairie* star, Michael Landon. In the
film's opening scene, Tony is brawling with his friend, Jimmy (Tony
Marshall), who unintentionally set Tony off when he came up from
behind him and gave him a friendly pat on the back. "I burn easily,"
Tony admits, "I say things. I do things, I don't know why. I try to
control them and it's too late. I've gone too far." Detective Sergeant
Donovan (Barney Phillips), who breaks up the fight, and Tony's girlfriend Arlene (Yvonne Lime) encourage him to seek professional
help to control his anger. He finally gives in and places himself in
the care of a psychiatrist, Dr. Alfred Brandon (Whit Bissell), who is
pleased to discover the belligerent youth is the ideal subject for his
latest experiment.

Dr. Brandon is one of the many scientists and doctors featured in horror and science-fiction films of the Cold War period who believes mankind is on the verge of destroying itself with nuclear weapons. His master plan is to save the human race by using hypnosis to regress Tony back to his primitive past and unleash his savage instincts. "The only hope for the human race is to hurl it back into his primitive dawn," he explains to his assistant, "to start over again. What's one life compared to such a triumph?" Apparently not the life of a troubled youth like Tony, who, Dr. Brandon quips, he is probably saving from the gas chamber. So after a few injections, short-tempered Tony starts to periodically transform into a hairy, fang-faced beast with an even worse disposition. He stalks and kills a classmate in the woods and, later at school, attacks a pretty, nubile gymnast in the middle of her workout.

Dr. Brandon and Tony's doctor/patient relationship serves a dual function for the film's presumably young audience. By having the desperate Tony seek professional help, only to become a psychotic doctor's "wolf-toy," the film taps into the fear, anxiety, and distrust many teenagers were feeling in the 1950s toward the older generation who didn't understand or trust them and were now able to blow up the world with the push of a button.[19] At the same time, Dr. Brandon suggests that his young patient's behavioral problems are not necessarily his fault. In addition to Tony's "disturbed emotional background," there are distinct "telltale marks" on Tony's body only the doctor would be able to recognize.

Dr. Brandon implies that Tony's antisocial behavior may be genetic or caused by a supernatural force, yet in the eyes of the other adults, he's just another ill-mannered, defiant juvenile delinquent in serious need of an attitude adjustment. As in most JD films of the period, there is some hint that it's the parents—in Tony's case, the absence of a mother and a neglectful father—who are at the root of Tony's problems. When Tony's dad (Malcolm Atterbury) learns about his son's hairy alter ego, he blames himself and admits, "Maybe I should have remarried." Maybe he should have because when he tries to counsel his son about his obvious problem with authority, he tells Tony (and the teenage audience) exactly what they don't want to hear: "Sometimes you just have to do things the way people want them done. That makes them happy and they'll leave you alone." In other words, whether you like it or not, just do what you're told.

Arlene's dad (John Launer) conveys the same message, but takes a more direct approach. In a scene that could be straight out of a Hollywood version of *Dating: Do's and Don'ts*, Tony arrives at Arlene's house for their date. He beeps his car horn, which angers Mr. Logan, who insists Arlene invite him in. Mr. Logan then starts in on Tony for not having a job after school, being disrespectful toward authority, and not calling on his daughter properly in her home.[20] By this time, it's hard not to feel sorry for Tony, who feels like everyone is coming down on him.

Tony Rivers was not the only teenager with an attitude problem. In the opening scene of *Blood of Dracula*, Nancy Perkins (Sandra Harrison) is being driven to her new boarding school by her step-mother and father, who she resents for getting married so soon after her mother's death. Upset that she is being sent away to school, Nancy suddenly grabs the steering wheel from her father and tries to run their car off the road. You don't need to be a medical expert to see Nancy is one flower short of an arrangement, yet Mr. Perkins (Thomas Browne Henry) chooses to ignore the warning signs and drops his suicidal daughter off at school.

At the Sherwood School for Girls, Nancy's antisocial behavior lands her in the clutches of her deranged chemistry teacher, Miss

Branding (Louise Lewis). As when Dr. Brandon first meets Tony, she immediately recognizes that Nancy is that "special kind of girl" she needs for her groundbreaking experiment that will also save mankind from its own demise. As she explains in her long diatribe to her faithful teaching assistant, the men who rule the world mistakenly search for power through the reckless development of the nuclear bomb, the fallout from which turns humans into "monsters—grotesque, misshapen, frightened fiends." She claims her fellow scientists will abandon their experiments once she unleashes a destructive power in a human being that's more terrible than anything man can create.

There's no question Miss Branding is a total loon, but her fears were not exactly unfounded. At the time, the testing of weapons was on the rise in both the United States and the U.S.S.R. In 1957 alone, thirty-two aboveground blasts occurred at the Nevada nuclear test site. In that same year, the two countries failed to reach an agreement that would have cut off the production and testing of weapons.

So, with the help of a magical antique Carpathian amulet, Miss Branding hypnotizes Nancy and unleashes her inner Dracula. While under her teacher's spell, she unknowingly starts knocking off her classmates until she finally realizes she's a vampire. In a scene brimming with lesbian overtones, she pleads with Miss Branding to end their "relationship":

Nancy: You've got to set me free!

Miss Branding: Free to do what?

Nancy: Free to be myself. I just left Glen, my boyfriend. You tried to stop him from seeing me.

Miss Branding: I didn't think it was important.

But Miss Branding refuses and insists her experiment is the only thing that is important:

Miss Branding: It's too late, Nancy. You and I, together, must go to the end of this experience.

Dracula and *Werewolf* both end tragically. Once Tony and Nancy realize they are responsible for killing their classmates, they both return to their respective "makers," who have no guilt about what they've done. Echoing Dr. Brandon, Miss Branding remarks, "The final result will justify everything." So it's only a matter of time before the teenage werewolf and little Miss Dracula turn the tables on them. Nancy kills Miss Branding and then dies when she is accidentally impaled on a piece of wood. Dr. Brandon also gets what he deserves: he's mauled by the teen wolf, who is then gunned down by the police.

Between the hocus-pocus and the carnage, there's an ample amount of screen time devoted to the normal stuff teenagers enjoy, like listening to music, dancing, and engaging in some good clean hi-jinks. An obvious attempt on the part of the filmmakers to cater to their young audience, these scenes not only grind the plot to a halt, they are painfully un-hip. One almost gets the sense that the filmmakers knew exactly what they were doing when it came to the horror and suspense, but were not as well-versed in modern teenage life. *Werewolf*, in particular, includes a rather long sequence at a "hangout" where all the guys and gals celebrate Halloween. There is a string of bad jokes and strained gags (a kid opens a door and a bucket of water falls on him) and a really awful song-and-dance number ("Eeny Meeny Miney Moe"). The film also establishes a precedent for casting actors who look like college graduates to play high-school students (Landon and Lime were both going on twenty-one at the time).

Blood of Dracula shared a double bill with another teen horror film, *I Was a Teenage Frankenstein.* Unlike the other two, the only teen in this film was the title character, who was actually assembled from body parts stolen off of other corpses (including a teenager who crashed his car while speeding). The focus shifts to the mad scientist, in this case Professor Frankenstein (once again played A.I.P.'s resident evil guy, Whit Bissell), who decides to replicate his ancestor's famous experiment involving the regeneration of dead tissue with the hope of creating, in his words, a perfectly normal human being able to walk among other humans undetected. His Nietzchean plan is to take selective breeding to the next level and create a race of intellectually superior human beings. The key to Professor F.'s plan is to perfect the human race by using the "ingredients of youth" to construct a teenager you can control.

Once his teenage creation comes to life, the mad professor discovers teenagers (especially the ones you make yourself) are not so easy to control. Bob, aka Teenage Frankenstein (Gary Conway), is anxious to get out of his creator's laboratory and have some fun. But when the impetuous youth wreaks havoc by showing his not-so-perfect face too soon in public, Professor F. has no choice but to dismantle his science project and ship the parts to England, where he can be reassembled. Just as Dr. Brandon couldn't control Tony the werewolf and Miss Branding's magic whammy can't overpower fang-faced Nancy, Professor F. is no match for the muscular Bob, who soon sends his creator off to a place where he will no doubt meet *his* maker.

By 1950s standards, *Teenage Frankenstein* is the most gruesome of the three A.I.P. films. At one point, Professor Frankenstein is shown using a buzz saw to remove damaged limbs from a corpse. Then there's the teenage monster's disfigured face, which we see again in close-up during the climax, which has an added shock value when the picture suddenly switches from black and white to color.

But what makes the film so entertaining is the campy script by Herman Cohen and Aben Kandel—the same writing team that penned *Teenage Werewolf*.[21] The humor is completely tongue in cheek, particularly Bissell's portrayal of Professor Frankenstein as an egotistical snob who is counting the days until he will be honored for saving all of mankind by perfecting the human race. His arrogance, impatience, and ironic lack of compassion for humanity are expressed through Cohen and Kandel's over-the-top dialogue, such as when he's scolding his loyal assistant ("In this laboratory there is no death until I declare it so!"); or reassuring his neglected fiancée, whom he later kills for being too nosy ("I think we should be grateful for the monster. Perhaps it's possible he's brought us closer together"). With his creation, he assumes the role of the controlling parent and insists on absolute obedience ("Speak! I know you have a civil tongue in your head because I sewed it back myself!") and makes Bob memorize Bible quotations and address his elders as "sir."

Dr. Frankenstein's demise didn't mark the end to the teen horror cycle. In an attempt to cash in on what proved to be for A.I.P. a profitable venture, other independent production companies tried their luck with the genre. Howco International Pictures' *Teenage Monster* (1958) is actually a horror/sci-fi/Western about a boy who gets zapped by a meteor and grows up to be a monster (but looks more like a really hairy guy in desperate need of electrolysis). *Teenage Zombies* (1959) is an amateurish, incoherent cheapie about a group of teenagers who stumble onto an island of zombies under the control of a mad scientist, Dr. Myra (Katherine Victor). In 1950s horror/sci-fi films, "zombie" was often the code word for "communist," so the plan is to dump the formula Dr. Myra is developing for one of those unnamed Eastern Bloc countries into the United States's water supply, thereby turning all of its citizens into slaves for the mighty Red Menace. Fortunately, the teenagers and democracy triumph in the end.

The best of the teen horror imitators was Allied Artists's *Frankenstein's Daughter* (1958), which tells the story of yet another member of the Frankenstein family. This time around its grandson Oliver Frank(enstein) (Donald Murphy), who is trying to repeat his granddad's famous experiment with the use of a drug that turns people into hideous monsters. Frank is not just a lunatic—he's also a total letch, whose victims include pretty young women who spurn his advances. He uses the drug on his colleague's pretty granddaughter, Trudy Morton (Sandra Knight), but she escapes with the help of her boyfriend Johnny (John Ashley), who manages to destroy Frank and his creature.

The film adheres closely to A.I.P.'s moviemaking formula. *Frankenstein's Daughter* was shot in only six days for $60,000 (and pre-sold for $80,000, thus turning a $20,000 profit before its release). There's also the usual mix of horror and teenage fun, complete with the obligatory party sequence and musical number. However, unlike its predecessors, the teens in this film—Trudy and Johnny—are not victims like Tony and Nancy, but emerge as the story's true heroes. Though somewhat accidentally, Johnny saves Trudy and manages to destroy Oliver, who is hit with a container of acid that was meant for the creature, which goes up in flames when it gets too close to a Bunsen burner.

While teenagers are generally victims in horror movies, they are usually the ones who save the day in sci-fi films. Unfortunately, they also spend most of their screen time trying to convince the adults that they really did see little green men (*Invasion of the Saucer-Men* [1957]); or a big, red, moving mass of flesh-eating Jell-O® (*The Blob* [1958]) or an oversize lizard (*The Giant Gila Monster* [1959]); or a very, very large, hairy spider (*Earth vs. the Spiders* [1958]). No one will listen to them because, after all, teenagers let their imaginations run wild and can't be trusted. Like teen horror movies, teen sci-fi films aimed to appeal to their young audience by exposing the distrust and narrow-mindedness of the adults, who are usually responsible for the film's high body count because they refuse to believe teenagers when they claim to have seen whatever creature happened to be menacing the Earth that day.

For example, *Invasion of the Saucer-Men*, which shared a double bill with *Werewolf*, used a blend of science-fiction and comedy to expose the foolishness of adults. The police presume anyone under the age of twenty-one is up to no good, so they don't believe the film's *über*-couple, Johnny (Steve Terrell) and Joan (Gloria Castillo), when they admit to accidentally running over a space alien with their car. At the time of their accident, Johnny and Joan were on their way to elope without the consent of her father. But we soon realize Joan's dad is wrong about Johnny, who is the only male character in the film clever enough to outsmart the aliens. Even the military, which, contrary to many cold war sci-fi films, is ill-prepared and totally inept when it comes to dealing with visitors from outer space. Once they locate the space-invader's empty flying saucer, the colonel in charge has no idea what to do. Fortunately, the ship blows up on its own and the matter is, once again, swept under the rug.

As for our heroes, Joan suggests to Johnny that they enlist the help of their friends. "They are not like our parents or the police," she explains. "They won't think we are drunk or crazy just because we're young." So with a little teamwork, the teenagers band together to disintegrate the remaining aliens by using their car headlights. Afterward, they bemoan the fact that the adults will never know about how they saved the world.

Still, *Invasion of the Saucer-Men* was clearly not meant to be taken seriously, though the people involved in the production disagree over whether the project started off as a comedy. Paul Blaisdell, who designed the aliens and other creatures for A.I.P. films, claimed that in the beginning it was a straight monster film, but "it sort of collapsed into comedy about three days into production."[22] Robert J. Gurney, Jr., who co-wrote the script, insists that when he first read Paul W. Fairman's short story upon which the film is based, "The Cosmic Flame," he told the producers he could only make it work by making a comedy out of it.[23]

But sometimes the laughs are not necessarily intentional. *The Giant Gila Monster* is an example of a cheesy, low-budget teen sci-fi film that goes to extreme lengths to establish its leading man, Chase Winstead (Don Sullivan), as the film's teen hero. Part rebel, part saint, Chase is designed to appeal to both teenagers and their parents. He's a whiz at fixing cars and something of a hot-rodder, but not the kind who speeds because he's too much of a good citizen to drive over the speed limit. Chase also has a French girlfriend (what she's doing in the backwoods of Texas remains a mystery) and is on the verge of becoming a recording star (not once, but twice, he picks up a mini-guitar and croons some awful pseudo-religious song about Jesus called "Laugh, Children, Laugh"). And, of course, he saves the town from the lizard with a thyroid condition by turning his car into a bomb and blowing up the giant creature. His courageous feat is enough to even impress Chase's biggest critic, who up to that point was convinced he was a bad influence on the other kids. But once he sees the boy blow up the giant lizard and save the town, he rewards him by offering him a job!

In light of their differences, how can one account for the appeal of teen horror movies versus teen-oriented sci-fi? The answer lies in the respective relationships within each genre between the teenagers and the grown-ups. In horror films, adults are the enemy: teenagers fall victim to demented, self-serving scientists with grandiose plans for saving the world from destroying itself. In sci-fi flicks, the evil forces teenagers battle are the product of either mankind's or nature's mistake or surprise visitors from outer space or another dimension. Yet equally menacing are some of the adult Earthlings, namely the authority figures who teenagers can't rely on for protection or help because they are blinded by their irrational mistrust of young people. So perhaps the true appeal of these films to a younger audience is the way in which they confirm the existence of a generation gap—a gap created by the older generation's distrust of and contempt for the younger, which will only continue to widen.

"You never dream it could happen to your kids"

In his 1955 study of juvenile delinquency, entitled *1,000,000 Delinquents*, Pulitzer Prize–winning journalist Benjamin Fine painted a bleak picture of what the future had in store for the youth of America. According to Fine, the number of juvenile-delinquency cases in the United States increased 45% between the years 1945 and 1953. In 1952 alone, approximately four hundred thousand children were referred to juvenile court. Fine predicted that if the number of cases continued to grow at this alarming rate, the United States would be home to one million juvenile delinquents within a year and 2.25 million by 1960.[24] "There is a good reason to think of delinquency as a national epidemic, a serious epidemic," Fine warned. "Unless this cancer is checked early enough, it can go on spreading and contaminate many good cells in our society."[25]

When *1,000,000 Delinquents* landed on bookstore shelves in 1955, public awareness of this so-called "national epidemic" was at an all-time high. The media nurtured the public's fears with newspaper headlines (TEENS WHO KILL FOR THRILLS) and front-page stories about gang violence and teens running wild in the streets. In addition to Fine's book, there were numerous studies and an endless stream of newspaper and magazine articles, which theorized, dissected, and analyzed the conditions and causes of juvenile delinquency.[26]

In addition to selling newspapers, the press's preoccupation with juvenile delinquency was due in part to the amount of attention the issue was receiving at the time from federal and state lawmakers and the U.S. Department of Justice. Throughout his forty-eight-year reign as FBI director (1924–1972), J. Edgar Hoover made juvenile crime one of the Bureau's top priorities. He frequently issued public statements and delivered speeches on the subject, which often sounded more like Sunday sermons than crime reports. "Reverend" Hoover's remarks were usually directed at parents, whose involvement, he believed, was crucial in order to stop the "plague of youthful lawlessness" from spreading. "The battle against juvenile violence," Hoover declared in 1958, "must be waged by the mothers, fathers and all adult citizens of America who share responsibilities for youth."[27]

There's no denying there is and will always be some "bad apples" (or as Hoover once called them, "snarling young thugs"), particularly in a teen population totaling over sixteen million. But why, in the mid-fifties, was juvenile delinquency suddenly reaching, as the U.S. Department of Justice claimed, epidemiological proportions?

The answer is complex because it starts with the very definition of "juvenile delinquency" and how it had changed over time. In the 1950s, the FBI's statistics regarding juvenile crime were gathered from major cities around the country. In addition to the obvious criminal acts (murder, rape, assault, burglary), there were certain "status crimes" (underage drinking, breaking curfew, driving without a license, sex delinquency, etc.), which were illegal depending on the suspect's age and the state where he/she lived.[28] As historian Charles

Gilbert argues, while the number of incidents involving juveniles may have increased, "the public impression of the severity of this problem was undoubtedly exaggerated."[29] The lack of a uniform definition, combined with the added attention law enforcement was giving to juvenile crime, and the interpretation of the youth of America's changing behavior as "criminal," were all factors that molded the public's perceptions and fostered their fears.[30]

Juvenile crime also became a priority for the U.S. Congress. In 1953, the U.S. Senate Subcommittee to Investigate Juvenile Delinquency was formed to study the issue and assess the effectiveness of current laws. Although juvenile crime was at the top of its agenda, the subcommittee eventually turned its attention to what some community leaders, educators, and politicians had been claiming was the real cause of the moral decline of America's youth since the end of World War II—teenage culture.

Comic books were the subcommittee's first target. In 1948, Dr. Fredric Wertham, a New York psychiatrist, launched a public crusade against both crime and horror comic books (with titles like *Crime Does Not Pay*, *Crime Patrol*, *The Vault of Horror*, and *Crypt of Terror*) and their makers, who he accused of putting "criminal or sexually abnormal ideas" into the minds of children and fostering racial hatred.[31] Wertham's initial attempt to get legislation passed to prohibit the publication and sale of comics with questionable content failed. Then, in 1954, his campaign was revived upon publication of his controversial book, *Seduction of the Innocent*, in which he accused the comic book industry of inciting their young readers to commit violent and immoral acts. Wertham was one of the many "experts" who appeared before the Senate subcommittee, which also heard testimony from members of the comic book industry. In the end, the subcommittee concluded that there was "substantial, although not unanimous agreement among the experts that there may be detrimental and delinquency-producing effects on the emotionally normal delinquent."[32] Meanwhile, the comic book industry, concerned the U.S. government would follow Wertham's advice and start regulating the content and sale of comics, formed the Comics Magazine Association of America, which issued a "Code of Standards" for both the content and advertising of comic books.[33]

Although Hollywood had been self-regulating film content since the Production Code was established back in 1930, the major film studios did not escape the watchful eye of the subcommittee. In June 1955, subcommittee co-chair Senator Estes Kefauver (D-Tenn.) traveled to the West Coast to hold a hearing on what he regarded as excessive violence, brutality, and sex in current movies and the danger they posed to the morals of America's youth.[34] While the studio executives who testified admitted to making some mistakes in terms of the amount of violence they've allowed in their pictures, they were adamant that there was no direct link between motion pictures and juvenile delinquency. As Frank Freeman, vice president of Paramount Studios, declared, the blame lay elsewhere. "When you wind it all up," Freeman testified, "you come right back to the foundation of our way of life—the home—and divorces and drinking."[35]

At one point, Senator Kefauver asked Dore Schary, vice president in charge of production at MGM, about a recent newspaper story that claimed a Nashville girl had set fire to a barn after seeing one of his studio's recent releases.

"There's no fire in the picture," Schary retorted, "You can't blame that on us."[36]

The film in question was *Blackboard Jungle*, a social drama released in March of that year which examined the problem of juvenile delinquency in inner-city schools. Based on the novel by Evan Hunter, the story is told from the point of view of an inexperienced, yet dedicated, teacher, Richard Dadier (Glenn Ford), who accepts a job at an all-boys vocational high school located in a rough urban neighborhood. Dadier's class is controlled by a smart-mouthed, devious thug named Artie West (Vic Morrow). He and his gang are an unruly bunch who carry switchblades, hijack trucks, and don't think twice about assaulting anyone, especially a teacher, who crosses their path.[37]

Comparing himself to a lion tamer, Dadier (or as his students mockingly call him, "Daddy-O") tries to figure out the best way to get through to his students. He rejects the methods used by his colleagues, who, in his mind, are either "clobberers" or "slobberers." The "clobberers" believe the only way to control their students is by force, which Dadier thinks is ineffective because they are so used to getting clobbered in the streets and at home. The "slobberers" are bleeding-heart liberals, like math teacher Josh Edwards (Richard Kiley), who thinks his students "aren't bad, just ignorant." In one of the film's most disturbing scenes, Edwards's theory is proven wrong when he's knocked down by Artie and his gang, who proceed to smash his collection of rare 78-rpm jazz records (along with his idealism) to bits.

So Dadier decides to "divide and conquer" his class by reaching out to the student with the most potential, Greg Miller (Sidney Poitier), in the hope that he will usurp the ruthless West's role as leader. Dadier gets some help from every teacher's best friend—the 16mm film projector—but instead of showing some preachy social-guidance film, he screens an animated version of "Jack and the Beanstalk." Afterward, the class discusses the moral of the story and debate whether Jack's actions—stealing the harp, slaying the giant, etc.—were justified. It's not so much what his students have to say that's important, but the fact that they are beginning to think for themselves. This message is not lost on Miller, so it's only a matter of time before he stands up to West, who tries to prove he's still in charge by pulling a switchblade on Dadier. But this time around only one other student backs up the gang leader up. West is defeated and his reign of terror finally comes to an end.

Blackboard Jungle was a box-office hit with audiences, thanks in part to the popularity of its theme song, "Rock Around the Clock," and the controversy it sparked in both the United States and abroad. The film was banned by local censor boards in both Memphis and Atlanta, where it was deemed "immoral, obscene, [and] licentious."[38] Objections were also raised to the depiction of a black student as the story's hero and the teenagers as rude and violent—behavior which they feared would be imitated by a young, impressionable audience.[39]

The film also made headlines when the Venice Film Festival pulled it from its lineup after Italian ambassador Clare Boothe Luce denounced the film for its negative portrayal of American schools. MGM's Dore Schary accused Luce of "flagrant political censorship" and called her a hypocrite for trying to "hide the fact that there is a juvenile-delinquency problem in this country."[40]

The administration at Bronx Vocational High School, which served as the basis for the fictional school in Evan Hunter's novel, were also less than enthusiastic about the way their school was portrayed. So they invited a contingent of school supervisors from the suburbs to inspect and evaluate their school. After a surprise inspection, they reported that the school's environment was "wholesome" and bore no resemblance to the school depicted in the film.[41]

MGM and the makers of *Blackboard Jungle* no doubt anticipated some of the negative criticism that would be leveled against them. The film opens with a statement clarifying the filmmakers' and the studio's intentions:

We, in the United States, are fortunate to have a school

James Dean:
The First American Teenager

On September 30, 1955, James Dean was killed when his Porsche Spyder collided with another car on a California highway. He was twenty-four years old. During his short career, Dean performed on television and the Broadway stage, and starred in three feature films for Warner Brothers—*East of Eden* (1954), *Rebel Without a Cause* (1955), and *Giant* (1956), which he completed two weeks prior to his death.

In comparison to other Hollywood screen legends, such as Clark Gable, Humphrey Bogart, and John Wayne, Dean's career was relatively short. By Hollywood standards, his rise to stardom was "meteoric." Now, fifty years after his death, Dean (and his image) remains one of the twentieth century's most enduring icons—a symbol of the angst, rebellion, and discontent of the "modern American teenager."

Although he received critical acclaim for his portrayal of the sullen Cal Trask in director Elia Kazan's screen version of John Steinbeck's novel, *East of Eden*, it was really his performance as Jim Stark in *Rebel Without a Cause* that struck a chord with his young fans. His iconic status was cemented with the release of *Rebel* four weeks after his tragic death. In the years that followed, Warner Brothers continued to receive thousands of letters from fans around the world.

Ironically, twenty-four-year-old Dean was well beyond his teen years when *Rebel* was shot between March and May 1955, yet he had plenty of experience playing troubled youths. Dean appeared in over twenty-five live television dramas, often in the role of a troubled youth or a young hoodlum.

But it's the image of Dean as Jim Stark—the young man in the blood-red jacket, white T-shirt, and blue jeans—that will endure.

system that is a tribute to our communities and to our faith in American youth.

Today we are concerned with juvenile delinquency—its cause—and its effects. We are especially concerned when this delinquency boils over into our schools.

The scenes and incidents depicted here are fictional. However, we believe that public awareness is a first step toward a remedy for any problem. It is in this spirit and with this faith that *Blackboard Jungle* is produced.

Ironically, *Blackboard Jungle* never fully delivers what the opening statement promises in the way of answering how and why some juveniles become delinquents. The only character to shed some light on the subject is a police detective (Horace McMahon) who tries, but fails, to get Dadier to cooperate in identifying the students who mugged him. As the detective recounts, these kids, who were five or six during World War II, were neglected because their fathers were at war and their mothers were working in the local factory. "No home life. No church life. No place to go," he explains. "They form street gangs . . . Gang leaders are taking the place of parents." The film doesn't dig much deeper when it comes to dealing with the root of their troubles. Ironically, the kids' parents are never shown and their home lives are never even discussed. So the film's resolution only confirms what Dadier believed all along—"they can't all be bad." It's just a matter of weeding out the "bad apples"—the Artie Wests of the world—from the rest of the bunch.

By the time *Blackboard Jungle* was released, the "juvenile delinquent" label was no longer reserved for bad boys like West. Any teenager who did not conform to so-called "normal" social behavior could be branded a juvenile delinquent. Hollywood took advantage of the more inclusive definition of the term, which accounts for the differences between *Jungle* and another commercially successful juvenile delinquent drama released by Warner Brothers that same year, *Rebel Without a Cause*.

Compared to the poor, ethnic, inner-city kids in *Jungle*, the clean-cut, white, middle-class suburban teenagers in *Rebel* are more *troubled* than trouble. As juvenile crime was so closely associated with urban youth, Warner Brothers realized they needed to convince potential ticket buyers that suburbia is also a hotbed of delinquency. A promotional segment for *Rebel* that aired on the TV series *Warner Brothers Presents* (1955–1956) addressed this very issue. In an obviously scripted exchange, Walter MacEwen, who is introduced as a member of "Warner's story department," shows series host Gig Young the source of inspiration for *Rebel*—newspaper headlines, such as SLUM YOUTHS' STOMP PARTY and STORE OWNER KILLED BY TEEN HOOD. "Slum kids started thinking," MacEwen explains. "We looked at some privileged homes far from the slums. Nice homes. Very respectable. And nice kids. Well-clothed. No slum kids here. But beneath the surface—"

"Trouble," says Young.

Rebel has all the elements a 1950s audience expected in a JD flick—defiant youth, switchblades, a drag race, etc. Yet director Nicholas Ray and screenwriter Stewart Stern chose to also focus on what's going on inside the heads of their three young protagonists, all of whom are in desperate need of their parents' attention, guidance, and love.

In the opening scene, three teenagers land in the juvenile-division police station: Jim (James Dean) for being drunk and disorderly, Judy (Natalie Wood) for walking around alone at night, and Plato (Sal Mineo) for shooting puppies with his mother's gun. In the course of their respective conversations with a juvenile officer, it becomes clear their home lives are at the root of their problems. Plato was abandoned by his father and is neglected by his mother, who has left her son in the care of her housekeeper. Judy is aching for her father's love, but he's having difficulty dealing with her burgeoning sexuality ("He called me a dirty tramp," she sobs, "my own father!"). Later, when she tries to kiss him on the cheek, he pulls away and slaps her in the face.

Jim also has "issues" with his father (Jim Backus), who he resents for allowing himself to be browbeaten by Jim's domineering shrew of a mother (Ann Doran). The lack of a strong father figure in his life has hindered Jim's emotional development and has left him feeling anxious, confused, and very angry. His Oedipal crisis grows more severe when he is forced to prove his manhood by competing in a drag race. When Jim goes to his father for advice, he finds him wearing an apron and sheepishly picking up a tray of food he dropped on the carpet before his wife sees it. A disgusted Jim literally picks his "feminized" father up by his apron strings and proceeds to ask him what it means to be a man. It's no surprise when his dad can't give him a straight answer. In a later scene, Jim grows so frustrated with his passive father that he starts choking him until his mother pulls him off.

With no father to lead the way, Jim is forced to find out what it means to be a man for himself. Before the drag race (known also as a "chicken" or "chickie" run), there's an "existential" exchange between Jim and his challenger, Judy's boyfriend Buzz (Corey Allen) that is a true expression of the confusion and angst plaguing the postwar adolescent. Standing on the edge of the cliff where Buzz will soon plunge to his death, Jim asks him, "Buzz? What are we doing this for?" Buzz answers, "We got to do *something*. Don't we?" After the race, a guilt-ridden Jim consoles Judy while hiding from Buzz's gang and the police. The couple is joined by Plato, who worships Jim and wishes he was his father. Plato gets the next best thing when he, his "dad" Jim, and his "mother" Judy spend a few quiet hours together in an abandoned house together as a "family."[42]

But Plato's feelings of contentment are short-lived. He falls asleep, only to wake up and find himself alone, surrounded by Buzz's boys. Thinking he's once again been abandoned by his "parents," the poor boy snaps, and despite Jim's efforts in the final scene to save him, he is gunned down by a police officer. A sobbing Jim lays at the feet of his father, who is at last ready, in his words, "to be as strong as you want me to be."

Unfortunately, the same can't be said for poor Plato. Like *Blackboard*'s Artie West, there's no place in society for the Platos of this world. The antisocial West got bounced out of Dadier's class because his behavior posed a threat to his fellow students and any chance they have of becoming productive members of society. As for Plato, the most emotionally damaged of the trio, he must be eliminated from the equation because his homosexual feelings for Jim cross over the line into what was still considered in 1955, at least by the Hollywood censors, as sexual perversion"[43]

If there are any real culprits in *Rebel*, it's the parents: Jim's, Judy's, and Plato's, who demonstrate just how much damage can be done by bad parenting. *Rebel* warns the parents in the audience: this could happen to your kids if you don't live up to your duties as a parent. Jim's mother drives this point home while she, Jim's dad, and a juvenile officer (Edward Platt), are riding around looking for Jim. "You pray for your children," she sobs. "You read about things like this happening to other families." The camera moves in for a close-up (which in a widescreen film like *Rebel* is a very BIG close-up) and, looking directly into the camera and out to the audience, she says, "You never dream it could happen to your kids!"

Blackboard Jungle and *Rebel Without a Cause* both grossed over $5 million, so it was only a matter of time before the rest of Hollywood was trying to capitalize on their success by churning out exploitation films about switchblade-wielding JDs, hot rodders, good girls gone bad, and clueless parents. Over thirty-five JD-themed films were produced between 1945 and 1960; approximately one-third of the titles were released in 1957, the genre's "peak year." MGM and Warner Brothers, along with the other major and minor studios, also produced and distributed low-budget JD films with titles that had an "A.I.P. ring" to them: *Teenage Rebel* (1956, Fox); *The Delinquents* (1957, United Artists); *The Green-Eyed Blonde* (1957, Warner Brothers); *High School Confidential!* (1958, MGM); *Life Begins at 17* (1958, Columbia); and *Live Fast, Die Young* (1958, Universal). Independent companies like A.I.P., Allied Artists, and Republic Pictures were responsible for the majority of these films, which met the two basic criteria for indie filmmaking: a low budget and a subject matter prime for exploitation. Low-budget meant no stars, yet the names and faces of several young performers who appeared in both indie and studios films—John Ashley, Yvonne Lime, Mark Damon, Tom Laughlin, and *Rebel* alums Sal Mineo, Corey Allen, and Dennis Hopper—were in time familiar to the genre's target teenage audience.

In terms of the quality of their writing and acting, the most memorable of the post-*Rebel* JD films were not produced by a major studio, but by an indie company, Allied Artists. *Crime in the Streets* (1956) and *Dino* (1957) were written by acclaimed television dramatist Reginald Rose, who is best known for his 1950 teleplay, *Twelve Angry Men*, which was remade as a feature film in 1957. Similarly, both dramas were first performed on television and later adapted by Rose for the big screen.[44]

Crime in the Streets stars future film director John Cassavetes as Frankie Dane, a neighborhood gang leader who is angry at anyone and everyone who crosses his path, including his overworked mother (Virginia Gregg), his kid brother Richie (Peter J. Votrian), and the director of the neighborhood teen center, Ben Wagner (James Whitmore), who reaches out to him. In Dadier's terms, Wagner is a "slobberer" who believes the key to turning troubled kids around is patience and understanding. "We try to remember that kids don't get that way without good reason," Wagner tells a frustrated father. "We listen, we sympathize, we talk."

But Frankie doesn't need a slobberer—he needs someone to talk straight with him. So Wagner lays it on the line and explains to Frankie in no uncertain terms why he has such a bad attitude: when his father abandoned the family, young Frankie was forced to become the man of the house while his mother gave all her love and affection to his younger brother. Feeling neglected, Frankie figured the only way to get anyone's attention was to become a delinquent juvenile.

Wagner's "diagnosis" is right on the money. When Richie interrupts his older brother just as he is about to stab a nosy neighbor, Frankie puts the knife under his little brother's throat. Once he realizes what he's doing and recognizes the contempt he has for his brother, Frankie finally breaks down and another JD is on the road to recovery.

Parents are also at the root of a troubled teenager's problems in *Dino*. Sal Mineo stars as a seventeen-year-old who returns home after a three-and-a-half-year stint in reform school for his involvement in a botched robbery that left one man dead. Dino's parole officer (Frank Mandel) convinces psychologist Larry Sheridan (Brian Keith) to treat the kid, who he describes as "quiet, but that real tense kind of quiet, like any minute—vroom!" Unlike Frankie Dane, it's no mystery that all of Dino's anger is directed at his father (Joe DeSantis), a mentally and physically abusive lout who makes no attempt to hide his contempt for his son.

The scenes between Dino and his father are particularly disturbing. After being used by his father as a punching bag, Dino gets closer to the breaking point as he holds a loaded gun to his sleeping father's head and comes close to pulling the trigger. But once Dino starts to transfer his anger for his father to his "head doctor" ("Stop fathering me!" he shouts), he opens up and admits feeling neglected by his parents. So Sheridan, like Wagner, gives his patient the cold, hard facts: his parents did the best they could and Dad is treating you the same way his father treated him. So Dino puts an end to the cycle of abuse by stopping his brother from participating in a robbery with a local gang by (ironically) knocking him unconscious.

In both *Crimes in the Street* and *Dino*, juvenile delinquency is a serious social problem that requires the attention of experts—juvenile officers, social workers, and psychologists—who must work in tandem and apply a little Freud so they can steer a troubled youth back on the right path. Environment is certainly a factor, as the *really* bad boys tend to be bred in bad neighborhoods, yet in the end it all comes down to a boy's relationship with dear old dad. The disturbance in a male teenager's transition to adulthood caused by a father's absence, neglect, or abuse can only be remedied with the help of a kind, understanding surrogate. It's only then that both Frankie and Dino are able to assume a similar surrogate role for their younger brothers.

In many of the post-*Rebel* films, bad parenting and an unstable home life continued to be the leading causes of juvenile delinquency. While these films are certainly not in the same league as *Jungle* and *Rebel* in terms of the writing, acting, and production values, they take themselves as seriously while hitting on some of the same themes. In

High School Big Shot (1959), a geek named Marv (Tom Pittman) is living below the poverty line because his alcoholic old man can't hold onto a job. So when Marv falls for the school tart, Betty (Virginia Aldredge), who only agrees to go with him if he gives her everything she wants, he does what every red-blooded American boy would do—plot a million-dollar heist. But when Betty's plan to double-cross him backfires, she ends up dead, Marv is carted off to jail, and his father, unaware of his son's crime, decides to make Marv's life easier by hanging himself!

Another of the many "high school"–titled films, *High School Caesar* (1960), stars John Ashley as Matt Stevens, a rich kid who, with the help of his lackey Homer and the rest of his minions, shakes down his classmates for their lunch money, steals and sells exams, fixes the student-body election, and covers up his involvement in the death of a fellow student who beats him in a road race. Despite the obvious successful political career that awaits him, Matt is not a happy camper. His parents spend most of their time in Europe, which the family butler thinks is understandable ("If I had a brat like that, I'd take off, too," he sneers). Matt takes his anger toward his parents out on his classmates, but when his manipulating and bullying go too far, he finds himself alone when the entire class, including Homer, turns on him. Now the High School Caesar is *really* alone. *Et tu, Homer?*

Even surrogate parents, particularly big brothers, don't fare too well. In *Date Bait* (1960), the clean-cut all-American Danny Logan (Gary Clarke), is being raised by his older brother Johnny, who offers him little in the way of guidance and support. When Danny comes home with a black eye, he couldn't be less interested and reminds him that just because he raised him, he's not going to fight his battles. Danny's rival, Brad Martinelli (Richard Gering) is also being raised by his brother Nico, who is overly concerned about his brother, who has just returned from a stint in rehab. Unfortunately, Nico is also part of the problem—he's a Mob boss who peddles dope, which Brad is still secretly sampling. Ironically, Johnny and Nico don't seem too bad compared to the father of the film's ingenue, Sue Randall (Marla Ryan). He objects to Danny, whom he refuses to let inside his house when he comes to pick Sue up for a date. He calls him "trash" and a "punk" to his face and insists Sue date a boy with "some background." Knowing her father will never approve of him, Sue and Danny run off and get married. When she returns home, her father, who's discovered what happened, punishes his daughter by grounding her and sending her up to her room. Being a good girl, she doesn't totally stand up to her dad, but instead goes up to her room and sneaks out of the window to be with her husband!

The reason why movie dads like Mr. Randall were so protective of their daughters is they knew just how easy it was for an innocent, vulnerable girl like Sue to fall in with the wrong crowd. Of course not all girls were innocent. Some even joined gangs with names like the Black Widows (*Teenage Doll*, [1957]) or the Hellcats (*High School Hellcats* [1958]) and ran wild alongside their male counterparts on movie screens across the country. The plot of the typical girl-gang film usually revolved around a "good girl," like Joyce Martin (Yvonne Lime), who falls victim to the Hellcats when they trick her into wearing pants to school by telling her it's "slacks day." Joyce's fashion faux pas sends her hysterically running out the front door of the school. Still, the Hellcats are impressed by the fact that she doesn't blow the whistle on them and invite her to join. She's uncertain at first, until her unhappy home life with her neglectful mother and uptight father (he berates her when she makes another fashion faux pas and walks around the house in her slip), forces her to seek out an alternative family.

As in male JD films, the finger always points back to the parents, particularly fathers. Judy's dad in *Rebel Without a Cause*, *Date Bait*'s Mr. Randall, and Joyce's dad in *Hellcats* all can't deal with their daughter's burgeoning sexuality. Of course, sometimes the parents aren't necessarily bad people—just clueless. That's the case in *The Violent Years* (1956), an exploitation film written by the infamous B- (or is it "Z-"?) movie director Edward D. Wood, Jr. In the campy plot, Mr. Parkins (Arthur Millan), who is editor in chief of the local newspaper, and Mrs. Parkins (Barbara Weeks), who devotes her time to various charities, have no idea their daughter Paula (Jean Moorhead) is a member of a notorious girl gang that knocks over gas stations and in one memorable scene terrorizes a young couple by tying the girl up with her skirt and then raping her boyfriend. When a heist goes bad, a now-pregnant Paula ends up serving a life sentence. She dies during childbirth, but when her parents go to court to gain legal custody of their granddaughter, the judge refuses their request because it's obvious they are unfit parents. "Juvenile delinquency is always rooted in adult delinquency," the judge explains to Mr. and Mrs. Parkins and the audience. Sounding like one of President George W. Bush's judicial appointees, he goes on to explain that "if all people would join this "Back to God" movement and train their children to respect the Ten Commandments . . . it would soon bring delinquency under control."

Amen.

"A safe and sane dance for all young people"

In addition to ushering in a new subgenre of teen movies better known as "the high-school film," *Blackboard Jungle* also earned a place in the history of modern American music when its theme song, "Rock Around the Clock," became the first rock 'n' roll song to reach

#1 on *Cash Box*'s music chart. Bill Haley and His Comets had first recorded the song back in 1954, but it didn't catch on until *Jungle* hit the theaters in April 1955. The tune held the #1 spot for a total of seven weeks (July 9, 1955–August 20, 1955) and, over time, "Rock Around the Clock" became the best selling single to date with fifteen million records sold.

Teenagers adopted "Rock Around the Clock" as their unofficial anthem because lyrics like "We're gonna rock, rock, rock 'til broad daylight," coupled with the song's connection to *Jungle*, were a declaration of teenage defiance and rebellion. While the success of *Jungle* certainly contributed to the single's popularity, it was the radio airplay it received on a national level—the first for a rock 'n' roll song—that helped turn it into a mega-hit. More importantly, the song helped to break through the self-imposed restrictions many radio stations around the country had when it came to playing what was commonly referred to as "race music" (or "sepia music," today known as "rhythm and blues"), which, along with jazz, swing, folk, country and western, and pop, were part of rock 'n' roll's musical roots.

Rock 'n' roll's strong musical ties to "race music" also made it a favorite target for some of the South's less open-minded citizens, who didn't appreciate rock 'n' roll's "jungle beat" and "tribal rhythms." In 1954, Alabama's White Citizens Council distributed a handbill warning that "rock 'n' roll will pull the white man down to the Negro level." A similar organization in New Orleans claimed "the screaming, idiotic words, and savage music of these records are undermining the morals of our white youth in America."[45] Then there were those who shared their opinion, but took a more "subtle" approach in deeming rock 'n' roll offensive and indecent because its roots were in "low class" music ("low class," in this case, meaning "black").

But it wasn't just small clusters of white, racist Southerners who objected to a new kind of music. Many parents thought rock 'n' roll was just another excuse for teenagers to get out of control. The suggestive lyrics and the way teenagers were moving their bodies on the dance floor led its detractors to conclude that rock 'n' roll promoted sexual promiscuity (gasp!).

Then there was the connection between rock 'n' roll and juvenile delinquency, which was planted in the minds of most people because "Rock Around the Clock" was used as the theme song for *Blackboard Jungle*. The press played a central role in promoting this connection with headlines like ROCK 'N' ROLL FIGHT HOSPITALIZES YOUTH and RIOTERS ROCK 'N' ROLL IN OSLO.[46] The latter headline, which appeared in the *New York Times* in September 1956, was one of the many newspaper stories about the outbreak of violence that occurred around the world during and after screenings of the film *Rock Around the Clock* (1956). Capitalizing on the song's title, the film is a fictional account of the discovery of Bill Haley and His Comets. According to the *New York Times*, there were riots during and/or after screenings of the film in places like Oslo, where thirty-three teenagers were arrested outside the theater for disturbing the peace; and Mons, Belgium, where the film was banned after teens stormed a police station with eggs and tomatoes.[47] Similar incidents occurred throughout England, where the press debated whether the film should be banned in places like Manchester and Bootle (near Liverpool) after young audiences started throwing objects and spraying water in the theaters. By comparison, reported incidents that happened in the United States in places like Minneapolis, Minnesota, and La Crosse, Wisconsin, were relatively minor and easily squelched.[48]

Rock Around the Clock is one of a dozen rock 'n' roll–themed musicals released between 1956 and 1959. Their major selling point to teenage audiences was the lineup of some of rock's top recording artists of the day, like Bill Haley, Chuck Berry, Fats Domino, Little Richard, and Frankie Lymon and the Teenagers. The films also featured Alan Freed, the Ohio disc jockey who coined the term "rock 'n' roll" (from the 1947 song "We're Gonna Rock, We're Gonna Roll") and became rock music's leading advocate. Freed produced and appeared as himself in several films, usually acting as a 1950s version of an MTV veejay and introducing the individual performers and groups to the film's teenage characters, who watch them perform live or at home on television.

For example, one of Freed's early musicals, *Rock, Rock, Rock* (1956), stars newcomer Tuesday Weld as a not-so-bright high schooler named Dorie who tries to raise enough money to buy a dress for the prom. Not exactly high drama—even for a teen movie—but it doesn't matter because the plot, along with the occasional song Dorie warbles (with some help from ghost singer Connie Francis), serves merely as filler in between the rock 'n' roll numbers. At one point, Dorie puts her prom crisis on hold and kicks back with a friend to watch Chuck Berry perform on Alan Freed's TV show, *Rock 'n' Roll Jubilee*. Freed also makes an appearance at Dorie's prom, where he introduces Frankie Lymon and the Teenagers ("I'm Not a Juvenile Delinquent"), Johnny Burnette ("Lonesome Train"), and singer La Vern Baker, who would later become the second woman inducted into the Rock and Roll Hall of Fame.

The rock 'n' roll films of the 1950s also did their part to help ease the tension rock music was creating between the younger and the older generations. For example, the plotline of *Rock, Pretty Baby* (1956) revolves around a father/son conflict between a devoted Dr. Daley (Edward Platt) and his rock 'n' roll-loving son, Tommy (played by a young, brooding John Saxon). Dr. Daley wants his son to follow in his footsteps and go into medicine, while Tommy wants to pursue a musical career. At the eleventh hour, Dr. Daley realizes he's been unfair—just in time to get Tommy to a local radio station to play with his combo in a big talent show. As for the musical numbers, there's no Bill Haley or Chuck Berry—just Tommy's band, which is comprised of Saxon on guitar, Sal Mineo (who received top billing) on drums, and songwriter/poet Rod McKuen on bass. Instead of Alan Freed, we get Los Angeles disc jockey Johnny Grant, who later became the Honorary Mayor of Hollywood. In fact, there isn't any real rock 'n' roll in *Rock, Pretty Baby*—at least not the kind promoted by Freed. What we get instead is a bland mixture of pop and jazz with a drumbeat. The fact that Henry Mancini, composer of such standards as "Moon River," served as the musical director of this Universal Studios production says it all.

While *Rock, Pretty Baby* takes the generational conflict over rock 'n' roll very seriously, two other films in 1956, *Shake, Rattle and Rock!* and *Don't Knock the Rock*, take a more satirical approach. *Shake* pokes fun at the small-minded attitudes of some adults who, in this case, band together to form SPRARCAY, which is an acronym for Society for the Prevention of Rock and Roll Corruption of American Youth. The leaders of their anti-rock campaign are the pompous Eustace Fentwick III (Douglas Dumbrille) and Georgianna Fitzdingle, who is played by Margaret Dumont, the heavyset character actress best known for her portrayal of the rich widows who are simultaneously insulted and wooed by Groucho in Marx Brothers comedies. When the SPRARCAYers launch a campaign to get a local TV dance show, *Rock, Roll & Shake*, off the air, the fate of rock 'n' roll is decided in a televised mock trial with the viewing audience serving as the jury.

In the aptly titled *Don't Knock the Rock*, singer Arnie Haines (Alan Dale) returns to his hometown, where he is greeted at the train station by his teenage fans, who give him a hero's welcome. But the mayor (and resident windbag) (Pierre Watkind), speaking on the town's behalf, tells Arnie that his music is "outrageous," "depraved," and "for morons." He then warns the singer he'll be kicked out of town if he and his band perform.

In both films, the conflict is resolved once the older generation understands that young people are not really that much different from the way they were back in the Roaring Twenties. The SPRARCAYers admit defeat when dance footage shot in the 1920s shows Mrs. Fitzdingle doing the Charleston. The same point is made by Arnie Haines, who, with some help from Alan Freed, presents a "Pageant of Art and Culture" for the grown-ups. In their tribute to the "art of the dance," the kids do the Charleston, which once again illustrates to the adults that teenagers haven't changed over time— just their style of dancing. In the end, the adults are convinced, to borrow Freed's words, that "rock 'n' roll is a safe and sane dance for all young people."

"Should a girl 'play house' before marriage?"

In the early 1960s, social scientists launched a serious investigation into the sexual practices of teenagers. They were following in the footsteps of Dr. Alfred Kinsey, whose published reports on male sexuality (1948) and female sexuality (1953) made it more acceptable, if not easier, for Americans to talk more openly about sex. In regards to teenagers, researchers were interested in learning more about their attitudes toward sex as well as what exactly they were doing (or not doing) when their parents weren't around. In his 1961 study of the "premarital intercourse experiences" of college students, Lester A. Kirkendall cited several reasons for the rising interest and concern over the sexual conduct and standards of young people: the increased opportunities unmarried couples had to be alone without a chaperone, the decline of parental and religious authority, the availability of contraception and automobiles, and the freedom "to acknowledge sex and sexual feelings."[49]

Of course the same double standard dating back to the Stone Age still governed male and female sexuality. As sociologist Ira L. Reiss explained in his 1960 study, *Premarital Sexual Standards in America*, premarital coitus was still considered "wrong" at the time for women and "excusable, if not right" for men. Women who indulged were bad; men who indulged were not.[50] Although abstinence from intercourse prior to marriage was still considered the "norm" for women, Reiss concluded that over 50 percent of women were not virgins on their wedding night and the majority who were had engaged in "deep kissing" or were the recipient of heavy petting (or what Reiss calls "breast manipulation").[51] More recent studies of sexuality in the 1950s estimated a 4 percent increase between 1956 and 1958 in the number of men and women who had intercourse by age eighteen.[52] Between 1956 and 1960, 39 percent of all women had sex before marriage, while a significantly lower number—22 percent—waited until their wedding night.[53]

Around the same time, the motion-picture industry started to loosen up a little about s-e-x. Since the Motion Picture Production Code was enacted in 1934, Hollywood was relatively chaste when it came to sexual themes and subject matter. The Code, which was enforced by the Production Code Administration (P.C.A.), prohibited couples on the silver screen from engaging in "lustful and open-mouthed kissing, lustful embraces, and suggestive posture and gestures." Although the Code acknowledged that "adultery and illicit sex" were sometimes necessary for the plot, they could not be "explicitly treated or justified or presented attractively." Above all, the Code demanded "the sanctity of the institution of marriage and the home shall be upheld." Consequently, "love triangles" required "careful handling" and "should not throw sympathy against marriage as an institution."[54]

By the 1950s, the Code was beginning to show its age. Although you still could not show an onscreen male character getting past first base, both single male and female characters—teenagers included— were starting to engage in premarital sex off-screen more frequently. Still, anyone who engaged in "illicit sex" (sex with anyone other than one's spouse) or an adulterous affair was forced to face serious consequences. Although these films were more for an adult than a teen audience, they paved the way for the treatment of sexual themes when more teen-oriented films would begin to address the subject in the early 1960s.

One adult drama that the P.C.A. believed required "careful handling" was the 1956 screen adaptation of Robert Anderson's play, *Tea and Sympathy*. The story focuses on the relationship between Tom Lee (John Kerr), a sensitive college student, and Laura Reynolds (Deborah Kerr), the wife of Tom's housemaster, Coach Reynolds. In the play, Tom is accused of being gay when he's seen skinny-dipping with a teacher, who is an alleged homosexual. Tom's attempt to repair his reputation by proving his manhood with the easiest girl in town is a disaster. So Laura, who is trapped in a loveless marriage and has a genuine, somewhat maternal affection for Tom, decides to restore the boy's self-confidence by offering him a little something extra with his afternoon tea. The final curtain comes down just as Laura and Tom are about to begin their illicit affair, which is signaled by the now oft-quoted line, "Years from now when you talk about this—and you will—be kind."

When adapting his play for the screen, Anderson was forced by

the P.C.A. to make several major script changes. The Code prohibited any inference to "sexual perversion," so the character of the gay
teacher was cut along with all direct references to homosexuality.
However, it's still clear in the film that the other guys think Tom, who
they nickname "Sisterwoman," might be queer because he walks like
a girl, is interested in the arts (he wants to be a folksinger), and
prefers playing tennis to contact sports.

The adulterous affair between Tom and Laura posed an even bigger problem. The P.C.A. believed the play was condoning adultery, so
Anderson and director Vincente Minnelli were forced to turn the
story into a flashback, which was framed by the return of a grown-up
Tom to his alma mater. Once Laura tells Tom to "be kind," Anderson
and Minnelli cut back to the present. The adult Tom then pays a visit
to Coach Reynolds, who gives him a letter Laura wrote to Tom after
their liaison. In it, she expresses her regret for what happened between
them as well as her guilt for destroying her marriage and her soon-
to-be ex-husband's life!

The new ending completely alters the meaning behind Laura's
"offering" of herself to Tom. In the play, it's an act of kindness between
two kindred spirits. Like Tom, Laura is a romantic; her affection for
him is genuine. Yet, she also has selfish reasons for sleeping with him.
Her husband is everything Tom is not: cold, hyper-masculine, and
unable to express his feelings. But the letter Laura writes to Tom not
only makes a moral judgment on what happened between them, she
essentially accepts the blame for her husband's lack of affection. It's
almost as if the film suddenly develops a case of amnesia and proceeds
to rewrite everything the audience had just witnessed. The ending may
have satisfied the P.C.A., but not Anderson, who had no choice but to
tack on the new ending. "I will never again give in," he later vowed.
"You become convinced you're saving the story, but you're not."[55]

Three years later, James Leo Herlihy and William Noble's play, *Blue Denim*, suffered a similar fate when it was adapted for the screen in 1959. Brandon de Wilde and Carol Lynley (repeating her stage role) starred as Arthur Bartley and Janet Williard, two high-school virgins who give in to their desires and are forced to suffer the consequences. Afraid to tell their parents she's pregnant and too young to get married, Arthur arranges for Janet to get an illegal abortion. While she is off taking care of their "problem," a guilty Arthur breaks down and tells his parents (MacDonald Carey and Marsha Hunt) what happened. At the eleventh hour, Arthur, his dad, and Janet's widower father (Vaughn Taylor), race to save Janet from the abortionist's knife. When Janet later overhears the adults talking about how their children have "put themselves in a straightjacket for the rest of their lives," she makes a noble sacrifice and leaves town without telling Arthur. Upon discovering Janet has gone to live with her aunt, Arthur catches up with her train and climbs aboard, just in time for a happy Hollywood ending.

Once again, the original ending was radically altered in accordance with the restrictions the Code placed on the subject of abortion (which was, of course, illegal at the time). In the play, Janet has an abortion and Arthur's parents hear the news from their daughter, who overheard her brother's telephone conversation. In the play's final moments, Arthur, unaware his parents know, decides he's going to tell his folks what happened. The ending violated the Code, which explicitly stated that "the subject of abortion shall be discouraged, shall never be more than suggested, and when referred to shall be condemned." Even the word "abortion," which appears in the play, was prohibited.

Just as *Tea and Sympathy* is not really about homosexuality, but the damage that can be caused by gossip and innuendo, *Blue Denim* is not a morality play about abortion, but a commentary on the lack of communication between parents and their children. Both of Arthur's parents are guilty of talking "at" rather than "to" their son. When he first attempts to discuss his problem with them, they are too self-involved to give him their full attention. While abortion was never the primary issue in the play, in the film it's turned into a big ugly secret ("It *is* the worst thing in the world!" Arthur cries. "She's gonna die! I've gotta stop! Help me stop it, Dad!"). The film has not one, but two "happy" endings: Janet's rescue from the abortion clinic (the staff look like they just stepped out of an old horror movie), and Arthur's final reunion with the mother-to-be. As Bosley Crowther of the *New York Times* observed, the filmmakers trimmed and crammed the play "into the mold of a Hollywood family picture, with the problem never permitted to assume such logic or credibility that it cannot be resolved with a conveniently 'happy ending'."[56]

Despite all of its flaws, *Blue Denim*, at the very least, told moviegoers something they already knew—some teenagers were indeed "going all the way."

But Arthur and Janet were not the only young screen couple to fall victim to their hormones. Sandra Dee, the fifteen-year-old ingenue whose name became synonymous with the word "virgin" thanks to roles like *Gidget* (1959) and Tammy Tyree in *Tammy Tell Me True* (1961) and *Tammy and the Doctor* (1963) (and years later the song from *Grease* mocking her virgin status, "Look at Me, I'm Sandra Dee"), was less than virtuous when she was paired with future teen idol Troy Donahue in *A Summer Place* (1959). It's love at first sight when Molly Jorgensen (Dee) meets Johnny Hunter (Donahue), but their courtship is complicated by Molly's hateful mother (Constance Ford), who has major sexual hang-ups, and her dad (Richard Egan), who leaves his wife after rekindling an old relationship with Johnny's mother (Dorothy McGuire). With adulterers for parents, it's only a matter of time before the young couple hit the sheets and she's in the family way. Like Janet and Arthur, they are full of shame and guilt for their "sins," yet are allowed to live happily ever after.

A *Summer Place* and *Blue Denim* both tackled what were considered at the time to be mature themes from the point of view of their young protagonists—a combination that widened their appeal to both teenage and adult audiences. Ironically, their respective happy endings contradicted the warning American teenagers had been receiving since the late 1940s about the hazards of getting married too young. The warning was in response to the dramatic rise in the marriage rate in the United States immediately after World War II. More Americans were getting hitched and they were doing it at a younger age, so impulsive teenagers harboring romantic notions about married life needed a serious wake-up call. Consequently, many self-help guides for teenagers included a chapter (usually at the end of the book) about marriage, though most advised their young readers to proceed with caution. For example, part four of Evelyn Millis Duvall's *Facts of Life and Love for Teen-Agers* (1957) is devoted to the various stages of a long-term relationship—going steady, getting engaged, and preparing for marriage—with an emphasis on the problems couples often encounter during the engagement period. The section also offers young couples a list of issues to think about and discuss (i.e., having children, financial matters, religious backgrounds) before taking the plunge, as well as advice on how to break an engagement. "Many [break-ups] were perhaps quite fortunate," Duvall writes, "for a broken engagement is far better than a broken marriage."[57]

There was also a series of social-guidance films produced in the 1950s that were designed to serve as a wake-up call for young couples who think they may be ready to tie the knot. In *Are You Ready for Marriage?* (1950), a pair of high-school lovebirds, Larry and Sue, want to get married, but Sue's parents won't give them their blessing. They seek help from a marriage counselor, who makes little sense when he tries to illustrate the complexities of male-female relationships using some contraption called a "psychological distancing board." But somehow it does the trick and Larry and Sue decide it's in their best interest to wait a few years and maybe get better acquainted.

But the subjects of love, premarital sex, and teenage marriage were not limited to films produced by McGraw-Hill and Encyclopedia Britannica. In addition to major studio productions like *A Summer Place* and *Blue Denim*, which were both released in 1959, A.I.P., Allied Artists, and other independent companies specializing in exploitation films tried to re-energize a sagging teenage market with a series of provocative dramas about you-know-what. As with JD dramas, there was some attempt to sell these films based on the presumable timeliness of their subject matter. In *Unwed Mother* (1958), teen pregnancy was treated like an epidemic ("Over twenty thousand girls each year live this story!"). The opening titles of A.I.P.'s *Diary of a High School Bride* (1959), which tells the story of a seventeen-year-old high schooler (Anita Sands), who marries a twenty-four-year-old law student (Ronald Foster) against her father's wishes, state that the film was made in response to an urgent social problem—high-school marriage—even though the teen marriage rate at the time was on the decline.

Young couples on the big screen who defy their parents and elope usually discovered they were unprepared for married life. As a result, they ended up as criminals (*Married Too Young* [1962]), or are terrorized by a psychopath (*The Young Captives* [1959]) or her jealous ex-boyfriend (*Date Bait*, *High School Bride*). In *Eighteen and Anxious* (1957), poor Judy (Mary Webster) not only loses her high-school husband before they get to tell their parents they eloped, she ends up pregnant and unable to find the marriage certificate. Once again, the parents are the real culprits. Judy's belligerent stepfather (played by *Rebel*'s Jim Backus) is your classic teen-hater ("They're a lot of juvenile delinquents!" he roars). Her late husband's parents are snobs who accuse her of trying to pull a fast one when she comes knocking at their door claiming to be their dead son's widow. But when the marriage certificate is found, which proves that Judy's baby is legitimate, they all change their tune and welcome Judy and their grandchild with open arms.

By the early 1960s, the rate of intercourse among teenagers in the movies was on the decline. But that didn't mean they weren't thinking or talking about it. But producers didn't seem to care if their teenage characters remained virtuous through the closing credits. Sex only had to be in the air (or, better still, suggested by the title) for them to cash in.

For instance, a film like *College Confidential* (1960) has sex written all over it. It was a sequel in name only to MGM's *High School Confidential!* (1958), which starred Russ Tamblyn as a narc who goes undercover at a high school to bust a marijuana/narcotics ring. As an exposé of this "insidious menace" plaguing America's high schools, the film (and the adults who made it) try so hard to be hip, it's painfully unhip (especially the annoying way the kids, who don't look a day under twenty-five, converse in jive talk). Today it's a camp classic—thanks to the participation of former Miss Palm Springs 1948 and Marilyn Monroe wannabe Mamie Van Doren as Tamblyn's tarty aunt/former lover, and the *The Addams Family*'s Uncle Fester, Jackie Coogan, as a drug kingpin.

In high school, the issue was drugs. In college, it was sex. Allegedly based on an actual case that rocked the nation, *College Confidential* was a 100 percent pure, bona fide, exploitation film that actually believed it had something important and relevant to say about the sexual mores of young people. In an odd bit of casting, comedian/composer/TV personality Steve Allen plays Professor Steve Macinter, who is conducting research on the sexual attitudes and activity of college students. When word gets out about his student sex survey, the parents hit the roof. To make matters worse, he invites his students to his house to screen some movies he shot of them, only to have someone switch his film with a stag reel. He's arrested and there's a big trial that's attended by a pack of real, live newspaper columnists (Walter Winchell, Louis Sobol, Sheilah Graham, and Earl Wilson as themselves), who are no doubt there to lend some credibility to this inane plot. The trial gives Professor Macinter, a defender of youth and liberal education, an opportunity to explain that today's college students are confused because "even though they're receiving an adult education, they're actually somewhere between adolescence and adult responsibility" (the same can be said for the film's producers). Consequently, the students, played by overage non-actors like singers Conway Twitty and Cathy Crosby, and *High School Confidential!* graduate Mamie Van Doren, never really come to their teacher's defense because, after all, this is 1960, not 1970—at this point in time only the teachers were ready to take on the establishment.

The same can't be said for the high-school students in *The Explosive Generation* (1961), one of the few intelligent films from the period that attempted to examine the sexual pressures plaguing America's teenagers. This time it's high-schooler Janet (Patricia McCormack) who raises the issue of sex in one of those progressive "let's talk about life" classes. When her teacher, Mr. Gifford (a pre-*Star*

Trek William Shatner) asks his students to suggest topics for discussion, she says she wants to know the answer to that age-old question: "How far does a girl have to go with a boy just to be popular?" Gifford instructs his students to write their thoughts on the subject on a piece of paper. Janet's boyfriend Dan (Lee Kinsolving) freaks out because he's afraid someone is going to find out they lied to their parents and spent the night together. When the parents, including Janet's motormouth mother (Virginia Field), hear that Mr. Gifford is encouraging sex talk in his class, they demand he be fired. Her father becomes hysterical when he learns that his daughter spent the night with Dan and calls a doctor to examine his little girl to make sure she's a virgin (a precaution also taken by Sandra Dee's heinous mother in *A Summer Place*).

When Mr. Gifford gets fired, the kids decide to take matters into their own hands and stage a demonstration. When that fails to get their favorite teacher reinstated, the entire school gives the teachers and the staff the silent treatment. The students sit silently in class, walk like zombies through the halls, and watch a basketball game without saying a word or showing any emotion. What they are demanding is academic freedom for their teachers and a guarantee that their First Amendment rights will not be violated. As Dan explains, "We want to be able to listen to anyone speak on any subject or issue so they can make up their own minds for themselves."

The Explosive Generation was advertised as an "adult motion picture for adults and teenagers" (producers recommended they go see it together) and it's apparent the ending was designed to please both groups. The principal (*Rebel Without a Cause*'s Edward Platt), agrees to their demands, yet insists they also get the consent of the parents, who are represented by Janet's mom. The big reveal is that Janet and Dan didn't do anything that night. So while the film made its by now familiar plea for communication between the generations, it also reinforced the equally familiar parent-prescribed moral values in regards to premarital sex.

Another film released in the same year, *Where the Boys Are*, was also "all talk" when it came to sex. A big hit for MGM in 1960–1961, *Boys* focuses on four Midwestern "coeds" looking for love amidst the sun, the sand, and the horde of teenagers who invade Fort Lauderdale, Florida, during spring break. Throughout the film, the four coeds—sensible, brainy Merritt (Dolores Hart), sexy Melanie (Yvette Mimieux), kooky Tuggle (Paula Prentiss), and the somewhat desperate Angie (singer Connie Francis, who sings the title song)—talk frankly about sex (that is, as frankly as you could in 1960). Foreshadowing the feminist movement and the change in sexual mores that would soon begin in the mid-1960s, the comedy asks a variation of the question Janet posed in *The Explosive Generation*: "Should a Girl 'Play House' Before Marriage?"

The outspoken Merritt raises the question in her "Courtship and Marriage" class and then, much to the horror of her old crone professor, answers it with an affirmative. Her critique of the course's outdated textbook and her use of modern-day expressions like "playing house," "making out," and "backseat bingo," land her in hot water with the dean. At the same time, it signals to the presumably young audience that this film is speaking their language.

Or is it? It's not long after the quartet arrives in Fort Lauderdale that they are paired off with their respective mates and are confronted with the question about "playing house." Tuggle tells a disappointed TV (Jim Hutton) that she most definitely won't be playing house until she's *really* playing house. "Girls like me weren't built to be educated. We were made to have children," she explains. "That's my ambition—to be a walking, talking baby factory—legal, of course. And with union labor."

Merritt turns out to be only liberated in theory. She is conflicted about losing her virginity to a rich, handsome Ivy Leaguer named Ryder (played by the terminally tanned George Hamilton). But just as she is about to go through with it, they are interrupted by a hysterical Melanie, who has just been date-raped in a hotel room. The shift in the film's tone is radical, but obviously the filmmakers believed they needed a crisis to hammer their message home about the danger of "keeping house" too soon. Merritt has the answer to her question, so when she and Ryder are reunited in the final scene, sex is no longer an option or an issue. They both admit they are in love and want to get to know each other better because good girls don't (and apparently neither did Dolores Hart, who gave up her acting career three years later to become a nun).

With its combination of fun, sun, and romance, *Where the Boys Are* ushered in a brand-new cycle of teen films that offered American audiences a sanitized and shrink-wrapped depiction of contemporary teenage life. In 1963, A.I.P. released *Beach Party*, the first in a series of *Beach Party* films that focused on the wild and wacky antics of teenagers who spend their summer vacation living it up on the California shoreline. The films paired actor/singer Frankie Avalon with former Mouseketeer Annette Funicello, who at the time was still under contract with Disney, as a young couple very much in love. But there was only one problem: she wants to get married and he only wants to pretend they are (wink, wink). The film's success at the box office (over $3.5 million) established Frankie and Annette as the genre's *über*-couple, who, by the time the last wave hits the sand and the end credits roll, are back together again—at least until next summer (and the next film).

The success of the *Beach Party* films was due in part to the surfin' craze that had actually started back in the 1950s when less expensive and lighter surfboards opened the sport up to anyone with a swimsuit. By the early 1960s, California surf culture had entered the mainstream, complete with its own language ("Hot dog," "Surf's up!" "stoked," and "bitchin'") and fashion ("baggies" were in). There was also the surfing music of Jan and Dean ("Surf City" [1963], "Ride the Wild Surf" [1964]), and the Beach Boys, whose list of surfing hits included "Surfin' Safari" (1962), "Surfin' USA" (1963), and "Surfer Girl" (1963). Their music turned America's attention to the Southern California coastline and those who never set foot on its sandy shores were led to believe that life on the West Coast was a twenty-four-hour beach party. The art of surfing was also popularized by the work of documentary filmmaker Bruce Brown, who is perhaps best known for his box-office hit *The Endless Summer* (1966), which followed two globe-trotting surfers in search of the perfect wave.

But before Frankie and Annette hit the beach, there was a surfer girl named Frances Lawrence, better known by her nickname, Gidget (a girl midget, because of her height). Sandra Dee was the first of three actresses to play the perky teen who learns how to hang ten with the boys so she can catch the man of her dreams, a surfer named Moondoggie (James Darren). With the help of Moondoggie's mentor, a career surfer nicknamed the Big Kahuna (Cliff Robertson), Gidget gets Moondoggie jealous without having to go all the way. Based on a book by Frederick Kohner, who modeled the title character after his teenage daughter, *Gidget* was the start of a profitable teen franchise for Columbia Pictures. The original *Gidget* (1959) was followed by two sequels, *Gidget Goes Hawaiian* (1961), starring Deborah Walley, and *Gidget Goes to Rome* (1963) with Cindy Carol, several made-for-TV movies, and two TV series, the first starring newcomer Sally Field.

"The Perfect Summer When the Urge Meets the Surge!"

If Gidget had spent her summers at home instead of traipsing around Rome, she might have joined the gaggle of bikini- and baggie-clad teenagers who surfed and Watusied through seven of A.I.P.'s *Beach Party* films. Between 1963 and 1966, Frankie, Annette, and the gang lived every American teenager's ideal existence in their own private world—a genuine teenage utopia with plenty of sunshine, surfin', and rock 'n' roll; and, best of all, no curfews, worries, cares, or parents.

Unlike their 1950s counterparts, the *Beach Party* teens lived a relatively angst-free existence. Except for a few minor romantic entanglements, they had no major heavy-duty, real-life problems. Money never seemed to be an issue, which explains why no one had a summer job. Their antiseptic, all-white world was immune from the social changes and political tensions that were rocking the rest of the nation during the early to mid-1960s, such as the Kennedy assassination, the cold war, and the civil-rights movement. Their moms and dads were neither seen nor mentioned, but their absence was never an issue because these kids were every parent's dream. They didn't drink, smoke, swear, get high, or break the law.

Although the *Beach Party* films were set in the present, their nostalgic, squeaky-clean view of teenage life was reminiscent of the pre–World War II Mickey Rooney-Judy Garland "let's-put-on-a-show" musicals. According to William Asher, who directed five of the Frankie-and-Annette films, that's exactly what he was aiming for. In a 2004 interview, Asher recalled telling executive producer Sam Arkoff how he wanted to make *Beach Party* (the first film) "a picture about kids who aren't in trouble. Who don't get into trouble. I don't want to see parents. I don't want to see any schools. I want to see them at the moment when freedom arrives. I don't want to see them doing anything but having a good time without any supervision."[58]

The lack of adult supervision was okay because sex was still a no-no, but that didn't stop the guys from taking leave of their senses every time a pretty girl in a bikini walked by. A.I.P. never shied away from using sex to sell tickets (the ad-line for *Muscle Beach Party* [1964] promised, "When 10,000 Biceps Meet 5,000 Bikinis . . . You Know What's Gonna Happen!"). Of course nothing ever did happen, which was an ongoing source of frustration for poor Frankie, who, in film after film, was continually trying be "alone" with Annette. In *Beach Party*, Frankie thinks he's going to be shacking up with Dolores (Funicello) for the summer, but she puts the brakes on before he even gets to first base. In the opening scene, he discovers that she purposely invited the entire gang to stay in their rented house (with boys on one side of the house, girls on the other, and blankets hanging in between them). But it doesn't matter because even when Frankie manages to get Dolores (who is renamed Dee Dee in the subsequent films) alone, there's no hanky-panky—just a romantic, innocent, walk on a moonlit beach (shot in a studio using rear-screen projection), which usually set the scene for a musical duet ("Because You're You" in *Bikini Beach* [1964], "I Think You Think" in *Beach Blanket Bingo* [1965]).

The various musical numbers in a typical beach-party film are performed in both the traditional Hollywood musical style (with one or more characters bursting into song) and as performances (usually at the gang's nighttime hangout). The inclusion of real musical performers in both A.I.P.'s beach films and their imitators is reminiscent of the Alan Freed rock 'n' roll musicals of the 1950s. In the Freed films, the plot merely provided the setting (high-school dance, TV show, etc.) for showcasing rock veterans like Chuck Berry and Bill Haley to do their thing. By comparison, the plots and characters of the beach party were more developed, though the performers who did appear, like "Little" Stevie Wonder, also entertained the kids at their nightly hangout.

The link between the beach-party films and the teen movies of the 1950s is not limited to the musical numbers. In film after film, the kids squared off against a motorcycle gang (known as "the Rats") led by Eric Von Zipper (Harvey Lembeck), a caricature of a 1950s juvenile delinquent who posed no real threat (except maybe to himself). Ironically, Lembeck was too old to have even been a juvenile delinquent in the 1950s—he was in his early to mid-forties when he appeared in the beach-party films.

But Lembeck certainly wasn't alone. Most of the young cast members were a little long in the tooth to be playing teenagers. When they were first paired in *Beach Party*, Annette was twenty-one and Frankie was twenty-four (and married with children). Many of the recurring supporting players, like Jody McCrea and John Ashley, were in their early thirties by the time the cycle came to an end. The one exception was Donna Loren, who was sixteen when she made her film debut in *Beach Blanket Bingo*.

The casting of twentysomething actors, a practice that would not change until the slasher films and teen sex comedies of the 1980s, was a strategy employed by the producers to broaden the genre's appeal to older filmgoers. The same could be said for the comics and film and television veterans who played the adult characters, who either befriended the teenagers or were trying to drive them off the beach. Included among the familiar faces were Morey Amsterdam (*The Dick Van Dyke Show*), Robert Cummings (*Love That Bob*), Elsa Lancaster, Paul Lynde, Dorothy Malone (Oscar winner for *Written on the Wind*), Don Rickles, and Mickey Rooney. *Pajama Party* (1964) and *How to Stuff a Wild Bikini* also featured a genuine Hollywood legend, silent-film actor/director Buster Keaton, whose work found a whole new audience in the 1950s thanks to television. He brought his brand of physical comedy to *Beach Blanket Bingo* and *How to Stuff a Wild Bikini* in the form of pratfalls and visual gags (like reeling in a bikini with his fishing pole). In fact, the climax of *Bingo* is straight out of a silent comedy. When the teenagers, Von Zipper and his gang, and the adults (Keaton included) team up to rescue singer Sugar Kane (Linda Evans) from the evil clutches of South Dakota Slim (Timothy Carey), who has her tied to a log down by the old sawmill ("Just like the *Perils of Pauline!*" Lynde zings), the race is shot in fast-motion like one of Mack Sennett's Keystone Kops comedies.

With their one-dimensional characters, formulaic story lines, banal music, and broad humor, beach-party movies became a prime target for critics, particularly Howard Thompson of the *New York Times*. Thompson described *Beach Party* as "harmless, eye-filling, and disarming," but was less kind when it came to the cast—"the dullest bunch ever, with the old folks looking sillier than the kids."[59] Thompson also called *Beach Blanket Bingo* "junk . . . for morons," and the final film in the A.I.P. beach cycle, *How to Stuff a Wild Bikini*, "the answer to a moron's prayers."[60]

Thompson's attacks against the films seemed to have been directed as much at teenagers in the audience as those up on the screen. But what he and other critics at the time didn't (and probably couldn't) recognize was the element of parody that was underlying the genre and its portrayal of American teen life as a fantasy. Beach-party movies are extremely self-conscious of their own artificiality—almost as if the filmmakers are winking at the audience and saying, "We know this is ridiculous, but at least we are having fun." Some moments even border on parody, particularly when they are rehashing the same convoluted plots as the teen films of the 1950s. They also repeatedly lampooned the older generation's skewed perceptions of the younger beginning with *Beach Party*, which featured Bob Cummings as an anthropologist conducting a study of "The Behavior of the Young Adult and Its Relation to Primitive Tribes," or as his sexy assistant Marianne (Dorothy Malone) likes to call it—teenage sex. Fortunately for her, the time he spends with Annette and the other kids has a positive effect on his own libido.

In *Bikini Beach*, a millionaire tries to discredit the younger generation by proving that his chimp Clyde (played by a short person in a cheesy monkey suit) is as, if not more, intelligent than a teenager. His reasons for showing the world that young people are feeble-minded with an abnormal preoccupation with sex is to drive them off the beach, which is close to the retirement home he's just built. As in *Shake, Rattle and Rock!* and *Don't Knock the Rock*, the films end with the old folks kicking up their heels with the teenagers on the dance floor.

Beach Party did boffo business at movie houses and drive-ins, so, once again, the Hollywood studios followed A.I.P.'s lead and started to churn out beach-themed films that stuck close to A.I.P.'s basic formula. Even their titles could be easily mistaken for A.I.P. films: Columbia's *Ride the Wild Surf* (1964), Paramount's *Beach Ball* (1965) and *The Girls on the Beach* (1965), and Twentieth Century–Fox's *Surf Party* (1964) and *Wild on the Beach* (1965).

Once the popularity of the beach films started to wane, both A.I.P. and the studios started tinkering with the genre in the hope of sustaining their young audience's interest. One approach involved adding elements from other genres to the *Beach Party* formula, which resulted in beach-party hybrids, like Fox's *The Horror of Beach Party* (1964) and A.I.P.'s *Dr. Goldfoot* series. Another strategy was to change the location and the time of year, as in A.I.P.'s *Ski Party* (1965) starring Frankie and Dwayne Hickman posing as chicks at a ski resort, Universal's *Wild Wild Winter* (1966), and Columbia's *Winter à Go-Go* (1966). But by then the sun had already set on Frankie and Annette for the very last time. The frivolity and sexual innocence of the beach-party cycle would soon be replaced by a new kind of reality.

"You're the One That I Want": Olivia Newton-John and John Travolta don period outfits for the Los Angeles premiere of *Grease* (1978). © Corbis

**PART
2**

You Say You Want a Revolution?:

Teen Movies as Counter-Counterculture (1965–1980)

"The shape of things to come"

"Be more! Sense more! Love more!"

"Where were you in '62?"

"You can't stay seventeen forever"

Never have the young been so assertive or so articulate, so well educated or so worldly. Predictably, they are a highly independent breed, and—to adult eyes—their independence has made them highly unpredictable. This is not just a new generation, but a new kind of generation.[61]

—*Time* magazine, January 6, 1967

The above issue of Time revealed the editors' choice for 1966's "Man of the Year," a title "bestowed" annually upon the individual who "for better or worse, has most influenced events in the preceding year." Unlike previous years, the magazine did not name a man (like "newsmaker" Adolf Hitler in 1938), or a woman (Queen Elizabeth, 1952), or a pair (Generalissimo and Madame Chiang Kai-shek, 1937), or a group (U.S. scientists, 1960).

The magazine chose instead an entire generation of Americans—nearly one half of the total U.S. population—who were growing in numbers and would one day soon be "the majority in charge."

Time's choice for "Man of the Year" for 1966 was "the man and woman of twenty-five and under."[62]

The magazine's decision was based, in part, on the sheer size of the country's youth population, which ballooned in the mid-sixties when the millions of babies born at the start of the postwar boom reached their teens and early twenties. According to *Time*, U.S. citizens twenty-five and younger "nearly outnumbered" those who were twenty-six and over. Young people seemed to be everywhere—in the streets and parks, on college campuses, even on TV—and there were more on the way. By 1970, the youth population was expected to total an estimated one hundred million.[63]

But the editors' decision was also based upon how the youth of America—"the most intensely discussed and dissected generation in history"—stood apart from their predecessors in terms of their independent spirit, diverse interests, and unpredictability. Raised in an era marked by prosperity and world peace, the "Now Generation," according to *Time*, was armed with a "unique sense of control" over its own destiny.[64] While young people's parents and grandparents relied on their elders for direction and guidance, these kids did their "own thing," which in the sixties included everything and anything from going to (and dropping out of) school, to protesting against (and fighting in) the Vietnam War, to "making the scene" and being one of "the beautiful people."

The youth of the late sixties were more outspoken than their ancestors, particularly when it came to questioning authority, speaking out against social injustice, and rejecting their parents' capitalistic and materialistic values. They believed no one over the age of thirty could be trusted; therefore, all adults should be seen and not heard. Of course that didn't stop parents from voicing their disapproval over the way their kids were wasting their days "tripping out," "getting it on," "tuning in," "turning on," and "dropping out."

While *Time*'s assessment of the twenty-five-and-under generation in January 1967 was generally positive and optimistic, the magazine's ongoing coverage of America's youth told another story. Since the mid-sixties, its pages were filled with stories about troubled teenagers and teenagers making trouble:

On July 4, 1965, drunken high school and college-aged youths partied a little too hard, resulting in $20,000 in damages, ninety injuries, and eight hundred arrests. In Ohio, the National Guard was called out to restore order to two resort towns, which were overrun by thousands of revelers who destroyed businesses and homes. ("That Riotous Feeling," July 16, 1965)

According to the FBI, individuals twenty-five and younger are responsible for over 70% of all major crimes (murder, rape, larceny) and approximately 30% of all traffic fatalities. ("On Not Losing One's Cool about the Young," December 24, 1965)

Young people are becoming a generation of "Acid Heads" as LSD use is on the rise on college and high-school campuses around the country. The medical community is alarmed by the number of young people seeking treatment for "post-LSD symptoms." ("An Epidemic of 'Acid Heads'," March 11, 1966)

Teenage marriage is on the rise in the U.S. 40% of American brides are between the ages of fifteen and eighteen. One half of teenage marriages end in divorce within five years. ("Teen-age Marriage," April 29, 1966)

Venereal disease is on the rise among high school and college-aged youths. The highest incidence of gonorrhea is in the twenty-to-twenty-four age range, with teenagers (fifteen- to nineteen-year-olds) in second. ("VD Detectives," September 1, 1967)

1960*speak*

acid: D-lysergic acid diethylamide, aka LSD

be-in: a public gathering

beautiful people: your fellow hippies

bum trip: a bad LSD experience

do your thing: to partake in whatever makes you happy

drop out: to withdraw from an activity (like school)

Establishment: those who are in power (the government, corporate America, etc.)

far out: to be really, really good or somewhat weird

get it on: have sex

happening: an organized gathering where people act spontaneously

make the scene: be part of the hippie movement

mellow: laid-back, usually as a result of drugs

pig: a police officer

trip out: to go on a hallucinatory trip or to see hallucinations

tune in: to intensely focus on something, particularly your inner self

turn on: to be sexually aroused

way out: something either good or bad that's beyond description

Source: Tom Dalzell, *Flappers 2 Rappers: American Youth Slang* (Springfield, MA: Merriam-Webster, 1996).

In addition to delinquency, drugs, marriage, and VD, some disapproving parents were also concerned about the threat long hair on boys and slacks on girls posed to traditional male and female gender roles.[65] "Boys look like girls, girls look like boys," *Time* snarled in 1965, "and the songs they sing are not of love and laughter, but sour, self-pitying whines about how awful things are in a culture that supplies them with about $12 billion worth of such essential equipment as cars, clothes, acne lotions, and hairsprays."[66]

The older generation's ambivalence toward the younger is evident in *Mondo Mod*, a 1967 exploitation documentary that claimed to capture the world of the American "Mods" (or "Moderns"). The Mod movement started in Britain back in the fifties, but didn't reach Yankee shores until the British music invasion of the mid-sixties, when groups like the Beatles, the Dave Clark Five, the Animals, and Herman's Hermits, came face-to-face with their screaming American fans.

Unfortunately, the only thing Mod about *Mondo Mod* is the title. Only one of the twelve segments that comprise the film is devoted to the fashions imported from London's Carnaby Street (like designer Mary Quant's miniskirt) that defined the British Mod movement. As for the music, none of the bands featured in the film are from "across the pond." Instead of the Fab Four, Dave Clark, and Peter Noone and his Hermits, we get the Gretschmen, who warble the film's obnoxious title song ("Mondooooo Modddd"); the Group, whose sound is as bland as their name; and the uninspired musical mumblings of Sam the Soul and the Inspirations.

Mondo Mod tries to sell its audience, who were presumably adults and younger folks not part of the Mod scene, on what they are repeatedly told is the fun and exciting world of the Mods (the fact that these kids are "free-spirited" is apparently enough to call them "Mods"). What the film actually showcases are the lifestyle trends of Southern California youth in the mid-1960s. Ironically, the film also reveals more about the older generation's attitudes toward the younger, who are rarely given a chance to speak for themselves. The guy who does all the talking is the film's narrator, Los Angeles deejay Humble Harve, who makes it clear to the audience from the start that what they are about to see is real and happening all around them:

All scenes were completely unrehearsed and are presented just as the eye of the camera caught them. Whether you approve or disapprove, they are real and they're happening now in the Mod world all around you . . . [the Mods] are an independent breed and to adult eyes this independence has made them highly unpredictable. *The Mods aren't simply a new generation, they are a new kind of generation*.

It's safe to assume the writer of *Mondo Mod*, Sherman Greene, subscribed to *Time* magazine.

To paint the Mods in a positive light, Harve points out that young people shelled out $18 billion in 1966 to maintain their "anything goes" lifestyle. "Their motto," he claims, "is spend it, man, 'cause there's always more." He even cites specific amounts that youths are willing to spend on music ($8–$10 a month on records) and to maintain their hairstyles ($15–$20 for women, $7.50 for men). In the segments devoted to various recreational activities, the audience is once again reminded how young people are contributing to the U.S. economy by buying motorbikes (six hundred thousand sold last year, with a 40 percent increase predicted for the future), Go-Karts (for under $1,000), and motorcycles ($1,300–$1,400 for the kind of "hog" driven by bikers whose club names contain words like "Angels" or "Devils").

While *Mondo Mod's* depiction of America's youth, like the *Time* article, is generally upbeat and positive, the film does include segments depicting teenagers engaging in questionable, if not objectionable, activities. One such segment focuses on the demonstrations held by high-school and college-age students on Los Angeles's Sunset Strip in the fall of 1966 in protest of the Los Angeles Police Department's (LAPD) enforcement of a 10 P.M. curfew for minors under the age of eighteen. The number of teenagers who roamed the famous street on Friday and Saturday nights had risen over the year, due in part to the opening of underage clubs like It's Boss, The Trip, and Pandora's Box. To prevent young people from clogging up the sidewalks, tying up traffic, and damaging personal property, the city was pressured by business and nightclub owners on the Strip to control the crowd by enforcing the curfew, which was enacted back in 1939, and not been enforced since the World War II era. As a result, arrests increased by 300 percent, and the tension between the LAPD and the "Strippies" continued to rise until some angry youths started fighting back by smashing windows and hurling rocks and bottles. Footage of the demonstration is included in *Mondo Mod*, followed by a short interview with Al Mitchell, owner of the Fifth Estate Coffeehouse and one of the organizers of the protests, who sheds some light on the situation. Mitchell explains that the "gulf" between the older generation and the younger has never been so wide. "There's going to have to be some compromise," Mitchell concludes, "and some meeting ground between the two generations that exist. The youth simply will not buy the world their elders have given them. They see too much hypocrisy in it."

When it was time for Hollywood to cash in on the counterculture, it's no surprise that the first in line was the same company that made a mint when they introduced American audiences to a teenage werewolf in the fifties, and the California coastline in the early sixties—American International Pictures. As their beach-party cycle was drawing to a close, producers James Nicholson and Samuel Arkoff recognized that young audiences wanted to see movies that would reflect "the exciting social changes, crises, rationalizations, and adjustments of society in our time."[67] That's exactly what A.I.P. and other companies were banking on when they started to make movies about the counterculture that emphasized its more "colorful" aspects—the hippie movement, San Francisco's Haight-Ashbury district (also known as Hashbury), the drugs (especially LSD), the demonstrations and sit-ins, etc.—and the ever-widening gap they created between the older and younger generation. On the surface, counterculture films like *The Love-Ins* (1967), *Riot on Sunset Strip* (1967), and *Wild in the Streets* (1968), may appear to be speaking the same language as "the beautiful people" (*The Love-Ins*'s marketing plan for distributors even included a "hippie dictionary" with the definitions of words like "grass," "head," and "narc"), but it was clear that the Establishment was the one doing all the talking. As Alan Betrock points out, "the real hippies found them to be inaccurate, juvenile jokes, and the rest of the kids didn't seem all that interested. They wanted something safe and secure in the face of a fast-changing world, or something that represented a complete fantasy. They didn't want reality, and for the most part that's what these films represented."[68]

Riot on Sunset Strip uses the Sunset curfew wars as a backdrop for the story of a troubled teenager and the tragic events surrounding her reunion with her estranged father. Incorporating real footage from the riots into a fictionalized story, *Riot* opens docudrama-style with an introduction to the teenagers on the Strip by an unidentified, authoritative male narrator who establishes that the story they are about to see will be told from the older generation's point of view:

These are not dangerous revolutionaries in a beleaguered city under martial law. These are teenagers on the Sunset Strip in Los Angeles, California, on a peaceful night. Irresponsible, wild, beat, protest youths with nowhere to go, nothing to do, no goal in life, just searching for one thing they demand through the ages—the right of self-expression and recognition. What you see here is happening all over the world and in every country the question is the same: What to do about the youth problem?

Don't look to *Riot* for any answers because what's going on along the Strip has little to do with the film's main plotline. The drama revolves around the reunion between a well-respected police lieutenant, Walt Lorimer (Aldo Ray), who is in charge of keeping the peace on the Strip, and his estranged daughter, Andy (Mimsy Farmer), who he abandoned and left in the care of his alcoholic ex-wife (Hortense Petra). During a police raid, he finds a half-naked Andy in a bedroom. She tells him she was drugged and raped by five guys. Later, at the hospital, Lorimer goes berserk and punches out two of her attackers, and when word gets out about the incident, it jeopardizes the lieutenant's reputation and his ability to keep the peace on the Strip. (The story line was actually loosely based upon a recent incident involving an LAPD officer who gunned down a man suspected of raping his daughter.)

Riot is also among the first of a string of A.I.P. films to include a scene in which a character drops acid. LSD was the drug of choice in the counterculture-themed films of the late 1960s because its reported widespread usage among the teenagers was making headlines and, as far as drugs go, hallucinogens are from a visual viewpoint more "cinematic" than marijuana. So when bad boy Herby (Schuyler Hayden), the movie star's son with the sexy eyes, slips a "sugar cube" into good girl Andy's diet cola, it's only a matter of time until she's off and flying. She goes into a trance and then suddenly breaks into a modern, slow-motion dance à la Twyla Tharp (too bad Tharp wasn't on hand to choreograph this spectacle).

It's not surprising that A.I.P. and legendary B-movie producer

Sam Katzman (*Teen-Age Crime Wave* [1955], *Rock Around the Clock* [1956]) were behind this obvious attempt to cash in on the counter-culture as well as the recent curfew wars, which occurred only five months prior to the film's release in March 1967. A press release for *Riot* overstating that the incident created a "world furor" plays it safe by claiming that neither the young people nor the business owners are 100 percent right.[69] When each side is given the opportunity to express their viewpoint to Lieutenant Lorimer (and the audience), the adults come across as less willing to compromise, while the "longhairs" (a pre-hippie term) are more articulate and level-headed. However, Katzman, who knows on which side his bread is buttered, makes it a point to say in the press release that he believes the "ten o'clock curfew is unrealis-tic as a horse-and-buggy on the Hollywood Freeway."[70]

Still, even with all the essential elements for a counterculture film in place—an acid trip, far-out chicks, oppressive adults, and some groovy music, in this case supplied by the Chocolate Watchband and the Standells—*Riot on Sunset Strip* fails to offer any insight into the mind-set of the younger generation. The big mistake the filmmakers made was to focus on a hackneyed father/daughter plotline (complete with a happy Hollywood ending) and exploit the more sensationalistic aspects of the counterculture (music, drugs, sex) while all the time ignoring what was *really* going on outside on the Strip. As one critic observed, the film "never explores the underlying issues . . . and is burdened, not enhanced, by incessant use of current teenage phraseology that some-how seems neither authentic nor contemporary."[71] In the film's final moments, the condescending narrator leaves the audience with a series of questions about what the future holds. "You can close down their clubs, impose curfew, punish their neglectful parents," he warns, "but one fact remains. Soon half the world population will be under twenty-five years of age. They must go somewhere. Where will they go?"

A.I.P.'s teen-oriented films of the late sixties seemed to have been preoccupied with the growing size of the twenty-five-and-under generation. While the first half of the decade was devoted to showing teenagers engaging in mindless fun on the beach, the latter half demonstrated what could happen if young people were in the majority and running the show.

"The shape of things to come"

In *Village of the Giants* (1965), a group of far-out teens who could be mistaken as refugees from the Strip turn into giants and terrorize a small town. The premise is loosely based upon H.G. Wells's 1904 sci-fi classic, *Food of the Gods*. In Wells's tale, two scientists create a powdered food that makes those who ingest it grow to six times their size. When the substance is fed to baby chicks and children, and accidentally ingested by wasps, rats, eels, and an assortment of bugs, the results are disastrous but the moral is clear: it's not nice to mess with Mother Nature.

In A.I.P.'s version, a similar substance, an orange sherbet-like concoction dubbed "Goo" is accidentally invented by a boy genius named Genius (no kidding), played by future Oscar-winning director Ron Howard back when he was still in his "Opie period." Unfortunately, the Goo lands in the hands of a pack of unruly teenagers who wandered into the sleepy town of Hainesville looking for a good time. We know this bunch of free-spirited kids are bad news because they drink beer, dance wildly in the rain, and use expressions like "groovy," "dig," and "nitty-gritty." Once they are "supersized," they kidnap the sheriff's bratty daughter and take over the town. Their leader, Fred (Beau Bridges), makes all of the townspeople turn in their guns and declares a nine o'clock curfew for all adults and "freedom of speech for all—they just have to approve of what you say."

The giants are outsmarted by our teenage hero, Mike, played by former Disney child star Tommy Kirk (*Old Yeller* [1957], *The Shaggy Dog* [1959]), who, at the age of twenty-three, was shown the door by Mickey Mouse when Uncle Walt learned that he was gay.[72] In the film's climax, Mike plays David to Fred's Goliath and nearly brings the giant down. Luckily, Genius arrives in time with the antidote that shrinks all of them down to size. Mike knocks Fred to his feet and tells him and his pals to hit the road.

For a film about giant teenagers (the advertising tagline read "No One Pushes These Kids Around Any More!"), it's ironic that the battle is not between the teenagers and the adults, but between the two types of teenagers: the square teens (Mike and his equally clean-cut friends) and the hip, yet troubled youths (Fred and his posse), who do drugs (or, rather, a drug substitute) and take over the town. Like the JD dramas of the 1950s, *Village* suggests that Fred's rebellious nature stems from his relationship with his parents, who are always telling him what he can and cannot do (with the emphasis on the latter). As Fred reveals to his hostage, Mike's girlfriend Nancy (Charla Doherty), "for the first time in my life I'm a big man—in more ways than one. You know how it is at our age. 'Don't do this. Don't do that. Don't! Don't! Don't! Don't! . . . Don't smoke. Don't drive too fast'." (Actor Lloyd Bridges must have forgotten to tell his son Beau, "Don't do a teen sci-fi film with a bad script and cheesy special effects.")

But all the Limburger aside, *Village* gave audiences some indication of the shape of things to come in terms of teen movies. There are obvious parallels between "Goo" and LSD, a hallucinogen that had been the subject of recent newspaper headlines and, therefore, was perfect for exploitation.

A second, and far more successful A.I.P. film that also played off of the audience's supposed fears that the younger generation were taking over was *Wild in the Streets*, a political satire that speculates what would happen if the 52 percent majority seized control of the country. The film follows the meteoric rise of a millionaire rock star named Max Frost (Christopher Jones), who, at the age of twenty-four, becomes the youngest president of the United States. Frost begins his political career by aligning himself with a California senator, Johnny Fergus (Hal Holbrook), who supports the lowering of the voting age to fifteen in exchange for the youth vote. Fergus is elected, but his plan backfires when an eighty-four-year-old congressman dies and Frost rallies his "troops" (as he calls them) and gets one of his entourage, a former child star turned hippie named Sally LeRoy (Diane Varsi) elected to fill his seat in the House of Representatives. Her first proposal is to amend the U.S. Constitution to reduce the required age to be a congressional representative, a senator, and the president to fourteen.

In one of the film's most memorable scenes, Max and his supporters spike the Senate's water cooler with LSD, so while they are all tripping, the Constitution is amended and Frost eventually becomes the youngest president in United States history. Once he is in the Oval Office, Max seeks revenge on the older generation by declaring thirty a mandatory retirement age and shipping anyone over thirty-five to a "Paradise Camp," where the old folks donning blue caftans are "neutralized" by being forced to drink liquid LSD. Those who aren't willing to submit, including Frost's overbearing mother-from-hell (Shelley Winters), are hunted down by Frost's army in Gestapo style and brought to the camp.

Wild in the Streets was based upon an *Esquire* magazine short story entitled "The Day It All Happened, Baby" by Robert Thom, who also adapted it for the screen. Around the time A.I.P. acquired Thom's script, another film entitled *Wild in the Streets* was shelved.

The company agreed to produce the film provided—in true A.I.P. fashion—they change the title to *Wild in the Streets* so they can use the artwork that had already been designed for the other film. Thom's script was shot in twenty days for a $700,000 budget, which was expensive by A.I.P. standards. Fortunately, *Streets* took in over $5 million and was nominated for an Academy Award for Best Editing.

Wild in the Streets's success can be attributed, in part, to good timing. The film hit the theaters in May 1968 when the antiwar movement was in full force, culminating with a violent face-off in August between the Chicago police and protestors outside the National Democratic Convention. Chicago's Mayor Daly reportedly feared some of President Frost's tactics might be put into practice and ordered barbed wire and guards placed around Chicago's reservoirs.[73]

The political satire no doubt also fulfilled the wish fantasy of many young people who believed it was time for a radical change in the system. Although he runs for president as a Republican, Max Frost dissolves the FBI, the CIA, the Secret Service, and the armed forces, and ships free grain to all the hungry countries on this planet. The irony is that Max rules the country like a fascist dictator, who, with the help of his Gestapo, denies those who are thirty-five and over their basic civil liberties and puts them in concentration camps. He has become in many ways, not better, but worse, than the self-serving politicians he ousted from office. In the end, Frost gets a glimpse, as the film's theme song suggests, of "the shape of things to come" when he tells a little girl his age (twenty-four) and she responds, "That's old." He then has a verbal confrontation with a young boy who, after Max walks away, turns to the camera and says, "We're going to put everyone over ten out of business."

The film is pure fantasy, but director Barry Shear utilizes a docudrama directing style that keeps the events grounded in the here and now. Like *Riot on Sunset Strip*, an unidentified male narrator tells the story. Shear also incorporates actual footage from protests on the Sunset Strip, college campuses, and the National Mall in Washington, and peppers the film with cameos by Dick Clark and newspaper columnists Walter Winchell, Pamela Mason, and Army Archerd.

For an exploitation film produced by a company that built its reputation on catering to young audiences, *Wild in the Streets* was generally well received by the critics—except for one. *Life* movie critic Richard Schickel couldn't understand why the public embraced the film instead of seeing it for what it is: "the veriest trash . . . entirely devoid of intrinsic interest, entertainment, or merit . . . made entirely by untrustworthy-over-thirties."[74] Arkoff and Nicholson disagreed. According to a marketing bulletin designed to sell the film to potential exhibitors, the film was being "heralded as American International's break from exploitation product to class filmmaking." But in the next sentence, the bulletin assures exhibitors that Arkoff and Nicholson "are not relinquishing their flair for ballyhoo, nor taking their sights off the most vital movie-going group, the youth trade."[75]

Wild in the Streets fared better at the box office than the five studio-produced films set against the student-protest movements that rocked college and university campuses around the country during the late 1960s. Universal's *The Activist* (1969), Columbia Pictures's *Getting Straight* (1970) and *R.P.M.* (1970), and from MGM, *The Strawberry Statement* (1970) and *Zabriskie Point* (1970) were all released within a nine-month period, between December 1969 and September 1970. *Getting Straight* and *The Strawberry Statement* were released shortly after the tragic killing of four students by National Guardsmen on May 4, 1970, on the Kent State University campus in Ohio, where protests were being held against the U.S. invasion of

Cambodia. As historian Aniko Bodroghkozy explains, despite the time-liness and relevancy of these films, the financially troubled Hollywood studios, which, at the time, were actively pursuing the youth market, were concerned about negative repercussions over the film's political content. Consequently, "the producers and filmmakers quickly tried to deemphasize the politically oppositional potential of some of these pro-ductions by focusing attention on individual character-driven elements of the movies."[76] Ironically, the "character-driven elements," namely the heterosexual couplings emphasized in their marketing campaigns, con-tradicted the radical politics of the story's backdrop.[77]

"Be more! Sense more! Love more!"

In the summer of 1967, also known as the "Summer of Love," *Time* devoted a cover story to those young men and women with "an almost childish fascination in beads, blossoms, and bells; blinding strobe lights and ear-shattering music; and exotic clothing and erotic slo-gans." "The Hippies: A Philosophy of a Subculture" took a closer look at the hippie movement, which was reportedly in full swing around the country and overseas in London, Paris, and New Delhi.[78]

The movement first attracted media attention when three thou-sand hippies gathered for the Love Pageant Rally in San Francisco's Panhandle Park on October 6, 1966—the day a California law ban-ning LSD went into effect. As one of the organizers, Allen Cohen, explained in his anonymous manifesto announcing the event, "A Prophecy of a Declaration of Independence," the purpose of the gath-ering was "to affirm our identity, community, and innocence from the influence of the fear addiction of the general public, as symbolized in this law."[79] The music for this cosmic journey was supplied by Janis Joplin and the Grateful Dead, who would be providing the "sound-track" for many a trip in the years to come.

Meanwhile, Down on Yasgur's Farm . . .

Exploitation films like *Riot on Sunset Strip*, *The Love-Ins*, and *Psych-Out* claimed to capture the world of the longhairs, hippies, and flower children, but all they could offer was a pale imitation. Their portrayal of the counterculture lacked the positive energy and *joie de vivre* that fueled the spirit and hope of a generation that really believed they were going to change the world for the better. Thankfully, their spirit was preserved on celluloid in three documentaries produced between 1967 and 1970.

D.A. Pennebaker's *Monterey Pop* (1968) captured the highlights of the three-day Monterey International Pop Musical Festival held on June 16, 17, and 18, 1967, at the Monterey County Fairgrounds in Monterey, California. The festival, which marked the start of the Summer of Love, featured thirty-six acts, including the Mamas and the Papas, Janis Joplin, the Who, the Grateful Dead, and Jimi Hendrix, who set his guitar on fire for the first time on a U.S. stage. Over two hundred thousand people were in attendance, and although the concert didn't initially make a profit, Pennenbaker's film and the sale of CDs continue to generate revenue for the Monterey International Pop Festival Foundation, which supports charities like the Haight-Ashbury and L.A. Free Clinics. An extended version of Pennebaker's movie was released on DVD by Criterion in November 2002.

Barry Melton, a member of the band Country Joe and the Fish, once said that if you think Woodstock was great, you weren't there—you saw the movie. What some consider the single most important event in modern American music history, The Woodstock Music and Art Festival was held on August 15, 16, and 17, 1969, on Max Yasgur's six-hundred-acre dairy farm in Bethel, New York (the festival retained the name of its original site, Woodstock, New York). Michael Wadleigh's three-hour-plus film beautifully captures the crowd of nearly half a million who listened to more than thirty musical acts, including performances by Joplin, the Dead, Hendrix, Jefferson Airplane, Ravi Shankar, Joan Baez, and Crosby, Stills, Nash, & Young. Although the film perhaps doesn't tell the whole story, Woodstock (1970) was a critical and financial success, winning the Oscar for Best Documentary and receiving two other nominations for editing and sound.

If Monterey Pop (1970) marked the beginning of the counterculture movement, then Gimme Shelter marked the end. The film, by Albert Maysles, David Maysles, and Charlotte Zwerin, chronicled the Rolling Stones's 1969 tour, which ended with a free concert at Altamont Speedway near San Francisco. While Monterey and Woodstock certainly had some problems, nothing compared to the violence that erupted at Altamont when the Hell's Angels, who were hired to control the crowd, got out of control themselves, resulting in the brutal murder of one audience member (which is captured on film and later screened for the Rolling Stones to get their reaction). The message of peace, love, and hope that started in Monterey had, over the course of two years, turned into something violent and ugly, marking the end of a decade and an era.

The rally's success spawned an even larger event held in Golden Gate Park on January 14, 1967. Twenty thousand people showed up at the "Human Be-In: A Gathering of the Tribes." For Cohen, the gathering was a "meeting of the minds" because it brought together two factions of the movement: the more politically minded Berkeley-based radicals, who were becoming more vocal in their opposition to the U.S. government's policies in Vietnam; and the hippies of Haight-Ashbury, a thirteen-block section (where Haight Street and Ashbury Street intersect) of midtown San Francisco that had become a mecca for the 1960s counterculture. At the time, there was tension between the police and the seven thousand or so flower children residing in the overcrowded neighborhood, most of them living communally in old Victorian houses. The population was growing by the day, so by the summer of 1967, "Hashbury" was firmly established as the nation's hippie capital.

"The Haight" also became a popular tourist attraction—a sort of counterculture Disneyland for anyone interested in seeing hippies in their native environment. One former resident recalls how Gray Line ran scheduled bus tours through the area, so those onboard could gawk at the flower children "as though they were freaks in a sideshow."[80] In a May 1967 piece for the *New York Times*, "Gonzo" journalist Hunter S. Thompson describes how local businesses were even catering to tourists by selling sandals and "Mod outfits" at prices few hippies could afford."[81]

The public's fascination with hippies and their lifestyle was fostered by the media, which often took a pseudo-anthropological look at their lifestyle and habitat with an emphasis on the more sensationalistic aspects, particularly the widespread use of marijuana and LSD.

Haight-Ashbury and LSD both get a "bum rap" in one of Hollywood's most straightforward indictments of the counterculture movement, Columbia Pictures's *The Love-Ins*. No doubt inspired by the Free Speech Movement that rocked Berkeley in the early sixties, the story revolves around a philosophy professor, Dr. Richard Barnett (Richard Todd), who resigns from his teaching position in protest over the expulsion of two of his students, Larry (James MacArthur) and Patricia (Susan Oliver) for publishing an underground newspaper on campus. Barnett is a firm believer in the freedom of expression, even when it involves taking a tiny pill containing D-lysergic acid diethylamide 25, better known as LSD. The crowds who gather to hear

Barnett speak start growing in size, along with his ego, and it's only a matter of time before some of his more enterprising followers are charging for tickets at the door.

Dr. Barnett's character is based on counterculture-guru psychotherapist Dr. Timothy Leary, who made headlines when he was fired from Harvard in 1963 when parents complained that he was conducting LSD experiments on his graduate students. He spent the remainder of the 1960s and 1970s in and out of prison, hiding from the authorities, and fighting the government's drug laws. He also developed a following among many members of the counterculture, who subscribed to Leary's basic philosophy of "tune in, turn on, and drop out." Similarly, Dr. Barnett also expresses his personal philosophy through a series of slogans ("Be more! Sense more! Love more!" and "Live! Let live! Live the way of life!"), which are repeated, right on cue, by his crowd of followers. It's too bad that Barnett doesn't practice what he preaches. When Larry and Patricia break up because he thinks Barnett is a phony, she eventually ends up in his bed and pregnant with his child. She realizes Larry was right when Barnett orders her to "get rid of it" because it will interfere with his movement.

What separates *The Love-Ins* from the other counterculture films is that the filmmakers let you know *exactly* what they think and feel about the Love Generation. Like the opening of *Riot on Sunset Strip*, the viewer's introduction to Haight-Ashbury is done in a pseudo-documentary style, shot from the point of view of a passenger aboard a trolley car, looking out at the hippie spectacle going by. The camera eventually picks up a "new arrival," the conservative (and much older) Dr. Barnett, and follows him as he walks down the street. The tourists on the trolley start snapping photos at the hippies, who wave back and start making animal noises. The tour guide at the front of the bus serves as the narrator:

We are now entering the famous Haight-Ashbury district, known as Psychedelia—the promised land of the Love Generation, the utopia of LSD, marijuana, and way-out music. It's estimated six to eight thousand teenagers, runaway kids, and dropouts from all over the world have moved in and are making this area their headquarters. Most of the hippies manage to exist by begging and borrowing from the very establishments they vigorously protest. But those who have occasional jobs share with those who don't.

Unlike the passersby on the tram, the viewer gets to stick around and get a closer look at what the film's trailer describes as a "dangerous and kinky world where drugs, love, and pot are spreading like an epidemic."

As in *Riot* and *Wild in the Streets*, the viewer also gets to go on an acid trip, only this time it's with "Alice" as she travels through the looking glass, down the rabbit hole, and into a psychedelic wonderland. When Patricia takes one too many tabs of acid, she goes on a trip inspired by Lewis Carroll's *Alice's Adventures in Wonderland*. With psychedelic lights flashing in the background, the surreal sequence is performed in the same manner as the "dream ballets" featured in the film versions of stage musicals like *Oklahoma* and *West Side Story*.

LSD and its effects were explored further in two A.I.P. films. *The Trip* (1967) stars Peter Fonda as Paul Grove, a TV-commercial director who, depressed over his divorce from his wife Sally (Susan Strasberg), asks his psychologist friend (Bruce Dern) to supervise his first LSD trip.

Nearly half of the film's eighty-five minutes is devoted to Paul's hallucinations, which combine symbolic imagery and psychedelic lights (cinematographer Allen Daviau's visual effects are kind of cool) with shots of Fonda running around various terrains (the beach, the mountains, etc.) wearing a puffy white shirt and a confused look on his face. Screenwriter Jack Nicholson and director Roger Corman, who reportedly went on a trip of his own before making the film, envision an acid trip as an incoherent narrative in which shots and sequences are jumbled. He claims that he wanted the film's position on LSD to be purposely ambiguous—parts of Paul's trip are positive (for instance, Fonda and Strasberg making love with psychedelic images being projected on their nude bodies), while others are horrific (witnessing your own death, being chased by men in black robes on horseback, etc.). Corman's vision was apparently undermined by the studio, which tacked on a disclaimer at the start of the film informing the audience that they are about to be involved in "a most unusual motion-picture experience" about a major social problem:

> Today, the extensive use in black market production of this and other such "mind-bending" chemicals is of great concern to medical and civil authorities. The illegal manufacture and distribution of these drugs is dangerous and can have fatal consequences. Many have been hospitalized as a result. This picture represents a shocking commentary on a prevalent trend of our time and one that must be of great concern to all.

Even the poster for *The Trip* implies that Paul's trip is a bummer by using the acronym LSD to stand for "Lovely Sort of Death."

An even stronger indictment of LSD, *Psych-Out* (1968) was produced by Mr. Squaresville himself, Dick Clark. Susan Strasberg stars as Jennie, a deaf girl who has run away to San Francisco in search of her brother, who she tries to track down with some help from members of a psychedelic band ("Mumblin' Jim") that includes Jack Nicholson (play-

Trippin' on $C_{20}H_{25}N_3O$

D-Lysergic Acid Diethylamide, also known as acid, LSD-25, and LSD, was created in 1938 by Swiss chemist Albert Hofmann as a stimulant to treat human respiratory and circulatory problems. Hofmann abandoned his study once the drug was proven to be ineffective. LSD was revived in the 1950s after Hofmann himself discovered that the drug is a hallucinogen with potential for treating schizophrenia and other mental illnesses. In 1947, Sandoz Laboratories started to market the drug, which was the subject of experiments conducted in the 1950s and the 1960s by the U.S. government and Harvard psychology professor Dr. Timothy Leary.

LSD and its effects were the focus of a series of exploitation films produced in the 1960s. In his study of the "short-lived life" of the LSD film, Harry M. Benshoff distinguishes between two general types of films. In the first group, which includes *Riot on Sunset Strip*, *Psych-Out*, and *Wild in the Streets*, LSD is linked to fascism, criminal behavior, and death. The second group's treats consists of campy comedies like *Skidoo* (1968) and *Mother Goose a Go-Go* (1967) (in which LSD cures a newlywed's impotency), and the sexploitation films like *The Acid Eaters* (1967) and *The Stewardesses* (1969).[82]

Teenagers were also warned about the dangers of LSD in a series of educational shorts, most of which try to simulate, through the use of moving lights and colors, what it's like to be on acid, only to have it turn into a less than groovy trip.

LSD-25 (1966): With an LSD tab serving as the narrator, this film reveals the wacky things kids do on LSD, like paint themselves green.

LSD Trip—Or Trap? (1967): Trap! A teenager tries to save his friend from a group of "acid heads," by writing him a letter telling him the facts about

LSD. On his way to mail it, he comes upon his friend, who, driving under the influence of a hallucinogen, has been killed in a car accident. Bummer.

LSD: Insight or Insanity? (1967): Insanity!—at least according to the film's narrator, Sal Mineo, who, with the help of scientists and medical experts, debunks the myths about LSD (it doesn't make you more creative) and warns young viewers about its dangers. Mineo doesn't appear on camera, but he sings a groovy song over the credits.

LSD: Trip to Where? (1968): Nowheresville, man.

LSD: Case Study (1969): In this classic anti-drug four-minute short, a teenager's first acid trip turns into a nightmare when the talking face that suddenly appears on her hot dog starts to scream when she bites into it. Talk about a bad trip!

ing the aptly named Stoney) on guitar. She falls for Stoney and gets caught up in the far-out scene, only to discover that her brother (Bruce Dern) is a raving lunatic known as "the Seeker" who is on a permanent acid trip. *Psych-Out* reveals the darker side of hippiedom. Although they preach peace and love, they can also be misogynistic, insensitive, and duplicitous. Stoney gets a lecture about honesty from his friend Dave (Dean Stockwell), who thinks nothing of moving in on Jennie when Stoney's back is turned and giving her a drink laced with LSD. Although Clark claims they were merely slipping an anti-drug message, there is certainly nothing subtle about a scene in which a guy (played by future film director Henry Jaglom) freaking out on LSD tries to cut off his hand with an electric saw! The film also has a Hollywood ending with Dave getting killed as punishment for his sins, but not before saving a freaked-out Jennie when she wanders into traffic.

A.I.P. probably thought that if they could sell LSD to the public, why not marijuana? Unfortunately, no one was interested in taking a "hit" off of *Maryjane* (1968), a dopey exploitation film reminiscent of the 1930s cult classic *Reefer Madness*. Teen idol Fabian stars as Phil Blake, a dedicated high-school art teacher/coach trying to uncover a marijuana ring at school, who makes the mistake of admitting to the authorities and the principal that he tried pot in college. This doesn't sit well with Police Chief Otis Mosley (Baynes Barron), who brands Phil with a big scarlet "M" across his chest. Suddenly, the other teachers won't talk to him, and he and the police chief make it their personal mission to put the former dope fiend behind bars. But putting Phil in jail won't stop the biggest dealer in the school, Jordan Bates (Kevin Coughlin), from leading his "gang" down the path of self-destruction. They are supposedly the bad kids in school, but even by movie standards, they are far too polite and well-groomed to pose much of a threat. When they are shown getting high, they laugh hysterically, everything starts to speed up, and their vision (and ours) becomes distorted. (Must have been some *really* good weed!) The writing team responsible for this mess was Richard Gautier, who was best known as Hymie the Robot on *Get Smart!*, and *Hollywood Squares* host Peter Marshall. One wonders if the two of them weren't sitting around getting stoned with Paul Lynde and Rose Marie in between *Square* tapings when they came up with the idea of doing a modern-day version of *Reefer Madness*.

"Where were you in '62?"

Nostalgia is defined as a bittersweet longing for someone, something, or some place in the past. Derived from the Greek root *nostros* (one's homeland) and *algos* (pain/longing), the term "nostalgia" was coined by a Swiss doctor, Dr. Johannes Hofer, in 1688. In his medical dissertation, Hofer described nostalgia as a medical condition "originating from the desire to return to one's native land" (what we might today call "homesickness") that at the time was afflicting students, domestics, and soldiers who were away from home. In addition to an obsessive longing for their native land, patients exhibited a variety of physical and psychological symptoms, including nausea, loss of appetite, fever, depression, and suicidal thoughts. Some even reported to have heard voices of a loved one coming out of another person's mouth. Apparently nostalgia was contagious because once Hofer identified the disease and its symptoms, an epidemic broke out throughout Europe. There were also reported cases of "feigned nostalgia" by soldiers wishing to return home.[83]

In modern times, homesickness is no longer considered an illness or disease. A homesick individual doesn't need to see a doctor or be treated with opium and leeches. He or she can usually get immediate relief by punching a few numbers into a cell phone and talking to a loved one back home.

The word "nostalgia" also has a completely different connotation. The term nostalgia is now defined as a longing for the past—a desire to return, for example, to a specific place, which is certainly possible, at a specific point in time, which, of course, is not. Consequently, nostalgia is often bittersweet. There can be a hint of sadness in even the fondest of memories because time travel only happens in science-fiction books. The past is inaccessible.

In the early to mid-1970s, a wave of nostalgia permeated American culture. Fashions from the 1940s made a comeback; women were once again wearing wedgies and platform shoes, fur scarves, and striped skirts. For men it was the "Great Gatsby" look: white hats and shoes, wide pants, slim jackets. Broadway paid homage to the Roaring Twenties with revivals of musicals from the period

(*No, No, Nannette* [1971], *Irene* [1973]) as well as musical tributes to the Ziegfeld Follies (*Follies* [1971]), the swing era (*Over Here!* [1974]), and 1950s rock 'n' roll (*Grease* [1972]). To varying degrees of success, prime-time television transported viewers back to the 1920s (*Chicago Teddy Bears* [1971]), the Great Depression (*The Waltons* [1971–1981], *The Manhunter* [1974–1975], *Paper Moon* [1974–1975], and the Eisenhower era (*Happy Days* [1974–1984], *Laverne and Shirley* [1976–1983]).

So how does one account for the public's fascination with the past? Why, to paraphrase entertainer Peter Allen, is "everything old" suddenly "new again"? As writer Gerald Clarke explained in his 1971 *Time* magazine essay, "The Meaning of Nostalgia," the current nostalgia craze is about more than making money. According to Clarke, this current preoccupation with the past would, in time, help Americans "dim or even erase memories of assassinations, wars, racial hatred and student riots from its vision of the '60s . . ."[84] In other words, nostalgia can help Americans forget the civil unrest and the tragic events of the past decade by being transported back to what they believed was a better place and time. Consequently, stage musicals, television series, and nostalgia-themed movies usually offered an idealized, and, therefore, distorted view of the past. Americans can forget about the turbulence of the mid- to late 1960s by revisiting those days when, as the older folks like to say, life was simpler and moving at a slower pace. But nostalgia has a selective memory. For most Americans who grew up in the 1950s, the decade was all about the hula hoop, Ozzie & Harriet, and James Dean, not Senator Joseph McCarthy, Emmett Till, and nuclear-weapons testing. We pick and choose the things we want to remember; the rest is left to the history books.

The Hollywood film industry's brand of nostalgia included a series of period films set in the 1920s (*The Great Gatsby* [1974],

At Long Last Love [1975], *The Great Waldo Pepper* [1975]), and the 1930s (*Paper Moon* [1973], *The Sting* [1973], *Chinatown* [1974]). In addition, there was a host of nostalgia-themed comedies and dramas with high-school and college-age protagonists, who were usually reaching an important crossroads in their lives. The narrative centers on an important moment or period in a teenager's life that serves as his or her entry point into adulthood.

Although the age of these characters range from the mid-teens through the early twenties, the nostalgic teen films of the early 1970s were not intended for a general audience. Their treatment of mature themes, such as sex, death, war, abortion, and homosexuality, made them more suitable for older ticket buyers. Under the new motion-picture rating system, established in 1968, the majority of these films were rated PG (Parental Guidance Suggested), though certain ones, like *Summer of '42* (1971) and *Buster and Billie* (1974), received an R (Children under 17 not admitted without parent or guardian) due to adult situations and nudity.

"You can't stay seventeen forever"

American Graffiti (1973) is the film that is credited, and rightfully so, with jump-starting the 1950s revival that would continue through the late 1970s. The virtually plotless narrative follows four friends— Steve (Ron Howard), Curt (Richard Dreyfuss), Terry, aka Toad (Charles Martin Smith), and John (Paul Le Mat)—over a fifteen-hour period on a Friday night in the fall of 1962. What's so special (and bittersweet) about this night is that on the following morning, Steve and Curt will be heading north to San Francisco to begin their freshman year of college. At various points in the evening, both guys have mixed feelings about leaving. Curt is afraid to leave his adolescence behind and start the next phase of his life, prompting Steve to remind him, "You can't stay seventeen forever." A few hours later, Steve has second thoughts about leaving his high-school sweetheart, Laurie (Cindy Williams), after she agrees to his suggestion that they see other people while he's away.

American Graffiti is loosely based on twenty-nine-year-old director George Lucas's experiences growing up in Modesto, Califor-nia. The story is set in early fall of 1962, a little over a year before the assassination of President Kennedy. The year is significant because, as Lucas explains:

[It was] the end of a political era, a sociological era, and a rock era. You have three eras coming to an end, and people have to change and the country has to change. You have to go from a warm, secure, uninvolved life into the later sixties, which was involvement, antiwar stuff, and a different kind of rock 'n' roll.[85]

During his high-school years, Lucas worked as a mechanic and entertained the idea of becoming a professional race car driver. *Graffiti* was inspired by Lucas's favorite activity on weeknights and weekends—cruising up and down the streets of Modesto in his car. As Lucas describes it, cruising was not just something kids did to pass the time, but "a significant event in the maturation of American youth. It's a rite of passage, a mating ritual. It's so American: the cars, the machines, the cruising for girls, and the whole society that develops around it."[86] Cruising also seems to have served as the structure for the film's loose-ly plotted narrative. Never knowing where their car will take them and who they will meet, the characters all land in places and situations they never expected: Toad gets the girl, a platinum blonde named Debbie (Candy Clark), while John, the king of cool, gets stuck riding around with a bratty preteen with a fresh mouth (Mackenzie Phillips, daughter of "Papa" John Phillips); Curt unintentionally helps a local gang, the Pharaohs, rob an arcade; and Laurie is nearly killed when she rides shotgun in a drag race and the car flips over and explodes.

The cast of *American Graffiti* was composed of mostly unknown actors; the one and only star of the film was the music. The sound-track includes forty-three golden oldies from the years 1955 to 1963. Some songs can be heard playing in the background, while others are featured more prominently, either to express the way a character is feeling or comment on the action, beginning with the opening song— the one that marked the birth of rock 'n' roll—"Rock Around the Clock" (which is appropriate, considering that the story takes place over the course of a mere fifteen hours). For example, when Curt first sees the beautiful blonde in the T-Bird (Suzanne Somers), who mouths to him the words "I love you," "Why Do Fools Fall in Love?" is playing on the car radio. As little Carol bids farewell to John, who gives her a peck on the cheek and something to remember him by, "Since I Don't Have You" plays over the radio. The film ends with the gang saying good-bye to Curt to the tune of "Goodnight, Sweetheart."

The rights to the music alone cost $90,000, more than 10 per-cent of *Graffiti*'s $775,000 budget. No one expected Lucas's little movie to gross over $50 million. The film's success proved that a film about teenagers could have a wide audience appeal. For those who can answer the question posed on the film's poster ("Where were you in '62?"), *American Graffiti* was a trip back in time. At the same time, the characters and situations still appealed to those who might have still been in diapers in '62.

The surprise success of *American Graffiti* marked the beginning of an all-out fifties/early sixties revival that would continue through to the late seventies, culminating with the release of the film version of *Grease* (1978), another blockbuster that grossed close to $100 million. While *Graffiti* and *Grease* are the two films that best exemplify Hollywood's contribution to the "nostalgia craze," there are other nostalgia-themed films produced during this period that paint a very different picture of the past.

The one film that was repeatedly compared to *American Graffiti* was the 1975 comedy-drama *Cooley High*. The film was distributed by A.I.P., which, at the time, was trying to exploit the urban, African-American film market with a string of "blaxploitation" horror and gangster films like *Blacula* (1972) and *Black Caesar* (1973). Amidst all the gunfire and blood there was this modest film about the friendship between two high-school students growing up in Chicago in 1964. Preacher (Glynn Thurman) is a well-read underachiever who aspires to be a Hollywood writer. His best friend, Richard "Cochise" Morris (Lawrence Hilton-Jacobs), is Cooley High's star basketball player. (Hilton-Jacobs would remain in high school for the next four years as one of Mr. Kotter's sweathogs on the TV sitcom *Welcome Back, Kotter* [1975–79]). The semi-autobiographical script was written by Eric Monte, who created the groundbreaking hit 1970s TV sitcom *Good Times*, which focused on an African-American family living in the Chicago projects. *Cooley High* later served as the basis for Monte's second series, *What's Happening!* (1976–1979), which is also a catchphrase repeated in the film.

On the surface, there are some similarities between the two films. Like *Graffiti*, *Cooley High*'s main characters are on the verge of adulthood, yet they are still not ready to stop partying, brawling, and screwing around. The film also features an oldies sound track with Motown hits by the Temptations, the Supremes, the Four Tops, Brenda Holloway, and Stevie Wonder. There's also a coda, which reveals the fate of both the male and female characters.

These similarities aside, to call *Cooley* a "black *American Graffiti*" diminishes the important role the film's setting and time period play in the lives of these characters. As Jack Slater observed in a *New York Times* article defending the film, *Cooley* "documents perhaps that last moment in American history—1964—when it was possible for young blacks to see color as simply one of the components of their personalities."[87] Slater adds that the film has "far more vitality and more variety than *Graffiti*," in which the kids seem "bored." At the same time, the film suggests that it's Preacher and Cochise's vitality in the form of joyriding and recklessness that is indirectly responsible for the sudden, tragic death of one of the characters. Still, there is something refreshingly honest about the friendship between the two main characters as well as the film's treatment of sexual themes. Unlike most teen films of this period, the characters aren't limited to talking about sex. Like real teenagers, they actually have it.

In his book *Yearning for Yesterday: A Sociology of Nostalgia*, Fred Davis identifies two types of nostalgia: "collective nostalgia," which encompasses all the sights, sounds, and objects from the past that are familiar and widely shared by the public, and "private nostalgia," which is specific to the individual (like the memory of the sound of your mother's laugh).[88] The nostalgia teen films of the early seventies can be divided along similar lines. The first group, the collective nostalgia teen films, which includes *American Graffiti*, *The Lords of Flatbush* (1974), *Cooley High*, *Grease*, *I Wanna Hold Your Hand* (1978), *September 30, 1955* (1978), *The Wanderers* (1979), and *The Hollywood Knights* (1980), are as much about the time period, which the filmmaker goes to great lengths to re-create, as the plot and characters. The setting and time period of most of these films are very specific: Chicago in 1964 (*Cooley High*), Brooklyn in 1957 (*The Lords of Flatbush*), the Bronx in 1963 (*The Wanderers*), and Hollywood in

1965 (*The Hollywood Knights*). The period is "authenticated" by the dialogue (words or catchphrases, current references), the art direction (scenery, locations, clothes, hairstyles), visual cues (a film title on a movie-theater marquee, a radio or TV program that's on in the background, etc.), and, of course, the sound track. Whether it's intentional or not, some filmmakers have a tendency to err on the side of excess and overstuff their films with iconography from the period, which usually results in a very self-conscious re-creation of the past.

Grease (both the Broadway show and the film) is a prime example of self-conscious nostalgia. *Grease* (as in "greaser") is a slang term from the late 1950s/early 1960s for a tough, white, working-class guy, who greased back his hair, liked to work on cars, and was assumed by most adults to be a hoodlum. It's also indicative of how the film/show defined the era primarily through popular culture and trends. For example, Rizzo (Stockard Channing) makes fun of Goody Two-shoes Sandy (Olivia Newton-John) by equating her to screen virgin Sandra Dee when she sings "Look at me, I'm Sandra Dee, lousy with virginity." Frenchy (Didi Conn) wishes she had a guardian angel to tell her what to do "like in those Debbie Reynolds movies." Sure enough, he appears in the form of fifties/sixties teen idol Frankie Avalon. To appeal to the audience members who were actually around in 1959, all the adults in the film are played by television veterans from the fifties and sixties, like Joan Blondell, Edd Byrnes, Sid Caesar, Dody Goodman, and Eve Arden, who does a variation of her wisecracking character from *Our Miss Brooks*.

The public's interest in "collective nostalgia" is put to the test when studios insist on producing a sequel to a successful nostalgia film. *Grease 2* was released in 1982 and suffered a similar fate as the sequel to *American Graffiti*, aptly titled *More American Graffiti*, which was released in 1979, six years after the original. Assuming the public wanted to see more of the same, the creative team behind *Grease 2* thought it was enough to pull the ole gender switcheroo. In *Grease* it's a member of the T-Birds, Danny (Travolta), who falls for Sandy (Olivia Newton-John), the virgin from down under, but this time around it's Pink Lady Stephanie (Michelle Pfeiffer) who has her eye on Michael (Maxwell Caulfield), who's also Sandy's cousin. After an energetic opening number ("Back to School") choreographed by Patricia Birch, who also directed, the film takes a quick nosedive. *Grease 2* is just a rehash of *Grease*, so after a while you start waxing nostalgic for the original instead of what looks and sounds like a bus-and-truck version of the stage show. No matter how much money the first one made, *Grease* was apparently *not* still the word.

Even the original cast of *American Graffiti* (minus Richard Dreyfuss) couldn't save *More American Graffiti*. George Lucas served as executive producer, but his involvement in the project was limited. The story takes place on the same day (New Year's Eve) in four different time periods between the years 1964 and 1968: John is now a race car driver (1964); Toad is fighting in Vietnam (1965); Steve and Laurie, who are having marital problems, get caught in the middle of a campus antiwar protest (1967); and, in the weakest segment, Debbie is a flower child in San Francisco (1968). Each story is shot in a different cine-matic style: John's segment resembles a fifities widescreen color film; Toad's is in 16mm (resembling the footage of Vietnam shown on the nightly news); Steve and Laurie's is in a pseudo-documentary style; and Debbie's is with multiple screens (a technique popularized by the docu-mentary *Woodstock*). The end result confirmed the decision made by Lucas's collaborators on the original screenplay, Gloria Katz and Willard Huyck, not to be involved in the project. "The story, when continued," Huyck explained, "is sort of sad and awful, very painful. Not only that, the period is more serious. No way I wanted to get involved with it."[89] Unlike *Grease 2, More American Graffiti* was not simply more of the same. The nation's political, social, and cultural climate changed radically after 1959, which warranted a more dramatic shift in the film's tone. So what seemed bittersweet and charming in the first film came off as superficial in the second.

The concept of a "private-nostalgia teen film" seems like a contradiction in terms. Can a person, place, or thing that has special meaning to one individual also mean something special to a theater full of strangers? One of the challenges writers who base their work on their own experiences face is how to effectively and artistically put their story onto the screen so it will be understood and appreciated by an audience. It's no surprise that so many writers who are up to the challenge choose to write about their teenage years and reflect upon those defining moments that occur between adolescence and adulthood.

The private-nostalgia teen films of the early 1970s were less concerned with re-creating the time period and more concerned with communicating the confusion and mixed emotions of their teenage protagonists. *Summer of '42* (1971), *A Separate Peace* (1972), *Ode to Billy Joe* (1976), and *Fraternity Row* (1977) all feature either voice-over narration by an adult who is reflecting back on his or her past (in *Ode to Billy Joe*, the title ballad sung by Bobbie Gentry is presumed to be the voice of Billy Joe's girl, Bobbie Lee (Glynnis O'Connor)). The opening narration signals that the story that's about to unfold is a bittersweet memory about losing one's virginity (*Summer of '42*), or losing a close friend (*A Separate Peace, Fraternity Row*), or a loved one (*Ode to Billy Joe*). The opening credits of both *Summer of '42* and *Ode to Billy Joe* consist of weathered photographs of the people and places that appear in the film. In *A Separate Peace*, which is based on the novel by John Knowles, the narrator, the adult Gene, returns to his old school (much like Tom Lee in the film version of *Tea and Sympathy*) and revisits the tree that then will play a central role in his tragic tale of friendship and betrayal.

Nostalgia is considered a conservative "mode" because it idealizes the past in order divert the public's attention away from current or recent events. But not all nostalgia films paint a rosy picture of yesteryear; some reflect on it as a means of critiquing current conservative values. For example, the 1974 film *Our Time* was released shortly after the Supreme Court handed down its historic 1973 decision in the case of *Roe v. Wade*, which legalized abortion in the United States. In the film, two young women, Abigail (Pamela Sue Martin) and Muffy (Betsy Slade), who are best friends and roommates at a strict, all-girls boarding school in 1955, are confronted with the issue when Muffy gets pregnant. She expects the worst when she arranges to have a backroom abortion. Much to her surprise (and ours), the abortionist is not some creepy old doctor, like the one Janet is rescued from in *Blue Denim*, but a handsome, sympathetic medical student (Robert Walden). He gives her tea, sympathy, and an explanation for why he performs abortions, which echoes the liberal argument that had been made for its legalization: "I think every woman should have a right to choose whether she wants to bring a life into the world." But the film confirms the necessity for making abortion safe and legal by having an illegal procedure that by all appearances seemed safe and easy be the cause of poor Muffy's death.

Another film that was misunderstood at the time of its release was *Ode to Billy Joe*, which solved the mystery surrounding the death of Billy Joe McAllister, who, in Gentry's song, inexplicably jumped off the Tallahatchie Bridge. In the film, Billy Joe (Robby Benson) jumps off the bridge because he had a homosexual experience with an older man, Dewey Barksdale (James Best), and is then impotent when his girlfriend Bobbie Lee is finally ready to sleep with him. Gay activists no doubt felt that a film about a young man hurling himself off a bridge because he had one homosexual experience was perhaps sending the wrong message. At the time, gays and lesbians were more visible than ever publicly fighting for the repeal of sodomy and anti-discrimination laws around the country. They would soon find themselves on the defense against the Christian Right and activists like Florida orange-juice peddler Anita Bryant, who successfully led a campaign to repeal a civil-rights law in Dade County, Florida, that prohibited discrimination on the basis of sexual orientation. But Billy Joe jumping off the bridge is only half the story. In the final scene, Bobbie Lee actually displays compassion and tolerance toward Dewey Barksdale, who was ready to turn himself into the authorities for being indirectly responsible for Billy Joe's death. Bobbie Lee talks him out of it, in part to protect Billy Joe, though her basic attitude is that nothing good will come of it if Dewey reveals what transpired.

America's obsession with the past eventually subsided, and teen movies shifted their attention back to the present just in time to tackle a whole new set of issues that teenagers were confronted with in the eighties.

Nicholas Ray (right)
directing Natalie
Wood and James Dean
on the set of *Rebel
Without a Cause*
(1955). © Corbis

Johnny (Troy Donahue)
and Molly (Sandra
Dee) go "all the way"
in *A Summer Place*
(1959). © Corbis

Fun in the sun: Annette Funicello and Frankie Avalon got the beach-film cycle rolling with *Beach Party* (1963). © Corbis

Where were you in '62?: An *American Graffiti* (1973) cast reunion in 2001 included (L to R, front row) writer Gloria Katz, writer/director George Lucas, writer Willard Huyck, and (L to R, back row) Charles Martin Smith (Toad), Richard Dreyfuss (Curt), Candy Clark (Debbie), Mackenzie Phillips (Carol), Bo Hopkins (Joe), Cindy Williams (Laurie), and Paul Le Mat (John). © Corbis

Boys will be boys: In *Porky's* (1982), Billy (Mark Herrier) (left) and Tommy (Wyatt Knight) get caught peeking into the girls' shower room. Photo courtesy of Twentieth Century–Fox. © Hulton Archive/Getty Images

In *Fast Times at Ridgemont High* (1982), virginal Stacy (Jennifer Jason Leigh) (left) gets sex tips from the more experienced Linda (Phoebe Cates). © Hulton Archive/Getty Images

Jennifer (Ally Sheedy) and David (Matthew Broderick) fall in love and save the world in the box-office smash *WarGames* (1983). Photo courtesy of MGM/UA Entertainment. © Corbis

Gen-Xers (L to R) Troy (Ethan Hawke), Lelaina (Winona Ryder), Vickie (Janeane Garofalo), and Sammy (Steve Zahn) shop for munchies at a local convenience store in *Reality Bites* (1994). Photo courtesy of Universal Studios. Photo by Van Redin. © Corbis

"Hello, Sid-ney!": *Scream* (1996) heroine Sidney (Neve Campbell) (left) receives another disturbing phone call as Tatum (Rose McGowan) listens in. © Corbis

Boyz n the Hood director John Singleton, who at twenty-four became the youngest film director to be nominated for an Academy Award, receiving a star on the Hollywood Walk of Fame in 2003. © Corbis

American Pie (1999) eaters (L to R) Jim (Jason Biggs), Oz (Chris Klein), and Vicky (Tara Reid) with director Paul Weitz. © Corbis

From tween to mean: Lindsay Lohan attending the Los Angeles premiere of *Mean Girls* (2004). © Corbis

The birth of the Brat Pack: *The Breakfast Club*'s (1985) (L to R) Judd Nelson, Ally Sheedy, Emilio Estevez, Molly Ringwald, and Anthony Michael Hall.
© Hulton Archive / Getty Images

"Like, Totally Serious":

"Nice, normal kids living ordinary lives"

"It *was* the bogeyman"

Boys Will Be Boys

Getting Serious

The Brat Pack

"Stubborn little troupers"

War and Peace

"I want my MTV!"

The teen films released before 1970 were mostly low-budget B-films produced by independent companies like Allied Artists and A.I.P. Like the other B-genres (the horror film, film noir, the Western, et al.), teenpics could be shot quickly and cheaply, didn't require a major star, and were relatively easy to market to young audiences. Once a cycle, like the teen horror films of the fifties or the beach-party musicals of the sixties, caught on with young audiences, the bigger studios sprung into action. Columbia Pictures, Twentieth Century–Fox, and Universal–International started producing their own teen exploitation films, which stuck relatively close to the "formula" in terms of plots, characters, and settings established by the indie companies.

The nostalgic teen films of the 1970s proved that teen movies didn't have to be wholesome and fluffy to be profitable. The success of *American Graffiti* took everyone by surprise (including Universal), but it wasn't the only "adult" teen film in the early 1970s to have moviegoers lining up in front of the box office. The coming-of-age drama *Summer of '42* was the surprise hit of 1971, earning $20.5 million in film rentals. Max Baer, Jr., who was best known to audiences as Jethro on *The Beverly Hillbillies*, struck it rich again ("oil that is, black gold, Texas tea") with a pair of indie hits in the 1970s. Baer produced, co-wrote, and played a supporting role in *Macon County*

Line (1974). Set in Georgia in 1954, the story focuses on two Northern boys traveling around the South before going into the service who are mistakenly accused of murdering the wife of a nasty sheriff (Baer). The film cost $225,000 and grossed $18.7 million at the box office. Three years later, Baer directed *Ode to Billy Joe*, which had a higher budget (around $1.1 million) and took in over $20 million at the box office. Another actor/director, Tom Laughlin, whose low-budget biker film, *The Born Losers*, made a killing at the box office back in 1967, repeated his success in 1971 with the sleeper *Billy Jack*, and its sequel, *The Trial of Billy Jack* (1974), which earned a combined total of over $70 million in rentals.

Hoping to repeat the success of *American Graffiti*, some studio executives decided to devote all their time and money to making low-budget films. Unfortunately, their strategy didn't pay off. MGM president James T. Aubrey, who strictly enforced a "make no movie over $2 million" rule, was forced to step down in November 1973, after a string of box-office flops, which included *The Man Who Loved Cat Dancing*, *Pat Garrett and Billy the Kid*, *Shaft in Africa*, *Slither*, and *Wicked, Wicked* (all 1973). Some executives, like Sid Sheinberg at MCA, Inc., were skeptical all along. "You can bleed to death from a series of small wounds," Sheinberg told the *Wall Street Journal*, "as easily as you can die of a large wound. What looks like safety with a group of smaller films is really illusory."[90]

Encouraged by the success of several mainstream genre films in the early 1970s, such as *Airport* (1970), *Love Story* (1970), *The Godfather* (1972), and *The Poseidon Adventure* (1972), the latter of which cost $4.5 million and grossed $143 million worldwide, studios started to put their money into big-budget movies, which had a better chance of turning a large profit. As film historian David A. Cook explains, "The conviction grew that the industry had experienced a cataclysmic market shift in which only a few films each year (perhaps one in ten) would make big profits, while the rest would break even or produce losses. History suggested that pictures with big budgets had the best chance of succeeding in a volatile market. . . ."[91] An August 1974 article in the *Wall Street Journal*, entitled "The Spectaculars," declared that "the big-budget, old-time cinematic spectacle filled with high-priced stars, throngs of extras, and eye-popping visual and aural excitement is back."[92]

Big-budget movies, known in the industry as "blockbusters," were still considered risky. Less than ten years earlier, Twentieth Century–Fox, the studio responsible for hits like *The French Connection* (1971) and Irwin Allen's *The Poseidon Adventure*, had almost gone under thanks to expensive flops like the $18 million *Dr. Doolittle* (1967) and the $14 million *Star!* (1968), a biopic starring Julie Andrews as Gertrude Lawrence. But this time around, the studios were planning to keep their budgets under control. Nineteen seventy-four's big-screen spectacular, *Earthquake*, cost Universal only $6.5 million, and Twentieth Century–Fox and Warner Brothers went "Dutch" on the $12.5 million tab for *The Towering Inferno* (1974).

The blockbuster approach to making movies, particularly those that were heavy on special effects, made fiscal sense considering the age range of their primary audience. According to a survey conducted in the early 1980s by the Motion Picture Association of America, three-quarters of movie admissions were purchased by individuals between the ages of twelve and twenty-nine. Although only 23 percent of the population was going to the movies regularly (more than twelve times a year), they were buying 86 percent of all tickets.[93] The number of tickets sold, coupled with the success of the blockbusters, indicated that the core of the American film audience was teenagers and twentysomethings. The realization that teenagers were a loyal and lucrative market would change the look and feel of Hollywood movies and open the doors for a series of teenpics—horror films, sex comedies, high-school dramas, et al.—that focused on the lives of contemporary American teenagers.

The backstory behind what critic Jonathan Bernstein dubbed "the golden age of teen movies" begins "a long time ago, in a galaxy far, far away" with the nationwide opening of a sci-fi flick called *Star Wars* on May 25, 1977.[94] The success of George Lucas's sci-fi adventure, which combined old-fashioned storytelling with technological wizardry, was unprecedented. By July 4, the film grossed over $30 million; two weeks later, that total had more than doubled. By mid-August, *Star Wars* had reached the $100 million mark faster than any other film in the history of Hollywood. *Star Wars* eventually surpassed Steven Spielberg's *Jaws* (1975) to become the highest-grossing film of all time. According to Lucas's biographer, Dale Pollack, the success of *Star Wars* was due to a combination of strong word of mouth; the film's wide appeal as escapist entertainment, which cut across ethnic and economic barriers; and the fact that in 1977 one out of twenty people had seen the film more than once.[95] Most of the repeat business was male teenagers and college-age students, who were willing to shell out another three bucks to take a ride on the Millennium Falcon for a second and sometimes even a third time.

The success of *Jaws* (1975) and *Star Wars* confirmed that the "blockbuster school of filmmaking" could potentially reap huge profits. To protect their investment, studios started to spend more money on marketing (Fox's campaign for *Alien* [1979] exceeded the film's $13 million budget by $5 million) and, whenever possible, put more emphasis on the "bankability" of a film's star or stars. In some instances, a big name over the title was not necessary and didn't guarantee big bucks at the box office (Sir Alec Guinness was the only name

The Top Ten Moneymakers of the 1970s and 1980s

Based on North American Film Rentals

1970–1979: Total Film Rentals

1. *Star Wars* (1977): $193.8 million
2. *Jaws* (1975): $129.5 million
3. *Grease* (1978): $96.3 million
4. *The Exorcist* (1973): $88.5 million
5. *The Godfather* (1972): $86.3 million
6. *Superman* (1978): $82.8 million
7. *Close Encounters of the Third Kind* (1977): $82.8 million
8. *The Sting* (1973) $78.2 million
9. *Saturday Night Fever* (1977): $74.1 million
10. *National Lampoon's Animal House* (1978): $70.9 million

1980–1989 Total Film Rentals

1. *E.T.: The Extra-Terrestrial* (1982) $ 228.1 million
2. *Return of the Jedi* (1983): $169.1 million
3. *Batman* (1989): $150.5 million
4. *The Empire Strikes Back* (1980): $141.6 million
5. *Ghostbusters* (1984): $132.7 million
6. *Raiders of the Lost Ark* (1981): $115.6 million
7. *Indiana Jones and the Last Crusade* (1989): $115.5 million
8. *Indiana Jones and the Temple of Doom* (1984): $109 million
9. *Beverly Hills Cop* (1984): $108 million
10. *Back to the Future* (1985): $105.5 million

Source: Susan Sackett, *Box Office Hits* (Rev. Edition). NY: Watson-Guptill, 1996.

actor in the *Star Wars* cast); yet it did, at the very least, improve a film's chances of having a strong opening weekend.

There were other factors that made a marketing executive's job much easier when it came to selling a blockbuster. Most blockbusters were genre pictures, like sci-fi (*Star Wars*, *Close Encounters of the Third Kind* [1977]) and disaster films (*Earthquake*, *The Towering Inferno*), so they were generally easier to market to a film-savvy public. The same was true for sequels as well as remakes, such as *King Kong* (1976) and *A Star is Born* (1976). Seven of the ten highest-grossing films of the seventies were followed by sequels (half of them by two or more sequels). In the eighties, *E.T.: The Extra-Terrestrial* was the only film in the top ten that was not followed by one or more sequels (both sequels to *Raiders of the Lost Ark* were also in the top ten).

The changes that rocked the film industry in the seventies were not limited to film production. The suburban drive-ins, which were the primary site of exhibition in the postwar period, were replaced in the sixties and seventies by multiplex theaters. Theaters with three or more screens became a staple of the outdoor shopping center and, beginning in the late seventies, the indoor shopping mall. More screens meant more choices, particularly for teenagers, who in the eighties divided their time between home, school, and the mall. After fiddling with the gag toys in Spencer Gifts, trying on jeans at Chess King, and hanging out in the arcade, teenagers still had enough money in their pocket to see a film. Historian Timothy Shary attributes the rise of "teenpics" in the eighties to the increased demand by young moviegoers. "Given the categorical choices offered by the multiplex theatre," Shary writes, "teens in the eighties were then able to go to the mall and select the particular youth movie experience that most appealed to them, and

Hollywood tried to keep up with changing teen interests and styles to ensure ongoing profits."[96]

Another reason for the influx of teen movies in the eighties was the success of several youth-oriented films, beginning in 1978 with *Grease* and the R-rated *National Lampoon's Animal House*. A predecessor to the "gross-out" teen sex comedies like *American Pie* (1999), *Animal House* is a nostalgic homage to fraternity living circa 1962, when having fun meant food fights, toga parties, getting laid, and raising hell (even when your house is on "double secret probation"). The campus comedy, which took in $70 million at the box office, launched the all-too-short film career of *Saturday Night Live*-er John Belushi, who died four years later from a drug overdose at the age of thirty-three, and elevated twenty-seven-year-old director John Landis to the A-list.

Four years later, American audiences were treated to an even cruder comedy about the horny hi-jinks of high-school students in the fifties. *Porky's* (1982) turned out to be the most successful (and the raunchiest) film to date in Canadian film history. It was also considered by the majority of critics, to quote *Variety*'s review, "one of the grossest [films] ever released by a major studio under an R rating." Twentieth Century–Fox didn't seem to mind having its name attached to a teen film that can best be described as one very, very long penis joke, and the film's R rating obviously didn't stop the seventeen-and-under crowd from sneaking into the theater. *Porky's* grossed over $100 million and spawned two sequels, *Porky's II: The Next Day* (1983) and *Porky's Revenge* (1985), which both put some extra change in Fox's pocket. The film would also inspire a glut of teen sex comedies, none of which came close to matching the success of the original film.

The teenpics of the eighties can be divided into three general categories: horror flicks, sex comedies, and "teen angst" films. These categories are by no means clear-cut. There is certainly plenty of overlap among the three in terms of characters, plots, and settings. For example, high school, the setting for most teen-angst dramas, also figures prominently in some slasher flicks and sex comedies. Slasher films are not about sex, though more kids get laid in horror films than in sex comedies. Unfortunately, sex is usually a prelude to getting knifed in the back or strangled to death.

The horror cycle of the eighties consisted mostly of slasher films in the same vein as *Halloween*, which, along with *Friday the 13th* (1980) and *A Nightmare on Elm Street* (1984), were the start of successful franchises that continue to this day (the recent *Freddy vs. Jason* [2003] pitted *Elm Street*'s and *Friday*'s killers against each other). But an overabundance of slasher titles in the early eighties, coupled with objections raised by critics over the genre's misogynistic portrayal of women, led to the genre's decline. Approximately one-third of the eighty-nine horror films produced in 1986 went straight to video.[97] Upon realizing that the genre's popularity was wearing thin, filmmakers injected more humor into the genre or made the murder sequences so graphic and excessive that films like *Slaughter High* (1986), *Return to Horror High* (1987), and *Sleepaway Camp II: Unhappy Campers* (1988) seemed more like parodies than the real thing. Filmmakers also added a little "spice" to the proceedings by utilizing "girls-only" settings like a cheerleading camp, a sorority house, or a slumber party that provided their young, nubile female characters the opportunity to flash their bare breasts to the predominantly male teenage audience. In addition to the "slasher comedies," there were also several comedies that were inspired by classical horror films like *The Wolfman* (*Teen Wolf* [1985], *Teen Wolf Too* [1987]) and *Dracula* (*Fright Night* [1985], *Once Bitten* [1985], and *Vamp* [1986]).

Another cycle of teen films that catered primarily to a young male audience was the teen sex comedy. The success of *Porky's* sparked a string of mostly low-budget comedies, which, as titles like *The Last American Virgin* (1982) and *Losin' It* (1983) suggest, were about guys obsessed with losing their virginity. With the exception of *Fast Times at Ridgemont High* (1982), the sexual desires of young women are rarely addressed, though older women offered their "services" to teenage male virgins on the road to manhood in films like the highly successful *Private Lessons* (1981) and its imitators, *Homework* (1982), *My Tutor* (1983), and *Class* (1983).

The "teen angst" film is the largest of the three categories because it encompasses a wide range of themes and genres, including romantic comedies, coming-of-age and juvenile delinquent dramas, musicals, as well as science, sports, and military-themed teen films. Although they are varied in terms of their subject matter, they all take the problems and pressures their teenage characters face very seriously.

"Nice, normal kids living ordinary lives"

In 1986, the Gallup Organization released the results of its latest Youth Survey, which measures the attitudes and behavior of young Americans. According to the 1985 survey, the beliefs and values of America's youth reflected the wave of conservatism ushered in by the 1980 election of Ronald Reagan. Although teenagers were, at first, critical of Reagan and the GOP during the economic recession of the early 1980s, they preferred Republican candidates to Democrats by a two-to-one margin. In the 1985 survey, President Reagan topped the list of men teenagers most admired.[98] The majority of teenagers also considered themselves religious. Ninety-five percent of the respondents indicated that they believed in God and 54 percent were likely to attend church (that's 14 percent higher than adults).

According to the Survey, fewer teenagers were experimenting and using marijuana. Twenty-three percent revealed that they had tried it, which is close to half of the percentage (41 percent) of those who admitted to doing the same back in 1979. Only 8 percent admitted to lighting up in the past month, a significant decrease from 27 percent back in 1979. The majority of teenagers also believed there should be tougher laws in place to prosecute people who deal and use drugs.

One of the more surprising results was in response to a question about homework: 40 percent of thirteen- to fifteen-year-olds and 50 percent of sixteen- to eighteen-year-olds admitted that they wanted their teachers to assign more homework.

"This is an exciting generation," remarked Youth Survey editor Robert Bezilla, "that seems able to combine the best of our old values and traditions and digest new movements and technology." Bezilla added that while American teenagers are often depicted in the news as defiant and troubled, most are "nice, normal kids living ordinary lives."[99]

In the affluent 1980s, money played a more important role in the "ordinary lives" of America's youth. One survey of college freshmen in the mid-eighties concluded that teenagers were more materialistic. Seventy percent of the respondents indicated that it is essential or very important to be "very well off financially" compared to 43.5 percent in 1967.[100] Teenagers were clearly eager to spend whatever money they had. According to a study by Teenage Research Unlimited, twenty-nine million teenagers spent an average of $80 a month on personal items in 1985 for a total sum of $28 billion.[101] Like the kids in *Fast Times at Ridgemont High*, many teenagers living in the suburbs were earning money after school and on weekends working at the local mall or for a fast-food chain. In May 1985, the Department of Labor reported that the jobless rate for white youth in April was 14.9 percent. For black teenagers, who resided primarily in urban areas, the rate was significantly higher—39 percent. President Reagan called joblessness among black teenagers "a national tragedy," and then in the same breath proposed a solution that would allow employers to pay young people a sub-minimum wage for the summer ($2.50 an hour instead of $3.35).[102]

The number of hours teenagers were working after school was also the cause for some concern. According to psychologists Ellen Greenberger and Laurence Steinberg, authors of *When Teenagers Work*, kids who spent more than fifteen hours per week behind a fast-food counter were more likely to fall behind at school. Flipping burgers and other mundane minimum-wage jobs could also potentially cause them to develop a negative attitude toward work.[103]

On the other hand, perhaps helping people "have it their way" was therapeutic for some teenagers in the 1980s, who, according to researchers, had some totally serious stuff on their minds. Gallup reported that four out of every ten teenagers felt peer pressure to go on dates and have boyfriends or girlfriends.[104] Less than a third said they felt pressure to have sex, though a worldwide poll conducted by *Teen Age* magazine the following year reported that sex is the most important issue facing American youth today, followed by drug abuse, alcoholism, suicide, teen pregnancy, and teen pornography and prostitution.[105] Compared to the other young participants in the poll from fifty-eight other countries, American teenagers also believed they will enjoy a higher standard of living than their parents and are in total control of their future.

But not all teenagers were so optimistic. Some of the data concerning drug abuse and teen suicide told an entirely different story. Drug use, particularly cocaine, was on the rise in the mid-eighties, prompting a Chanel-clad First Lady Nancy Reagan to generously take time out of her busy social calendar to launch her highly publicized "Just Say No" campaign.[106] According to the U.S. Department of Justice, 13.1 percent of sixteen thousand high-school students surveyed in 1985 admitted to using cocaine within the last year. But apparently some kids heard Nancy's message because the percentage of cocaine users dropped dramatically to 5.3 percent in 1990.[107]

Another alarming statistic was the suicide rate among American youth, which reached six thousand per year by 1989—three times as many as thirty years ago.[108] In 1987, teen suicides were second to accidents as the leading cause of death in the United States for fifteen- to twenty-four-year-olds.[109] Teenage suicide also became a front-page story in the eighties when a series of "cluster suicides" (suicides in the same community within a relatively short period of time) occurred around the country. In 1986, three youths in Omaha who attended the same school committed suicide within a five-day period. Between February 1983 and February 1984, seven teenagers in Plano, Texas, and five teenage boys in Westchester and Putnam counties in New York killed themselves. In 1987, two nineteen-year-old boys and two teenage sisters in Bergenfield, New Jersey, were found dead in an idling car parked in a closed garage filled with carbon monoxide. They left a note asking they be given a joint funeral and burial.[110] The only thing the experts could agree upon was that there is no one single, clear-cut reason why a teenager would choose to take his or her own life. The proposed list of possible causes includes bad grades, a break-up with a boyfriend or girlfriend, divorce, and rock-music lyrics.[111]

Echoing the protests launched against rock 'n' roll back in the fifties by concerned parents and religious leaders, the lyrics of current rock 'n' roll and heavy metal music came under attack in the eighties. In 1985, a group of concerned Washington wives, led by Tipper Gore, wife of Democratic senator Al Gore, expressed their concerns to a Senate subcommittee, which held hearings to determine what if anything should be done to regulate the sale of music with obscene or objectionable lyrics to minors. Ms. Gore was one of the founding members of the Parents Music Resource Center, which advocated the placement of warning labels on CDs. Among the recording artists who defended their First Amendment rights as artists before the subcommittee were Twisted Sister's Dee Snider, Frank Zappa, and John Denver, who came under attack back in 1973 when his song about the beauty of the Colorado Rockies, "Rocky Mountain High," was interpreted as a "pro-drug" song. Recording artists and record executives were also afraid some stores would refuse to sell certain CDs and deejays might choose not to play certain songs. When Congress passed the Children Protection and Obscenity Enforcement Act in 1988, which made retailers liable for the content of every song they sold, the RIAA (Record Industry Association of America) gave in and agreed to put "Parental Advisory: Explicit Lyrics" stickers on their product. As some predicted, the "Tipper Stickers" made it all the easier for young consumers to find CDs with explicit lyrics and opened the door for state legislators to start regulating the sale of music to minors.

The U.S. government's interference in the lives of young people was not limited to song lyrics. At a time when teenagers were more sexually active than ever, the Reagan administration put the youth of America at risk for unwanted pregnancies, STDs, and AIDS by publicly opposing the distribution of contraception to teenagers. Reagan disagreed with the findings of a congressionally chartered study recommending "contraceptive services should be available to all teenagers at low or no cost." Secretary of Education William Bennett dismissed the recommendation made by the panel's chairman, Dr. Daniel Federman of Harvard Medical School, to distribute condoms and pills at school-based clinics as "a dumb policy . . . that will damage our schools and our children."[112] When White House spokesman Larry Speakes was asked by a reporter how the president expects teenagers to avoid getting pregnant, he borrowed a phrase from Nancy Reagan's drug campaign and replied, "Just say no." Such ignorance, which pervaded public policy during the Reagan years, prompted Faye Wattleton, president of Planned Parenthood, to point out that "Just saying no prevents teenage pregnancy the way 'Have a nice day' cures chronic depression."[113]

Wattleton and every parent in the country had reason to be concerned because more teenagers were having sex and at a younger age. The percentage of men who had sexual intercourse by the age of eighteen increased from 64 percent in 1980–1982 to 73 percent in 1986–1988. In 1988, 25 percent of sexually experienced teens between the ages of fifteen and nineteen had sex several times a week, 19 percent had it once a week, and 33 percent had it two to three times a month.[114] With the advent of AIDS education, the use of contraception improved between 1982 and 1988, yet only 53 percent of young people between seventeen and a half and nineteen years of age admitted to using a condom the last time they had sex. Even in the middle of a health crisis, when sexually active teenagers were putting themselves at risk by not practicing safe sex, the so-called religious right (an oxymoron if there ever was one) was advocating abstinence-only sex education. They believed teaching kids about birth control was encouraging them to engage in sexual behavior, a conclusion for which there is no evidence.

"It *was* the bogeyman"

On October 28, 1978, American film audiences came face-to-face with a menacing, knife-wielding, masked killer named Michael Myers. "[He has] no reason, no conscience, no understanding," explains his doctor, Sam Loomis (Donald Pleasance), "of even the most rudimentary sense of life or death, good or evil, right or wrong." His intended victim in the first film in the *Halloween* series is a studious high-school student named Laurie Strode (Jamie Lee Curtis), who we later learn in the film's sequel, *Halloween II* (1981), is Michael's younger sister. But the siblings' reunion is not a happy one. Michael terrorizes Laurie for nearly half an hour before Dr. Loomis arrives on the scene and saves her. Laurie, who is understandably in a total state of shock, then utters the now famous line, "It *was* the bogeyman." *Halloween* and the genre it spawned, the slasher film, would not only tap into our childhood fears of the bogeyman, but takes us places and show us things that were more horrific than anything a child could possibly imagine.

The victims in most slasher films are teenagers, who at the time are usually in a highly vulnerable place both emotionally and physically, so they are often set in an isolated location, like a summer camp (*Friday the 13th* [1980], *The Burning* [1981], the *Sleepaway Camp* series [1983, 1988, 1989], *Cheerleader Camp* [1987]), or a less remote setting where a teenager's anxiety level can be high, like at school (*Student Bodies* [1981], *Night School* [1981], *Slaughter High* [1986], *Cutting Class* [1989]). And when there's a maniac on the loose, a high-stress situation, like taking an exam or pledging a fraternity, can be all the more stressful (*Final Exam* [1981], *Hell Night* [1981], *The Initiation* [1984], *Rush Week* [1989]), or throw a wet blanket on a holiday celebration (*April Fool's Day* [1986], *Don't Open 'Til Christmas* [1984], *Silent Night, Deadly Night* [1984]) or a day or evening that's supposed to be a fun or special occasion (*Prom Night* [1980], *Graduation Day* [1981], *Happy Birthday to Me* [1981], the *Slumber Party Massacre* films [1982, 1987, 1990]).

The slasher film also tapped into the fear and anxiety (both the real and the media-induced) that permeated American teenage life in the eighties. Teenagers seemed to enjoy watching one of their own being chased through the woods by a madman or hacked to death with a butcher's knife. Watching a slasher film, particularly when it's well-crafted, can be a cathartic experience, which probably accounts for their popularity with teenagers, who are always looking for a legitimate outlet other than sports for relieving some of the stress they feel on a daily basis. Perhaps the teenager sitting in the audience might think his or her problems are not so bad compared to what the kids up on the screen are going through. Or maybe they force teenagers to face some of their repressed childhood fears, like being abandoned by their parents, who are seldom around in slasher movies (and when they are, offer their kids little help or protection).

Slasher films have been criticized for their misogyny. They take their audience on an emotional roller-coaster ride at the expense of one or more female characters, who are hunted down, battered, and bruised, all for the audience's entertainment. But feminists have also recognized that unlike other action-oriented genres, the lone survivor in most of these films—the one who has the smarts to escape, fight back, and often defeat the killer—is a female. Sally (Marilyn Burns) in *The Texas Chainsaw Massacre* (1974), Laurie in *Halloween*, Alice (Adrienne King) in *Friday the 13th*, and Nancy Thompson (Heather Langenkamp) in *A Nightmare on Elm Street* are all what feminist critic Carol Clover calls "the final girl":

The image of the distressed female most likely to linger in memory is the image of the one who did not die: the survivor, or Final Girl. She is the one who encounters the mutilated bodies of her friends and perceives the full extent of the preceding horror and of her own peril; who is chased, cornered, wounded; whom we see scream, stagger, fall, rise, and scream again. She is abject terror personified. If her friends knew they were about to die only seconds before the event, the Final Girl lives with the knowledge for long minutes or hours. She alone looks death in the face, but she alone also finds strength either to stay the killer long enough to be rescued (ending A) or to kill him/her (ending B). But in either case, from 1974 on, the survivor figure has been female.[115]

The first and unquestionably the best of the slasher films, *Halloween* established the subgenre's basic ingredients that the film's countless imitators would soon follow: a young, highly intelligent female protagonist, a homicidal maniac, a pack of horny and/or sexually active teenagers, and one very sharp knife or ax. One reason why filmmakers initially stuck so close to the formula is that *Halloween* is a genuinely creepy and scary movie. The second reason is purely financial. *Halloween* cost approximately $325,000 and subsequently earned $18.5 million in film rentals and grossed around $47 million at the box office, making it at the time the most successful independent movie to date.

While *Halloween* is credited (and rightfully so) for ushering in a whole new subgenre of the American horror film, its roots are in the psychological horror films of the 1960s, such as Alfred Hitchcock's *Psycho* (1960), which is best remembered for the forty-five-second montage of Curtis's mom Janet Leigh getting hacked to death in the shower; and *Peeping Tom*, the 1960 cult horror classic that nearly ended the career of A-list British director Michael Powell. The killer in *Peeping Tom* is a deeply disturbed young German (Carl Boehm), whose father, a behavioral psychologist, used him as a human guinea pig in his experiments on scopophilia ("the desire to look"). Now

Mark is the one doing the looking as he uses the camera his father once used on him to photograph his female victims as he sticks a spike through their throats.

Another inspiration for the eighties slasher films were horror movies like *The Bad Seed* (1956), *The Other* (1972), and *The Omen* (1976), which all focused on demonic children who will use any means necessary to get what they want. Teenage killers were also featured in three films in the mid- to late seventies. The title character in George Romero's *Martin* (1978) thinks (and acts like) he's a vampire. In *Massacre at Central High* (1976), David (Derrel Maury), a psychotic transfer student, goes after a pack of so-called "cool kids" who terrorize the school. In Brian De Palma's successful screen version of Stephen King's *Carrie* (1976), a high-school outcast with telekinetic powers seeks revenge on her classmates who tease and humiliate her by turning their high-school prom into a bloodbath.

Unlike Carrie's tormentors or the ill-fated "cool kids" in *Massacre*, *Halloween*'s Michael Myers's three victims—Annie (Nancy Loomis), Lynda (P. J. Soles), and Lynda's boyfriend Bob (John Michael Graham)—have no connection to the killer and haven't done anything wrong, though critics have suggested that perhaps their early demise was punishment for their "vices," namely getting high and getting laid. While driving herself and Laurie to their respective babysitting jobs, Annie pulls out a joint and lights up in the car (Laurie takes a hit too). She later drops off the kid she is sitting for with Laurie to go get her boyfriend so they can do you-know-what (her car never makes it out of the driveway because Michael is in the backseat waiting for her). Lynda and Bob are both killed after having sex, a motif in slasher films that critics have interpreted as the price you have to pay for engaging in premarital sexual relations (of course there are just as many victims, if not more, who don't have it). In *Friday the 13th* an unknown killer terrorizes a group of unsuspecting counselors in an isolated camp. Jack (Kevin Bacon) and Marie (Jeannine Taylor) get what they deserve immediately after doing it in an empty cabin. In Part II, Jason kills Mark (Tom McBride) and Vicky (Lauren Marie-Taylor) prior to their planned rendezvous. He makes a human shish kebab out of Jeff (Bill Randolph) and Sandra (Marta Kober) while the couple is in a postcoital embrace. In Part III, it's Debbie (Tracie Savage) and Andy (Jeffrey Rogers) who meet their maker after taking a tumble in a hammock.

Many critics found the genre's mindless mixture of sex and violence objectionable. Variety described *Friday the 13th* as "low budget in the worst sense—with no apparent talent or intelligence to offset its technical inadequacies . . . [the film] has nothing to exploit but its title." *Chicago Tribune* film critic Gene Siskel and his *Sneak Preview* co-host, *Chicago Sun-Times* critic Roger Ebert, gave *Friday* more than two thumbs down. Both critics were appalled by the gratuitous and excessive violence, so in October 1980, the duo devoted an entire show to the subject of "Extreme Violence Directed at Women," during which they demonstrated with film clips how the camera in slasher films often took the killer's point of view when stalking his or her victims. The real problem lies in how the acts of violence in these films were aimed at the independent, sexually liberated female characters (like Lynda in *Halloween*). Siskel, the more analytical of the two, sees the victimization of "independent" women in these films as a "primordial response" to the "growth of the women's movement in America in the last decade."[116] "The women in these films are typically portrayed as independent, as sexual, as enjoying life," Siskel explained, "and the killer, typically—not all of the time but most often—is a man who is sexually frustrated with these new aggressive women, and so he strikes back at them. He throws knives at them. He can't deal with them. He cuts them up, he kills them."[117]

Siskel also took issue with the top brass at Paramount Pictures for their decision to distribute a film as violent and exploitative as *Friday the 13th*. He called for a public boycott of Paramount's films, but apparently neither the studio nor the public listened or cared. *Friday the 13th* made a bundle at the box office, so in 1981 Paramount released the first in a long line of sequels and the Canadian-made *My Bloody Valentine*. In fact, with a record number of theatrical releases, 1981 turned out to be a banner year for the slasher film.

Ironically, both Siskel and Ebert had nothing but praise for the film that started it all, *Halloween*. Siskel called John Carpenter's film a "beautifully made thriller—more shocking than bloody—that will have you screaming with regularity." He justifies putting his thumb up by posing a rhetorical question to his readers: "What can be so good about a film involving a young man attacking young women?" Answer: "*Halloween* does not pander to the violence-prone. This film is only meant to thrill."[118] As Ebert, who is also a fan, explained in a 1982 article for *American Film* magazine entitled "Why Movie Audiences Aren't Safe Anymore," *Halloween* is superior to *Friday the 13th*, *Prom Night*, *Terror Train* (1980), and other slashers because Michael Myers is an established character, not some "faceless, usually unseen, unknown killer" who stalks innocent "people."[119]

The so-called "innocence" of the stalker's victims has been called into question by those who believe that teenagers get knocked off in slasher films as punishment for their "immoral" behavior. But not all of these teens are killed simply because they let their hormones get the best of anything. The killer targets them because they are linked, directly or indirectly, with a crime that had been committed in the past. In *Friday the 13th*, Mrs. Voorhees avenges the death of her son Jason, who drowned twenty years ago because two counselors were off

1981: The Year of the Slasher

In addition to the first in a long line of sequels for *Halloween* and *Friday the 13th*, 1981 offered horror fans an odd assortment of slasher films, many of which featured unknown actors who would go on to make a name for themselves in cinema and/or on television.

Bloody Birthday: Creepy slasher about a trio of evil tykes who go on a murder spree. No explanation is given for their behavior, except that they were all born during an eclipse. The eclectic cast includes Academy Award winner José Ferrer (*Cyrano de Bergerac*), Susan Strasberg, and MTV host/songstress Julie Brown ("The Homecoming Queen's Got a Gun").

The Burning: Cropsy, a caretaker at a boy's camp, is permanently disfigured by some campers when a prank backfires. Five years later, he's back to wreak havoc on Camp Stonewater. Sound familiar? The film marks the screen debuts of Jason Alexander (*Seinfeld* [1989–1998]), Fisher Stevens (*Short Circuit* [1986]), and future Academy Award–winner Holly Hunter (*The Piano* [1993]). Bob Weinstein, cofounder and co-owner of Miramax, collaborated on the story with director Tom Maylam.

Final Exam: It's exams week at Lanier College and a pretty coed named Courtney (Cecile Bagdadi) is finding it difficult to concentrate when there is a madman on the loose. Will Courtney survive? Will she pass history?

Graduation Day: Campy, cheesy slasher about a young woman who returns home to investigate the mysterious death of her sister, a high-school track star. Cast includes "scream queen" Linnea Quigley, future letter-turner Vanna White (as Doris, a high-school cheerleader), and Vanna's uncle, actor Christopher George, as a high-school track coach named George Michaels.

Happy Birthday to Me: Another birthday-themed slasher film starring Melissa Sue Anderson, best known as Laura Ingalls Wilder's blind, older sister Mary on *Little House on the Prairie.* Anderson plays Ginny, who belongs to a clique at a private school. Her friends are murdered one by one, but she's determined not to let it interfere with her upcoming eighteenth birthday party. Veteran film actor Glenn Ford plays Anderson's psychologist.

Hell Night: Whatever possessed Linda Blair to play a sorority girl who is forced to spend the night with three other pledges in an old house where there's a deformed killer running amok? Trapped in hell is right.

fooling around and didn't hear his cries. She murdered the counselors the following year and now, twenty years later, she figures the best way to keep the camp from reopening is to kill off the new staff, whom she also blames for her son's death. "You let him drown! You didn't pay attention!" she cries at a very confused Alice (Adrienne King), the only surviving counselor and the film's Final Girl. Then, in a Norman Bates moment (with the roles reversed), Mrs. Voorhees starts to engage in a little mother-and-son exchange with herself. In Jason's high-pitched, little boy voice, he tells his other half, "Kill her, Mommy! Don't let her get away!" In Part II, Jason comes back from the dead to avenge his mother's death. His first stop—Alice's house.

The guy who is keeping all the neighborhood kids up nights in *A Nightmare on Elm Street* is Freddy Krueger (Robert Englund), one of the walking dead who appears in his young victims' dreams and then proceeds to stalk and brutally kill them. The first to be shredded by Fred is Tina (Amanda Wyss), who falls asleep after having hot sex with her boyfriend Rod (Nick Corri). Rod is accused of the murders, but never gets a chance to clear his name. He falls asleep in his cell and with Freddy's help, hangs himself with a bedsheet. After Freddy liquefies hunky boyfriend Glenn (Johnny Depp), "final girl" Nancy (Heather Langenkamp) is left all alone to battle Freddy.

Like Mrs. Voorhees, Krueger's motives are clear. In his former life Freddy was a child murderer who was released by the authorities on a technicality. Some of the more civic-minded residents of Elm Street, led by Nancy's mother (Ronee Blakely), took justice into their own hands and doused the creep with gasoline and burned him alive. So now he's back and seeking revenge on their offspring. After a game of cat and mouse, Nancy defeats Freddy by wishing him away. "You're just a dream. You're not alive," she says, "You're nothing. You're shit." By confronting her fears, Nancy restores order to *Elm Street* (until the final tag, which opens the door for a sequel, in which Nancy helplessly watches Freddy attack her mom).

As with Michael's and Jason's victims, the kids who live on Elm Street are guilty by association. They are being punished for the mistakes, indiscretions, and acts of violence committed by the older generation who, with the exception of maybe *Halloween*'s Dr. Loomis, are ineffectual when it comes to helping teenagers battle these demons.

Sometimes it is personal, such as when the killer is seeking revenge on a specific group of people because they humiliated him (*Terror Train*) or were responsible for his sister's death (*Prom Night*). Jealousy is sufficient enough for most female killers, like the mascot who literally stabs a cheerleading squad in the back (*Cheerleader Camp*) or the actress who wants a part so badly she eliminates her competition (*Curtains* [1983]). But not all killers have a clear motive. Sometimes he or she might be just your run-of-the-mill violent schizophrenic who was let out of a mental institution prematurely (*Cutting*

Class) or a serial killer like Russ Thorn, who, the audience is told via a newspaper headline at the opening of *The Slumber Party Massacre* (1982), is an escaped "mass murderer of five."

Although the *Halloween*, *Friday*, and *Nightmare* franchises would continue into the 1990s, the genre had overstayed its welcome by the mid-eighties and many titles, *The Forest* (1983), *The Ripper* (1985) and *Half Past Midnight* (1988), could only be seen on video. Producers also started to make slasher films, like *Blood Cult* (1985), specifically for the home video market. Most of these films were cheaply produced with cheesy effects, a bad script, and amateurish acting. There was some effort made to inject more humor into their titles—*Student Bodies*, *Return to Horror High*, *Cutting Class*—or by making the killings' violence so excessive that it becomes campy.

A good example is the *Sleepaway Camp* trilogy, which started in 1983 as a more or less standard slasher film with a rather shocking and highly original ending. Five years later, two sequels were produced back-to-back and released theatrically, *Sleepaway Camp II: Unhappy Campers* in 1988, and *Sleepaway Camp III: Teenage Wasteland* in 1989. The killer in both films is an intolerant, moralizing counselor named Angela (Pamela Springsteen, sister of Bruce), who in what is considered the slasher tradition, kills anyone who doesn't measure up to her high moral standards (which is essentially anyone). The methods Angela uses to dispose of some of her fellow counselors combine the traditional means (slashing throat, stabbed in back, decapitated with machete, drilled in the head) with the more unconventional and, depending on your sense of humor, comical: drowning in an old outhouse (yuck!), firecracker exploding in a kid's nostrils (ouch!), shredding a head with a lawn mower (nasty!), throwing battery acid on a counselor's face (that burns!), and inhaling industry chemicals instead of cocaine (yikes!).

But slasher films were not the only teen films to mix elements of horror and comedy. There's nothing dark or terribly horrific about *Teen Wolf* (1985), which doesn't quite qualify as a remake of *I Was a Teenage Werewolf* because the only thing it borrows from the fifites classic is its premise. Michael J. Fox plays Scott Howard, a mediocre high-school basketball player and all-around nice guy who doesn't have much luck with girls until he discovers that he is descended from a long line of werewolves (his father is one too). But this father and son are not the kind of wolves who prey and ravage innocent people. He is still the same sweet old Scott, except he's covered with hair. As his father predicted, his problem works to his advantage and improves his game on the basketball court. But once he realizes that people only like him for his wolf-side, he proves—in one of those "feel good" endings involving the big championship game—that he's a winner even without his fangs.[120]

There are some genuinely scary moments In *Fright Night* (1985), which stars Roddy McDowell as a veteran character actor named Peter Vincent, who at one time was famous for playing a vampire killer in horror movies, but has since been reduced to hosting a local *Creature Features*–style TV program, from which he is fired. "The kids today don't have the patience for vampires," Vincent moans. "They want to see some mad slasher running about and chopping off heads." Having learned all there is to know about vampires from his movie days, Vincent once again assumes his onscreen persona when he's hired by a teenager (William Ragsdale), who is convinced his new neighbor (Chris Sarandon), is a vampire.

Some horror-comedies also added a little sex into the mix. In *Vamp* (1986), two fraternity pledges (Robert Rusler and Chris Makepeace) set out to find a stripper for a fraternity party. They end up in a strip joint where they encounter the head vamp, played by the entertainingly bizarre Grace Jones. In *Once Bitten*, Jim Carrey has a similar encounter with model/actress Lauren Hutton. She is a four-hundred-year-old vampire who is in danger of looking her age unless she drinks the blood of a male virgin three times. As Hollywood was still in its *Porky's* phase, the big twist is that it's not his neck she has to bite.

Boys Will Be Boys

According to Hollywood, there is no one single subject that pre-occupies the minds of the American male teenager more than sex. It doesn't matter if a guy is a virgin or has a few notches on his belt, life—when it all comes down to it—is all about getting laid.

Hollywood is well aware that most guys devote more of their waking hours thinking about you-know-what than actually doing it. So producers seized the opportunity to fill in that gap of time between "thinking" and "doing" and, in the process, take full advantage of the male teenager's hunger for a little titillation. Following the success of *Porky's*, a series of low-budget sex comedies were produced in the 1980s for a young male audience. While some sex comedies attempt to address the fears, self-doubt, and anxiety that often plague a teen-ager on the brink of manhood, the majority of them, like the male teenager characters themselves, have only one thing on their mind.

When Hollywood first acknowledged in the fififties that premarital sex was a fact of life, the treatment of sexual themes, particularly when teenagers were involved, was regulated by the Hollywood Production Code. The teens who were sexually active in dramas like *Blue Denim*, *Tea and Sympathy*, and *A Summer Place* all paid the price for their indiscretions, but once the Code was replaced by the current ratings system in 1968 movies were generally less chaste and apologetic when it came to sexual matters.

In *The Graduate* (1967), twenty-year-old Benjamin Braddock (Dustin Hoffman) is seduced by the wife of his father's business associate, Mrs. Robinson (Anne Bancroft). Although he insists he is not a virgin, his nervousness and awkward behavior, particularly just as they are about to hit the sheets, suggest otherwise. Their May-December affair, which is purely sexual, is soon complicated by his affection for her daughter, Elaine (Katherine Ross). Although *The Graduate* is best remembered for Mrs. Robinson's seduction of the somewhat nerdish Benjamin (and the Simon & Garfunkel song bearing her name), the box-office hit is not so much about sex as it is a commentary on sixties America and the younger generation's rejection of the elder's middle-class values, which are summarized in one word that's offered as a piece of advice to Benjamin at his graduation party—"plastics."

The young man-older woman scenario is also at the center of the 1969 Canadian comedy *The First Time*. A predecessor to the "I wanna get laid" comedies of the eighties, the film focuses on a teenager named Kenny (the doe-eyed Wes Stern), who makes the mistake of lying to his friends and telling them he regularly frequents a brothel in nearby Niagara Falls while he's staying with his grandparents in Buffalo. Before you know it, his pals Tommy (Wink Roberts) and Mike (Ricky Kelman) are in town and rarin' to go. Their search for the fictional brothel is sidetracked when they meet a beautiful British woman, Anna (Jacqueline Bisset) in a go-go bar. They mistake her for a prostitute, when in fact she was just using the pay phone to call the married man she's dating. After helping Anna cross the border into the States, they spend the day together sightseeing. Thinking it's time for them to each have their way with her, the guys let her take a nap in their hotel room. She finally realizes what they are up to as the guys start to come in one by one. Tommy and Mike both chicken out. The naive Kenny thinks she slept with the other two, so he is upset when she rejects him ("What's wrong with me?" he asks). But when Kenny shows his sensitive side and comforts Anna over her breakup with her married fella, she does what every red-blooded American (and Canadian boy) dreams about and makes him a man.

For a late-sixties comedy about getting laid, *The First Time* is, like its three young protagonists, a bit sheepish about the subject of sex. You never believe that these three fresh-faced, clean-cut teenagers, who all look as if they just stepped out of a Disney movie, have sex on their minds. Even when they enter the go-go bar and stop to ogle at one of the dancers, you suspect that the actors aren't entirely sure how they are supposed to react. The love scene between Stern and Bissett, who were actually only three years apart, is strictly for the kiddies, which is not surprising considering that director James Neilson's credits include TV's *Bonanza* and the Disney films *The Moonspinners* (1964) and *The Adventures of Bullwhip Griffin* (1967).

There is nothing remotely Disneyesque about *Porky's*, the Canadian comedy that popularized, for better or worse, the teen sex comedy in the eighties. Like *The First Time*, one of the subplots of *Porky's* revolves around the quest of one of the central characters, Pee Wee Morris (Dan Monahan), to lose his virginity. The film is set in a Florida beach community in the fifties, which adds a touch of nostalgia to a moment that's considered a turning point in any boy's life. The period setting also puts some distance between the audience and the characters, which in some instances is necessary to make their raunchy humor and hearing a word like "pussy" coming out of a teenager's mouth more palatable.

Porky's is hands down the raunchiest of them all. Like poor Pee Wee, who starts each day measuring his "morning wood" and recording any change in growth on a chart he hides under his bed, the film is obsessed with both male and female genitalia. The film's big scene, which is teased by the image on the film's poster of an eye peeking through a hole into the girls' shower, involves *Porky's* resident prankster, Tommy (Wyatt Knight), putting his "thing" through the hole, only to have it nearly torn off by the school's castrating gym teacher, Miss Balbricker (Nancy Parsons), who is better known as Beulah Ballbreaker. In the film's funniest moment, Miss Balbricker tries to convince Angel Beach High's harried Principal Carter (Eric Christmas) to allow her to inspect Tommy's—to use the principal's "less personal" term—"tallywacker" so she can identify him as the culprit. Parsons, a very talented and accomplished stage actress, manages to keep a straight face as she ignores the roar of laughter coming from the two male coaches as she nudges the principal closer and closer over the brink of hysteria.

Every few minutes, Pee Wee reminds his friends (and us) just how desperate he is to pop his cherry. The big moment arrives during the film's credit sequence when Pee Wee gets his seven minutes in heaven with Wendy (Kaki Hunter), who is supposedly the easiest girl in school (it's later revealed she's only been with two guys before Pee Wee and is actually in love with the little horn-toad). It all happens off-screen, so it's pretty anticlimactic (pun intended). But perhaps that's because Pee Wee couldn't compete with the far more entertaining climax that preceded it: the total destruction of Porky's, a roadside strip joint/whorehouse whose portly redneck proprietor (and namesake) humiliated the boys of Angel Beach High by disposing of them via a trapdoor into the lake that surrounds the establishment after they had paid their $30 in the hope of scoring.

Writer/director Bob Clark's screenplay consists of a string of mostly unrelated sexual gags that usually involve some form of sexual humiliation (e.g., a naive female freshman is coaxed by the older girls to ask Meat (Tony Ganios) how he got his name). Clark, who would go on to direct the far superior *A Christmas Story* (1983), admits his film is "vulgar" and "outrageous," but adds that it's also honest. "That's how we grew up," Clark explained in a 2003 interview. "Every single one of those stories is true. Everything in *Porky's* was collected from high schools around the nation, because I realized that high schools are the repository of our ritual of our sexual coming-of-age, which is an important part of what life is about."[121]

What Clark is really saying is that high school is a repository for adolescent male sexuality, which positions the male as the active/aggressor and the female as the passive/object. An alternative reading might go so far as to suggest that because the male teenage characters' preoccupation with sex is so extreme and their behavior so excessively lewd, the *Porky's* trilogy is on some level making fun of adolescent male sexuality, even if it's at the expense of the undeveloped female teenage characters.

Along with all the teenage sexual hi jinks, Clark does attempt to address more serious themes, like racism and anti-Semitism. One of the gang, Mickey (Rick Wilson), is a redneck whose friends don't approve of his use of the "n" word (African-Americans are conspicuously absent from *Porky's*). Another guy, Tim (Cyrill O'Reilly) addresses his anti-Semitic remarks to Brian Schwartz (Scott Colomby), the new Jewish kid in school. Brian rags on Tim for calling him a "kite" (he means "kike"), though in the end Brian eventually sees the error of his ways and stands up to his racist, abusive father. Of course one can't help wonder—if they are so socially conscious, why wouldn't they be a little more sensitive and respectful toward women?

The sequel, *Porky's II: The Next Day*, not only toned down the sexual content a bit, but dealt more extensively with racism as well as current issues like censorship and religious fundamentalism. In a speech to a religious group in Dallas on August 22, 1980, soon-to-be-elected president Ronald Reagan stated where he stood on the First Amendment. "When I hear the First Amendment used as a reason to keep traditional moral values away from policymaking, I am shocked. The First Amendment was written not to protect the people and their laws from religious values, but to protect those values from government tyranny."[122] After Reagan's election, conservatives and the religious right across the country voiced their objections to what their kids were learning in public schools (even the president supported the teaching of creationism alongside evolution). By 1985–1986, the People for the American Way recorded 130 examples of attempts to censor classes, textbooks, and library books (a 33 percent increase from the previous year), mostly from the conservative right, though some attempts were made on the political left in California.[123]

In *Porky's II*, the same brand of religious fundamentalism threatens Angel Beach's Shakespeare festival when a crazed Southern fundamentalist preacher named Bubba Flavel (Bill Wiley) declares Shakespeare obscene. In one of the film's funniest moments, Reverend Bubba starts spouting Shakespearean verse to prove it's obscene. Principal Carter not only stands up to him, he starts quoting verses from the Bible to prove that it also contains suggestive phrases. In the end, the gang succeeds in exposing Reverend Bubba and the politicians as hypocrites and humiliating members of the local chapter of the Ku Klux Klan, who object to a Native American Indian student playing Romeo.

Most of the teenage sex comedies inspired by *Porky's* offered the same male adolescent treatment of sexuality. The teenagers in *Zapped!* (1982), *Getting It On* (1983), *Private School* (1983), *Screwballs* (1983), and *Revenge of the Nerds* (1984) all indulge in the same antics as the *Porky's* gang, so there's plenty of leering at bare-breasted young women through windows and peepholes into girls' bedrooms, locker rooms, and shower rooms, sometimes with the help of strategically placed cameras.

Of course getting laid, especially for the first time, is always the priority. The "virginity films" like *The Last American Virgin* (1982) and *Losin' It* (1983) both feature a trio of guys (why do they always seem to travels in threes?). Written and directed by Boaz Davidson, *Virgin* is an American version of Davidson's 1978 Israeli coming-of-age film, *Lemon Popsicle*. It is an odd entry in the genre that follows the antics of three high-school friends—Rick (Steve Antin), the cocky stud; David (Joe Rubbo), the happy-go-lucky fat kid; and Gary (Lawrence Monoson), the sensitive romantic. Every time they try to score, something happens: parents arrive home early, a hooker gives them crabs, a jealous husband returns. The film also takes all the "dick jokes" tossed around in *Porky's* to the next level with a scene in which an entire gym class lines up with full erections in order to determine who has the longest tool (and "wins the pool").

Midway through the film there is a dramatic shift in tone when Karen (Diane Franklin), the girl Gary pines for, falls for the much cooler Rick. But when Karen tells Rick she's pregnant, he dumps her. Fortunately, good-guy Gary is there to pick up the pieces. He pays for Karen's abortion, takes care of her while she is recovering, and finally tells her he loves her. They kiss. Gary buys a ring for her birthday, only to find the love of his life kissing Rick in the kitchen during her party. In what is hands down the most downbeat ending of any American teen movie, Gary rides away with tears streaming down his face. The end. So what is Davidson's message? Don't trust your best friend? Don't help a friend in need? Don't tell her how you feel? How about "life *sucks*"?

Set in the early sixties, *Losin' It* is a much slicker comedy starring Tom Cruise as a clean-cut honor student named Woody who heads down to Mexico with his two best buddies, Spider (John Stockwell) and Dave (Jackie Earle Haley), and Dave's little brother, Wendell (John P. Navin, Jr.) in Dave's '57 Chevy. Along the way, they stop at a convenience store to steal munchies and end up giving a lift to the owner's unhappy wife, Kathy (Shelley Long), who decides to join them across the border to get a quickie divorce. When they arrive in Tijuana, Woody finally gets a chance to lose it to a less than attractive hooker, but he chickens out, and ends up scoring with Kathy, who considers him a kindred spirit ("You're like I am, Woody, you need romance," she tells him as they slow-dance). Like Pee Wee's "big finish," Woody's first time is left entirely to the viewer's imagination as director Curtis Hanson cuts away from the motel room just as he and Kathy are about to "hook up."

Tom Cruise has the unique distinction of losing his virginity not once, but twice in the same year. Four months after the release of *Losin' It*, Cruise played another nice guy/virgin in writer/director Paul Brickman's *Risky Business* (1983). The film opens with a dream sequence that establishes the two issues weighing heavily on the mind of high-school senior Joel Goodsen (Cruise): sex and college. In his dream, Joel goes into his neighbor's house where a young, nubile, naked woman invites him into the shower. But when he enters the stall, he gets lost in the steam and suddenly finds himself in a classroom where students are taking their college boards. His face suddenly grows pale when he realizes he's three hours late and there's only two minutes left for him to complete the entire exam.

Like any white, upper-middle-class kid growing up on Chicago's North Shore, Joel is worried about his future. Mom and Dad have their hearts set on their only son going to Princeton, but Joel knows he's not Ivy League material. His sex life, like his academic record, is nothing to write home about. Joel is still a virgin, horny as hell, and tired of being the model son, yet he admits to his friend Miles (Curtis Armstrong) that he won't take any chances because he's afraid of making a mistake and screwing up his life. Miles offers him a piece of friendly advice: "Every now and then say, 'What the fuck!' 'What the fuck!' gives you freedom," Miles explains. "Freedom brings opportunity. Opportunity makes your future."

With his parents away on vacation, opportunity arrives in the form of a streetwise, blond prostitute named Lana (Rebecca De Mornay), who immediately solves Joel's virginity problem, and then proceeds to turn his world upside down. As a result of a series of mishaps and semi-major disasters, mild-mannered Joel suddenly finds himself running from an angry pimp named Guido (Joe Pantoliano), watching his father's Porsche sink to the bottom of Lake Michigan, getting suspended from school, and turning the Goodsen family home into a brothel to raise the cash to fix his father's car. Despite all the problems and obstacles he encounters, Miles's words were right on the money. Freedom brings opportunity, which opens the door to Joel's future. Standing on the other side of the door is Mr. Rutherford (Richard Masur), an admissions officer from Princeton who arrives at the Goodsen residence the same night Joel is hosting a "mixer" for his friends and Lana's "associates." After reviewing Joel's high-school record, Rutherford informs him his stats are "respectable" and "solid" but "not quite Ivy League." Once again Joel seizes the moment. He puts on his signature pair of Ray-Ban sunglasses and shares his new mantra ("What the fuck!") with a confused Rutherford. His surge of cockiness is soon replaced by self-doubt, until Lana reminds him of all that he's accomplished in the past few days: he's making good money, providing his friends with a service, and he's got a girlfriend to boot.

Rutherford takes Joel's advice. He sticks around for the party and obviously enjoys himself enough to put in a good word for Joel who, much to his amazement, is offered fall admission to Princeton.

In a decade marked by consumerism and a national obsession with wealth, social status, and material success, *Risky Business* offered a semi-satirical look at how capitalism permeated contemporary American life, particularly the value system of our nation's youth. Next to sex, Joel and all of his pals are only interested in making money—lots of it. They base their college and career choices on the dollar amount they will be earning straight out of college. Once Joel adopts a "What the fuck" attitude, he transcends his average high-school record and transforms himself into a successful entrepreneur, which in this case is a fancy word for "pimp." Brickman doesn't address the fact that entrepreneur Joel's new business venture is illegal and in the minds of some people morally objectionable (and sexist) because those issues don't factor into the equation—just as long as what he's practicing is good, old-fashioned American capitalism.

His first major business venture turns out to have a few glitches. He is forced to turn over most of his profits to fellow flesh-peddler Guido and assume responsibility for a tiny scratch on his mother's precious Steuben egg (which, along with Dad's coveted Porsche, epitomizes eighties materialism). Still, for Joel, the cost outweighs what he gets in return: four years at Princeton (as a business major, a definite step in the right direction toward financial success), and an experienced, older woman who wants to make love to him while riding the "L" around the city. Joel also learns that his newly adopted "what the fuck" attitude is not necessarily something invented by his generation. When his father gives him the good news about Princeton, he reminds Joel that what he's been telling him about taking chances ("Sometimes you just got to say, 'what the heck'") is true. Like father, like son.

One can imagine Joel (or any of his friends) eventually going to work for Gordon Gekko, the ruthless millionaire played by Michael Douglas in Oliver Stone's *Wall Street* (1987), and adopting his mantra, "Greed is good." But compared to Stone's heavy-handed exposé on the lack of ethics among greedy capitalists, Brickman's satire is subtle, perhaps even too subtle for an adult audience (*Business* was rated R). Joel's admittance to Princeton is certainly ironic, yet the film lacks the film's clear moral message that is typically delivered in teen films by someone who is older and wiser before the end credits roll. Unlike Stone, who has a tendency to repeatedly hit his audience over the head with his message, Brickman lets the story's ironic moments speak for themselves. In the end, what Brickman is trying to say about capitalism in the eighties is ambiguous. As *New York Times* critic Janet Maslin observes, the film's "deadpan humor" at times "borders on dangerously dead seriousness" and the film's "moral concerns" are overshadowed by Brickman's excessive visual style.[124]

Whether it happens on camera or off, Cruise's Woody and Joel get to fulfill what Hollywood apparently believes is at the top of every red-blooded American teenage boy's wish list: the chance to make it with an older woman. The first film of the eighties to evoke the spirit of Mrs. Robinson was *Private Lessons* (1981), a low-budget comedy ($2.8 million) that grossed over $26 million at the box office. Dutch actress and former Miss World Sylvia Kristel, who played *Emmanuelle* in a series of soft-porn films in the seventies, before graduating to fully clothed roles in *The Concorde: Airport '79* (1979) and *The Nude Bomb* (1980), stars as an au pair named Nicole who is blackmailed by a nasty chauffeur (Howard Hesseman) into seducing their employer's fifteen-year-old son, Philly (Eric Brown), and then pretending to die during intercourse. Hesseman then plans to bilk the boy out of his savings by pretending to be his confidant and helping him dispose of the body. Brown, who was seventeen at the time, looks like he's thirteen, so there is something kind of creepy about a naked Kristel exposing herself to a nervous kid and asking him to join her in the bathtub and her bed. Fortunately, she's the sexy au pair with a heart of gold. In the end she teams up with Philly to get his money back.

But Philly wasn't the only lucky teenager in the eighties to receive some private instruction by an older woman. Before she became known to television audiences as *Dynasty*'s Alexis Morrell Carrington Colby Dexter Rowan, Joan Collins appeared in a low-budget, low-grade, coming-of-age teen sex comedy called *Homework* (1982). In a tawdry little scene, at least by teen film standards, Collins seduces her daughter's boyfriend, a virgin named Tommy (Michael Morgan), who is one of those sex-obsessed high-school students who fantasizes about magazine centerfolds and his sexy, young teacher. When Tommy finally gets his chance to do it with a prostitute, he can't perform, which is not the case when Collins puts the moves on him while he is standing on a ladder helping her hang a picture. The most interesting aspect of the scene is the reversal of roles. Instead of having the female be the object of the male character's gaze, it's Collins who is gazing at Michael's ass and crotch. What follows is less creepy (and less explicit) than *Private Lessons* and adds up to less than two minutes of screen time.

By comparison, *My Tutor* (1983) is a much slicker film that features a full-blown affair between Bobby (Matt Latanzi), a rich kid who needs to pass his French exam in order to go on to college, and his gorgeous, blond tutor Terri (Caren Kaye). Up to this point, Bobby's sex life was limited to daydreaming, watching Terri skinny-dip in the family pool, and peeking into her window at night. He soon discovers French is not Terri's only specialty, which makes Bobby's lecherous father (Kevin McCarthy) jealous. Bobby and Terri look like they are closer in age than the May-December couples in *Private Lessons* and *Homework*, so it seems like even less of a big deal when they hit the sheets.

The teen sex comedies of the eighties typically feature young female characters that are usually introduced as either a potential conquest or love interest of the young male characters. What's noticeably missing from the majority of these films is the female point of view. In most instances, female sexuality is defined in male terms, so women are reduced to being passive objects that exist solely to be leered at and pawed by the males.

The one exception is also the best teen comedy of the eighties. *Fast Times at Ridgemont High* (1982) is based on writer/director Cameron Crowe's account of his experiences posing as a student at his old high school. The film, like Crowe's book (which is more character- than plot-driven), takes a slice-of-life approach to American high school from multiple perspectives. The film is in a league of its own because it is the first film to truly capture that modern-day teenagers were really growing up, as the title suggests, much faster than their ancestors without passing judgment over them. Caught up in the consumerist culture of eighties America, these kids devote most of their time after school working at the mall and dealing with adult problems, which Crowe and director Amy Heckerling treat in an adult manner. Bradley (Judge Reinhold) is an ambitious senior who works after school at fast-food joints that require him to wear ridiculous costumes. His somewhat shy, virginal sister Stacy (Jennifer Jason Leigh) works in a pizza parlor at the mall with her more sexually experienced friend Linda (Phoebe Cates). Mark "Rat" Ratner (Brian Backer), is a virginal and equally shy movie usher with a crush on Stacy. His best friend is the fast-talking, double-crossing Mike

The Brat-Pack Films

Taps (1981): When cadets Hutton, Cruise, and Penn are told their military academy is slated to close, they spring into action and seize the school. George C. Scott has a chance to play Patton again as the academy's old warhorse commander. Good performances (Cruise really lets loose as a psycho marine), but it's not entirely clear what the film is saying about schools like Bunker Hill Academy. Are they obsolete or are they the last bastion of values like honor and duty?

The Outsiders (1983): Francis Ford Coppola directed this arty adaptation of S. E. Hinton's popular young adult novel about a group of tough, working-class teens ("the Greasers") in the 1950s who square off with a bunch of rich kids ("the Socs"). Coppola gives the film the look and feel of a 1950s melodrama. It's great to look at, but, unfortunately, the visuals overshadow the material and the actors. The cast includes Brat Packers Lowe, Estevez, and Cruise in supporting roles and two younger performers, C. Thomas Howell and Ralph Macchio, as the poetic Ponyboy Curtis and his best friend Johnny.

Red Dawn (1984): The Brat Pack's second string—Jennifer Grey, C. Thomas Howell, Charlie Sheen, Patrick Swayze, and Lea Thompson—star in this celebration of American militarism and paranoia. The Russians start World War III by invading the United States and it's up to a bunch of midwestern teenagers to save the day! This is the first film to be released with the new PG-13 rating (due to violence), which carries a warning for parents that "some material may be inappropriate for children under 13."

The Breakfast Club (1985): Estevez, Nelson, Ally Sheedy, Molly Ringwald, and Anthony Michael Hall star as the jock, the juvenile delinquent, the basket case, the princess, and the brain who discover they are not so different when they are forced to spend a Saturday together in detention.

St. Elmo's Fire (1985): A record number of Brat Packers (six if you include Demi Moore, seven if you add Mare Winnigham) teamed up to play recent college graduates who struggle with relationship and career problems. The film's superficiality is part of its charm, which made it one of those movies people love to trash, but can't resist watching it for the umpteenth time whenever it aired on pay cable (which was often).

Other titles include *Class* (1983), in which McCarthy sleeps with Lowe's mom (Jacqueline Bisset), but it's okay because she's nuts; *Pretty in Pink* (1986), starring Ringwald as the poor girl who falls for rich kid McCarthy; *About Last Night . . .* (1986), a watered-down version of David Mamet's *Sexual Perversity in Chicago* with Lowe and Moore as discontented lovers; *Blue City* (1986), in which Nelson tries to find out, with help from Sheedy, who killed his father; and *Wisdom* (1986) (pronounced Wis-dumb), written and directed by Estevez, who also costars with Moore as a pair of Robin Hood bandits; and *Fresh Horses* (1988), which re-teams the stars of *Pretty in Pink*.

Damone (Robert Romanus). The one exception is surfer dude Spicoli (Sean Penn), who is stoned 24/7 and living in his own world.

Unlike *Porky's*, *Risky Business*, and the *Private Lessons* clones, the female characters (Stacy and Linda) are not merely the projection of some adolescent male sexual fantasy, but three-dimensional characters with their own sexual desires. In fact, in one of the film's funniest scenes (see "Memorable Movie Moments of the 1980s"), Crowe and director Amy Heckerling take a jab at the male-dominated genre by interrupting Brad's very private fantasy about Linda. More importantly, *Fast Times* doesn't pass judgment on Stacy and Linda for being sexual active. At the time, it was rare to see two young female characters supporting, rather than competing with, each other, and talking about sex (including, in another memorable moment, blow jobs) in an open and honest manner. Heckerling also keeps it real by capturing the self-doubt and awkwardness that are often part of a teenager's early sexual experiences. There is nothing romantic about virginal Stacy's encounter with Ron, the sexy stereo salesman (D. W. Brown), in a grungy baseball dugout, or with her fling with Damone, who prematurely ejaculates before she even gets started (and gets her pregnant). There is also a radical shift in the film's tone when Stacy goes, without any support from Damone, to have an abortion, which is also treated in a nonjudgmental fashion.

Fast Times hit the movie theaters just as public attitudes toward sex and drugs were beginning to change with the growing awareness of AIDS and the increased use of cocaine and crack cocaine, which, in addition to Nancy Reagan's "just say no campaign," the Reagan administration responded to with a declaration of war on drugs. The abortion issue was also heating up again thanks to President Reagan, who vowed during his presidential campaign to nominate judges who would overturn *Roe v. Wade*. Fortunately, Sandra Day O'Connor, who conservatives were counting on for her swing vote, didn't meet their expectations. Although the majority of post-*Fast Times* teen films would approach teen problems with the same degree of seriousness, they would also begin to reflect some of the more conservative values and attitudes that were prominent during the Reagan era.

Getting Serious

The teen films of the eighties were not all about getting slashed or laid. By the mid-fifties, teen slasher movies and sex comedies wore out their welcome, though both old and new titles could be watched over and over again on video and premium-cable channels like Home Box Office and The Movie Channel. Hollywood started to take teenagers and their problems and pressures they faced at school and at home more seriously in a host of teen dramas and comedy-dramas that focused on contemporary teenage life. What separates the "teen angst" films of the eighties from the teen films from all three decades that preceded them is they don't trivialize the issues that are important to teens. In other words, teen problems were now being treated as real problems.

The writer/director who set the tone for the eighties teen films was John Hughes. While working as an advertising copywriter, Hughes wrote articles for *Playboy* and *National Lampoon* before taking over as editor of *Lampoon*, which opened the door for him to write screenplays. His first, *National Lampoon's Class Reunion* (1982) was barely released, but he made a name for himself with two major back-to-back hits: *National Lampoon's Vacation* (1983) and *Mr. Mom* (1983). In 1984, Hughes wrote and directed *Sixteen Candles*, the first of six teen films produced over a three-year period. In addition to *Candles*, Hughes wrote and directed *The Breakfast Club* (1985), *Weird Science* (1985), and *Ferris Bueller's Day Off* (1986). He also wrote *Pretty in Pink* (1986) and *Some Kind of Wonderful* (1987), which were both directed by Howard Deutch.

In the world of John Hughes, teenagers have a specific label stamped on their foreheads which indicate their social position in the high-school caste system. In *The Breakfast Club*, considered by many as the best of his teen comedies, he assigns a label to each of his five protagonists: Andrew (Emilio Estevez) the jock, Brian (Anthony Michael Hall) the brain, Allison (Ally Sheedy) the basket case, Claire (Molly Ringwald) the princess, and Bender (Judd Nelson) the juvenile delinquent. When they are forced to spend one Saturday afternoon together in detention, their respective labels begin to fade as they let down their defenses and start to open up. The big revelation is that they share many of the same emotions, fears, and insecurities. Yet, with no referee (like most teachers and principals in Hughes's films, Mr. Vernon (Paul Gleason), their proctor is ineffectual and off doing his own thing), they are never really on equal ground. Bender, the tough guy/stoner, is the one who is really in control. He is the most brutally honest, which means he is also the cruelest, even resorting to name-calling (in almost the same breath, he calls Brian a "dork," "a parent's wet dream," and a "neo-max-zoom dweebie") and reducing Claire to tears by taunting her about being a virgin, a tease, frigid, etc. At times he even gets the others to join in. He's also the one you are supposed to feel the most sorry for because he is verbally and physically abused at home. Obviously you need a Bender in the mix to get things going, but once everyone starts to open up, all the mean things he says to the other characters are too easily forgotten. When Hughes insists on pairing his teen characters off in the film's final moments, he does a great disservice to his female characters. Claire is verbally abused and berated by Bender throughout the film, yet she suddenly has a change of heart and visits Bender in solitary confinement for a little lip action (talk about low self-esteem). Hughes also insists on giving Allison, with a little help from Claire, a *Pretty in Pink* makeover to "fem her up" a bit so she'll look less like a "basket case" and more like a suitable mate for Andy (so much for accepting one another's difference). As for Brian, he's left alone to write the essay they were assigned at the start of the day: in one thousand words, describe who you think you are:

The 1980s:
Memorable Teen Movie Moments

Fast Times at Ridgemont High (1982): Two memorable moments featuring Linda (Phoebe Cates). While dining in the school cafeteria, she teaches Stacy (Jennifer Jason Leigh) the art of fellatio on a carrot, much to the delight of a nearby table of male onlookers. In the second, she accidentally walks in on Brad while he's in the middle of a fantasy about her and doing the five-knuckle shuffle.

Risky Business (1983): While his parents are out of town, Joel (Tom Cruise) dances up a storm in his underwear to "Old Time Rock & Roll."

The Karate Kid (1984): With a little help from his mentor, Mr. Miyagi (Pat Morita), an injured Daniel LaRusso returns to the match and defeats Johnny Lawrence (William Zabka).

Ferris Bueller's Day Off (1986): Ferris takes time out from his day off to serenade the good people of Chicago while riding atop a parade float singing "Twist and Shout."

Dirty Dancing (1987): Johnny Castle (Patrick Swayze) and Frances "Baby" Houseman (Jennifer Grey) have the time of their lives on the dance floor.

Dead Poets Society (1989): In the film's final moment, Todd (Ethan Hawke) and his classmates pledge their allegiance to their departing English teacher, Mr. Keating (Robin Williams), who was recently fired, by standing on their desks.

Say Anything . . . (1989): Distraught over being dumped by Diane (Ione Skye), Lloyd (John Cusack) stands outside her window with his boom box, which he holds over his head as it's blasting Peter Gabriel's "In Your Eyes."

Dear Mr. Vernon:

We accept the fact that we had to sacrifice a whole Saturday in detention for whatever it was we did wrong. But we think you are crazy to make us write an essay telling you who we think we are. You see us as you want to see us—in the simplest terms, the most convenient definitions. But what we found out is that each one of us is a brain, an athlete, a basket case, a princess, and criminal. Does that answer your question?

Sincerely yours,
The Breakfast Club

In the world according to John Hughes, teenagers, like the members of *The Breakfast Club*, begin to bond once they are ready to overlook their differences and recognize that they share many of the same problems, insecurities, and fears. There are moments when his approach works, such as the heart-to-heart talk at the dance in *Sixteen Candles* between Samantha Baker (Ringwald) and "Farmer Ted" aka "The Geek" (Hall). They are sitting in a shelled-out car in an auto mechanics classroom. He's trying to score (he needs her panties to win a bet) and she's upset because her family forgot her sixteenth birthday. Anthony Michael Hall, who is by far the most naturalistic of the male Hughes actors, manages in both *Sixteen Candles* and *Breakfast Club* to turn potentially stereotypical roles into complex characters, particularly brainy Brian, who unexpectedly emerges as the most emotionally raw member of the quintet.

The Brat Pack

In June 1985, *New York* magazine featured a cover story about a group of young movie stars who, in the words of journalist David Blum, "have top agents and protective public-relations people . . . legions of

fans who buy them drinks and follow them home. And, most important . . . [they] sell movie tickets."[125] Blum dubbed them the
"Hollywood Brat Pack," because like the Rat Pack of the 1960s, which
included Frank Sinatra, Dean Martin, Peter Lawford, and Sammy
Davis, Jr., they made movies together and when they weren't working
they were "on the prowl for parties, women, and a good time." Blum
spent an evening at Hard Rock Café in Los Angeles with three of its
illustrious members: Rob Lowe (the one with "the most beautiful
face"), Judd Nelson ("the overrated one"), and the Pack's unofficial
president, Emilio Estevez. His article paints the young actors in a less
than flattering light as they sit and hold court at their table at the
Hard Rock or take advantage of their celebrity status to get in to see
a movie without paying or into a club without waiting on line.

Blum suggests that the Brat Packers spend much of their time
together, but except for running into Timothy Hutton—whom they
later disparage for his recent string of bomb movies—the journalist's
interaction is limited to Lowe, Nelson, and Estevez (though *Bright
Lights, Big City* author Jay McInerney joins up with them at one
point). While the three underrated female members (Molly Ringwald,
Ally Sheedy, Demi Moore) are barely mentioned, Blum has plenty to
say about the other guys, including Hutton ("the only one with an
Oscar"), Tom Cruise ("the hottest of them all" after *Risky Business*),
Matt Dillon ("the one least likely to replace Marlon Brando"),
Nicholas Cage ("the ethnic chair"), and Sean Penn, the "most gifted
of them all" and the "natural heir to Robert DeNiro's throne."

While some of them did work together in a series of teen-oriented films in the eighties, they were hardly a "pack" in the Rat Pack tradition and, as director John Hughes pointed out, the "brat" label was
entirely unfair. In a 1986 interview with Molly Ringwald published in
Seventeen magazine, Hughes explained how the young actors were

"hit harder because of their age." "[Brat Pack] suggests unruly, arrogant young people, and that description isn't true of these people. And the label has been stuck on people who never even spoke to the reporter who coined it."[126]

Whether their reviews were pro or con, the critics had strong opinions, perhaps more than on any teen film to date, about *The Breakfast Club*. Most of the negative criticism took Hughes's film to task for its lack of veracity. Jay Carr of the *Boston Herald* commended Hollywood for making "more of an effort to reflect the range and depth of the emotions teens feel." But this was apparently not the case with *The Breakfast Club*, which he described as "lifeless and formulaic." "[T]here isn't a moment that rings true," Carr claimed, "when it moves from lethargy to a contrived erosion of . . . social barriers."[127] The *San Francisco Chronicle*'s Paul Attanasio—who would later pen the screenplays for *Quiz Show* (1994), *Disclosure* (1994), and *Donnie Brasco* (1997)—pointed out that even though Hughes's film and Rob Reiner's romantic comedy, *The Sure Thing* (1985), don't follow the teen-sex genre formula, the characters "have nothing to do with real kids." Attanasio also accused *The Breakfast Club* of wearing its "themes on its sleeve" and was dissatisfied that the characters solved their identity crisis "by deciding to have no identity at all."[128]

The critics who liked the film felt the exact opposite. They praised Hughes for his fresh, honest treatment of teenagers and their problems. Gene Siskel called his fellow Chicagoan a "savvy chronicler of contemporary teenage life" and the film "a breath of cinematic fresh air, taking on a very adolescent problem and offering, in a dramatic way, a possible solution."[129] *Time* magazine's Richard Corliss also believed Hughes's film was a step in the right direction for teen-pics, which he complained are all the same. But Corliss considered films like *The Breakfast Club* and *Sixteen Candles* a cut above the rest because they are intelligent and the director understood "how the ordinary teenagers, the ones who don't get movies made about them, think and feel."[130]

The Breakfast Club also figured prominently in newspapers and magazines which analyzed and discussed the accuracy of the American cinema's depiction of teenage life at a time when teenpics were being released in record numbers between 1985 and 1988. For example, in May 1985, Siskel sat down with four real, live teenagers and asked them to name their favorite and least favorite teen films. They all admitted they were fans of *The Breakfast Club*, yet they were also quick to point out some of the problems they have with the film and the teen genre in general:

- Kids always seem to hate their parents and blame them for their problems
- Female characters are limited to supporting roles
- Ugly girls are smart, pretty girls are dumb
- Male characters are only interested in sex
- Minorities, particularly Hispanics and African-Americans, are invisible

Two years later, a similar article by freelance writer Patti Hartigan appeared in the *Boston Globe*. Hartigan spoke informally with a total of sixty teenagers, who once again raised objections about how young men being portrayed as sex-crazed and adults—parents and teachers—as "cartoon characters who are either too lenient or too strict."[131] There was also a consensus that "teen-age sex and romance are too easy for the actors on the screen, that the sexual encounters have none of the sweaty palms, the awkward gestures for real life, none of the emotional trauma and physical pain."[132] Once again, objections were also raised over what was perceived as the privileging of white, upper-middle-class suburban kids in films like *Sixteen Candles* and *The Breakfast Club*, yet the latter was still respected by teenagers two years after its release.

Class differences present a major obstacle for two high-school students in *Pretty in Pink*, the first of two high-school comedy-dramas written by Hughes and directed by Howard Deutch. Molly Ringwald stars as Andie, the smart girl from the poor side of town who catches the eye of an affable rich kid named Blane (Andrew McCarthy).

On their first date, Blane takes Andie to a party hosted by his best friend, Steff (James Spader), a rich, obnoxious creep who had recently made a play for her and was promptly told to get lost. She feels uncomfortable with Blane's friends, especially Steff's girlfriend Benny (Kate Vernon), who ranks numero uno on the list of the all-around meanest, bitchiest high-school blondes in a eighties teen film (and one of the oldest—both Vernon and Spader look more like college graduates than high-school seniors). Andie's friends don't exactly welcome Blane with open arms, particularly her best friend Duckie (Jon Cryer), who is in love with Andie and doesn't like Blane because he's a "richie." And so the big question looms: can the couple overcome their differences or will Blane give into peer pressure and dump Andie before the prom?

Hughes's script for *Some Kind of Wonderful* is a variation of *Pink* with more complex characters. This time around it's a middle-class guy, Keith (Eric Stoltz), who is smitten with a middle-class gal, Amanda Jones (Leah Thompson), who hangs with the rich kids because she's going out with the school's resident super-rich, philandering asshole, Hardy (Craig Sheffer) (why don't any rich kids in Hughes films have normal names?). But when Amanda breaks up with Hardy, she's persona non grata among her rich friends (then they weren't really your friends, were they, Amanda?). In a plot that defies all logic, Keith squanders his college savings to take Amanda on an *über*-date with his best friend, a tomboy drummer named Watts (Mary Stuart Masterson), who steals the movie. Like Duckie, she also has a major crush on her friend to the point where she makes a masochistic gesture and agrees to chauffeur Keith and Amanda when they go on their date, which culminates with a party at Hardy's house, where the ex-boyfriend is planning to kick Keith's ass. Fortunately, Keith gets help when the school's head juvenile delinquent (Elias Koteas) crashes the party. There's no violence—Hardy just exposes himself as the jerk he is. Meanwhile, Keith has a major revelation, no doubt induced by all the excitement (this all happens over the course of about ten minutes)— he's in love with Watts!

Some Kind of Wonderful and *Pretty in Pink* share the same basic premise: a pair of lovers can only be together by overcoming their differences, which, in the case of both films, are a matter of economics. This is familiar territory, yet one of Hughes's strong points as a writer is his ability to treat his young characters and their problems with respect. He never trivializes their problems, and they are often more in touch with their emotions than the average grown-up. Unfortunately, inasmuch as he tries to keep it real, he takes the economic caste system that no doubt does exist in some American high schools to an extreme; and then uses the teens' differences to demonize the rich kids (Steff, Benny, and Hardy are caricatures of arrogant spoiled brats) while simultaneously turning the Andies and Amandas of the world into victims. Granted, this was the height of eighties affluence, when greed was good and conspicuous consumption became the new religion (at least until the New York Stock Exchange took a nosedive on October 19, 1987). Fortunately, Hughes's women are usually much thicker-skinned and far more in touch with their feelings than the males, so rich jerks don't pose much of a threat. Although he comes around in the end, Blane is a far too passive character and Keith is too wrapped up in himself to notice his best friend is in love with him. Perhaps if all these characters, from both sides of the economic lines, spent a Saturday in detention together, they might find out just how much they have in common.

"Stubborn little troupers"

In addition to the typical problems and pressures teenagers encounter on a regular basis, the young characters in 1980s teen movies also faced obstacles and challenges that were far from ordinary. In the *Rocky* tradition, teenagers became Hollywood's new underdogs who beat the odds and emerged victorious by using either their physical strength and skill or their brainpower.

In a short piece published in the *Los Angeles Times* in July 1986, critic Patrick Goldstein criticized Hollywood for turning films into commercials that sell young viewers "swollen self-righteous teen dreams." According to Goldstein, "professional teenagers" like Rob Lowe and Michael J. Fox were stealing the spotlight with their "kiddie machismo" while female actors were treated like "sexual cannon fodder." More importantly, the teenage characters they were playing were no longer "rebels without a cause," but "stubborn little troupers triumphing over adversity in every imaginable pursuit."[133] Goldstein's list of examples included *Flashdance* (1983), *Footloose* (1984), and *Crossroads* (1986), along with four sports-themed teen films: *The Karate Kid* (1984), *Vision Quest* (1985), *Youngblood* (1986), and *American Anthem* (1986).

Goldstein makes two valid points. With the exception of *Flashdance*, the majority of these films have a male protagonist, so female actors were usually reduced to playing the leading man's devoted girlfriend. Secondly, these teenagers were not "rebels without a cause" because these films were set in the 1980s, not the fifties. What these films were selling was a Reagan-induced sense of individualism, which, as critic Robin Wood explained around the same time, was all about the individual hero "whose achievements somehow 'makes everything all right,' even for the millions who never make it to individual heroism (but every man can be a hero; and in the begrudging generosity of contemporary liberalism, even every woman)."[134]

But there is another problem with Goldstein's list of films (he states there are a "few hundred other examples"). While the protagonists in each of these films struggle to triumph over adversity, they are not, as Goldstein implies, all doing it simply for their own personal gain. In other words, these films do not all promote the same brand of individualism, and the battles that they wage against their opponents and oppressors are not all the same.

The sports cycle of teen films, which was going strong in the eighties thanks to the box-office success of *The Karate Kid*, began in the late seventies with a series of films that would establish the genre's basic formula. These films focused on the relationship between a coach and his/her players, who are usually the underdogs in their league or division in variations of a standard plot where the coach whips them into shape in time to win the big game. Sometimes the coach is a fish out of water, as in the T & A comedy, *Coach* (1978), which stars blond beauty Cathy Lee Crosby as an Olympic medalist who is hired sight unseen to coach a boys basketball team (her name is Randy, so they thought she was a he). Randy eventually wins the respect of her players and leads them to victory. A sign of just how much times have changed, Randy also falls for one of her players

(Michael Biehn), but their sexual relationship doesn't raise any eyebrows (or even make the nightly news).

The eighties version (minus the student/coach sexual relationship) is *Wildcats* (1986), starring Goldie Hawn as a track coach who accepts a job coaching football at an inner-city high school. The filmmakers evidently thought the fish-out-of-water premise was enough to sustain a feature-length film because not much happens; that is, until the "big game" when the team faces its across-town rivals (guess which side wins?). Still, it's hard to dislike Hawn, even when she has nothing to do, and the cast includes some familiar faces (Woody Harrelson, Jan Hooks, LL Cool J, and Wesley Snipes) who at the time were at the start of their careers.

Another comedian tried his luck at coaching in *Fast Break* (1979), a formulaic sports comedy that should have been titled *Mr. Kotter Goes to College*. Gabriel Kaplan, fresh from his five-year stint as a history teacher on the TV sitcom *Welcome Back, Kotter*, stars as David Greene, a wisecracking coach hired by Cadwallader College, a second-rate, all-white Nevada school, to turn their losing basketball team into champions. Before heading west, Mr. Kotter—I mean Mr. Greene—recruits four players from the inner city, one of whom is nicknamed "Swish" because he's a little "light in his Nikes"; that is, until the big reveal: he is actually a she (sigh of relief). Then again, it's not much of a reveal if you take a look at the advertising tagline on the poster, which reads: "Gabe Kaplan's having a ball! His dream team's got a preacher, a jailbird, a pool shark, a muscleman. And the best guy on the team is a girl." *Where's Horshack when you need him?*

Not all coaches have the body of Coach Crosby or the sharp wit of Coach Kotter. One of the best of the '70s sports pix, *One on One* (1977) tells the story of a small-town high-school basketball star who is recruited to play for Western University in Los Angeles, where athletes are showered with gifts and special favors. Unfortunately, Henry (Robby Benson, who co-wrote the script with his dad, Jerry Segal), doesn't quite fit in with the team and butts heads with his hard-nosed coach (J. D. Spradlin) over his militaristic methods. Hoping Henry will give up his scholarship, the coach makes the player's life miserable, but with the support of his tutor (Annette O'Toole), he hangs in there and in another one of those "feel good" Hollywood endings, emerges a winner. The plot is a bit predictable, yet Benson is a likable underdog who brings the right mixture of sensitivity, idealism, and perseverance. As *New York Times* critic Vincent Canby pointed out, Benson/Henry's "clean-cut naïveté masks a surprising moral strength, which, even if it's not very common, is something we'd like to believe in."[135]

Along similar lines, Tom Cruise is convincing as Stef, a small-town high-school football player with coach problems in *All the Right Moves* (1983). Stef's future depends on getting an athletic scholarship—it's the only way he can go to college and it's his ticket out of the Pennsylvania steel-mill town. When he makes the mistake of talking back to Coach Nickerson (Craig T. Nelson) and questions his calls, the coach not only kicks Stef off the team, but bad-mouths him to recruiters, leading to the loss of his college scholarship. There is no final "big game" scene, yet the film's happy Hollywood ending, in which Nickerson offers Stef an apology and a scholarship to Cal Poly, comes out of nowhere.

Most teen athletes in movies have something to prove and so, with the support of their coach, they push their bodies and minds to the limit. It doesn't matter if it's an individual sport like wrestling (*Vision Quest*) or a team sport (ice hockey in *Youngblood*), it usually all comes down to defeating one opponent, who is bigger, meaner, and usually plays dirty. The stakes are even higher when our hero is, as Goldstein suggests, a "stubborn little trouper" like a skinny kid who enters a karate competition in *The Karate Kid* and an undersize high-school football player in *Lucas* (1986).

Academy Award–winning director John Avildsen, who took home his gold statuette for *Rocky*, was the perfect choice to direct *The Karate Kid*, the story of a teenager, Daniel (Ralph Macchio), who trains for a karate competition with a Japanese master, Mr. Miyagi (Noriyuki "Pat" Morita). Short and skinny Daniel is no match for his muscular opponents, who are also his enemies outside the ring. The film's final scene is the championship match between Daniel and the school bully (William Zabka), whose sensei (teacher) is a sadist who believes you do whatever it takes, including fight dirty, as long as you win.

There are definite parallels between *Rocky* and *The Karate Kid*: Rocky and Daniel are both underdogs, both films end with the championship match, etc. Yet the real heart of *The Karate Kid* lies in the friendship between Daniel and Mr. Miyagi, who Oscar-nominee Morita doesn't turn into a cliché (every word out of his mouth is thankfully not a proverb or ancient saying) or take too seriously. In fact, Morita's sitcom training (he played the owner of Arnold's, the gang's hangout on *Happy Days*) is put to good use when Miyagi makes an occasional unexpected remark. For example, when Daniel manages to make it to the final round, he says, "Wouldn't it be great if I won?" Mr. Miyagi replies, "Be great if you survive."

In *Lucas*, the smallest and youngest kid in a midwestern high school, literally risks his life when he goes out for the football team to impress the girl of his dreams. Writer/director David Seltzer uses high-school football as a backdrop for his story of a brainy fourteen-year-old (Cory Haim), who falls for a cheerleader, Maggie (Kerry Green), who is in love with a football player and Lucas's friend, Cappie (Charlie Sheen).

Lucas is one of the best teen dramas of the eighties—a smart and touching film about what it's like to be different. In Lucas's case, what it means to be short, highly intelligent, younger than the other kids (he "accelerated"), a bit disheveled in appearance, and interested in bugs and classical music instead of pep rallies and football games. He's the kid it's easy for everyone to pick on, but he still refuses to fade into the background because he's not only smart, he's got chutzpah. When he's barred from playing football until his parents give their consent, Lucas begs the coach to let him in the game. When the coach refuses and calls him a pissant, the kid strikes back: "Don't call me that! Don't you call me a pissant, you dumb fucking jock! . . . You heard me, pencil brain! I mean, who are we kidding here? Who is the pissant? The second-rate coach of a third-rate team or me?"

David Seltzer's screenplay beautifully captures the angst and awkwardness of unrequited love and the lengths young people will go simply to capture another person's attention (and heart). The characters talk and act like real people, thanks to a terrific ensemble of young actors, which also includes Winona Ryder (her film debut) as a shy girl in love with Lucas, and Courtney Thorne-Smith as the cheerleader who dumps Cappie. Green is a gifted actress who, in essence, is playing two roles: she is Lucas's devoted friend, who turns to him for support, yet must let him down easy once his feelings are known. At the same time she is the young woman who is in love for the first time. Sheen gives his most subtle performance as the caring jock who is caught between Maggie and Lucas, who he really cares about.

War and Peace

In March 1983, President Ronald Reagan, aka the Great Communicator, referred to the Soviet Union as the "evil empire." Later that month, he announced the United States's plans to develop a system called the Strategic Defense Initiative (S.D.I.), nicknamed Star

Wars, that could intercept in space a strategic missile headed toward the United States. The estimated cost would be in the billions and it was still questionable whether such a system could actually work. As absurd as it sounded to some, the Soviet threat became more of a reality six months later when Korean Airlines Flight 007 strayed off course into Soviet airspace, where it was shot down by a Soviet fighter jet, killing all 269 passengers and crew. The cold war was on and the tension between the United States and the Soviet Union continued to mount until President Reagan entered negotiations with Soviet prime minister Mikhail Gorbachev in the mid-eighties. Finally, at a summit held in Washington, D.C., on December 8–10, 1987, Reagan and Gorbachev put their John Hancocks on the Intermediate Nuclear Forces (INF) Treaty, which required both countries to eliminate intermediate-range weapons from their nuclear arsenals.

During this period in history when Soviet–U.S. relations were strained, teenagers were worried, and justifiably so, about the threat of nuclear war. According to a study conducted by psychologist Jerald G. Bachman and his colleagues at the University of Michigan at Ann Arbor, the percentage of high-school seniors worried about nuclear war rose from 7 percent in 1975 to 30 percent in 1980.[136] In 1983, just over half of the 1,500 high-school students surveyed by the National Association of Secondary School Principals identified a nuclear disaster or the threat of World War II to be the most important world problem. But when asked if "nuclear weapons are necessary to protect the U.S.," 53 percent of the teenagers surveyed said they "mildly" or "strongly agreed" with the statement.[137]

Concern about a nuclear threat was not limited to American teenagers. A 1986 poll conducted for *Teen Age* magazine asked teenagers (between the ages of thirteen and twenty) from fifty-nine nations if they believed there would be a nuclear war in their lifetime. Two out of five teenagers outside the United States answered "yes," while the percentage of teenagers in the United States who agreed was lower (28 percent).[138]

The threat of nuclear war becomes a reality (or, at the very least, a simulation) in *WarGames*, a major hit at the box office in the summer of 1983. Before he became the poster child for truancy as *Ferris Bueller*, Matthew Broderick played David Lightman, a computer geek (but the cool kind) who is bored with school and would rather be playing video games in an arcade or on his home PC. To impress a classmate, Jennifer (Ally Sheedy), he pulls a Ferris Bueller and hacks into the school's computer to change their grades (Ferris did the same to reduce his number of absences) and then into a company's computer system to try one of their new games. But what he doesn't know is he's hacked into the U.S. Defense Department's monitoring system, so when he starts playing Thermonuclear Nuclear Warfare with the computer and starts launching Soviet missiles toward Las Vegas and Seattle (his hometown), he's put the United States on a full-scale alert. David is tracked down by the feds and accused by the guy in charge, Dr. McKittrick (Dabney Coleman), of being a spy (in one of the film's many plot holes, he's brought to computer headquarters). What only David understands is that the computer is continuing to play the game until someone wins, but with the help of the computer's inventor (John Wood), David essentially saves the planet from total destruction.

Although it does not have the satirical tone of Kubrick's *Dr. Strangelove* (1964), *WarGames* does make you wonder exactly whose finger is on the button (*WarGames'* General Jack Beringer [Barry Corbin] could be mistaken for *Dr. Strangelove*'s cigar-chomping General Buck Turgidson [George C. Scott]). Besides being a well-crafted and entertaining film, its not-so-subtle message—when it comes to nuclear war, the only winning move is not to play—was certainly timely, considering what President Ronald Reagan, always the jokester, said the following year during what he thought was a microphone check: "My fellow Americans, I'm pleased to tell you today that I've signed legislation that will outlaw Russia forever. We begin bombing in five minutes."

Although the threat of nuclear war is a serious subject, John Badham's direction is not heavy-handed. He was also fortunate to have Broderick and Sheedy, two terrific young actors who, as David and Jennifer, react to the crisis they inadvertently create as real teenagers would, with just the right mixture of fear and excitement. For instance, when David realizes he almost started World War III, boyish Broderick has that "scared little kid" expression on his face that teenagers often have when they know they've done something bad and are about to get into big trouble. David may be smart, but he's by no means perfect. He can escape the feds by rewiring an electronic door à la *Mission: Impossible*, yet he doesn't know how to swim. When he is forced to admit this to Jennifer, his anxieties about the impending apocalypse begin to surface:

> *David:* I can't swim. . . . I never got around to it, okay? I always thought there was going to be plenty of time. . . . I wish I didn't know about any of this. I wish I was like everybody else in the world and tomorrow it would just be over. There wouldn't be any time to be sorry about anything. (pause) Oh, Jesus. I really wanted to learn how to swim.

WarGames also gets high marks for not pushing Sheedy's character in the background or reducing her to the typical "girlfriend" role. She not only gets in on the action, but at times she is even more levelheaded than David when it comes to figuring out their next move.

While *WarGames* delivers a clear message about the futility of nuclear war, the filmmakers' position on new technology is ambivalent. On the one hand, the film serves as a warning of what could happen if we put the fate of all mankind in the hands of a computer or, as General Beringer says, an "overgrown pile of microchips." The general and McKittrick debate this issue early in the film after one of several men responsible for turning the key that launches the nuclear missiles refuses to do so during what was later revealed to be only a drill. At the same time, it's ironic that the film's "no-nuke" message is not delivered by a human, but by the Defense Department's computer (nicknamed Joshua), which, in the end, proved to be more humane than the men who operate it.

At the time of its release, *WarGames* also signaled how the current nuclear arms race with the Soviets was being fueled by the same ignorance, paranoia, and hawkish mentality that ran rampant during the cold war in the fifties. The photo of Reagan that hangs on the wall next to the lighted sign indicating the United States's current DEF-CON (Defense Readiness Condition) level was a less-than-subtle reminder of the president's role in resurrecting the cold war. It's also painfully clear just how removed the current administration was from reality when, in a moment straight out of an anti-communist propaganda film from the fifites, an FBI agent characterizes David, who he suspects of espionage, as "intelligent but an underachiever, alienated from his parents, has few friends—the classic case for recruitment by the Soviets."

But the reason why these middle-aged white guys are so threatened by teenagers like David has nothing to do with communism. It was the realization that in the field of new technology, young people were becoming increasingly more knowledgeable and more adept at operating new technology than adults. David could not only break into the system, he can speak the computer's language and understand its "thinking" patterns better than McKittrick, who was the protégé of the computer's inventor, Dr. Falkan (John Wood).

While the adults in *WarGames* are threatened by David's knowledge and skill, a mercenary scientist exploits the minds of his brilliant students in *Real Genius* (1985). *Valley Girl's* (1983) Martha Coolidge directed this tale about a bunch of brainiacs who are recruited by a sleazy scientist/TV science guy, Jerry Hathaway (William Atherton) to help him build a laser that, unbeknownst to them, will be used by the military as a weapon. The students involved in the project include a fifteen-year-old freshman, Mitch (Gabe Jarret), and his roommate, Chris (Val Kilmer), a senior physics whiz and class clown. Chris takes Mitch under his wing because he wants to make sure he and his egghead pals don't graduate without having a little fun. The first half of the film is devoted to young Mitch's adjustment to college life and his off-the-wall roommate's antics (like turning the dorm into a skating rink and hosting a beach party, complete with a pool, in the auditorium).

In the second half, they complete Hathaway's laser project, and then realize its potential as a deadly weapon. They also discover that Hathaway used his students as free labor and pocketed the grant money he received from the government to renovate his new house. So they get revenge by reprogramming the laser so it will zap Hathaway's house, which is completely destroyed when the popcorn kernels they filled it with start to pop.

Real Genius is a funny film about smart people. Unlike another comedy about overachievers, *Revenge of the Nerds* (1984), in which a bunch of nerds, geeks, and other social outcasts form their own fraternity act just as sexist, crude, and offensive as their jock rivals, *Real Genius* doesn't feel the need to lower the IQs of its characters (and audience) when it's time for them to have some fun.

While the adults in *WarGames* who work for the Defense Department are just carrying out orders, the government officials in *Real Genius* are downright demonic. Director Coolidge has fun with the opening sequence, in which a bunch of good old government boys in suits sit around and discuss the laser (code name: the Crossbow Project), which they claim is not intended for warfare, but for peacetime. "So it's both immoral and unethical," one of them quips as the rest of the guys start to chuckle. When one of the men (the only African-American) decides he can't be a part of this and excuses himself, it's decided that he will need to be "liberated" ("As in 'liquidated'?" asks another).

But the biggest surprise in *Real Genius* is Val Kilmer, who is best known for his dramatic roles (like Jim Morrison in *The Doors* [1991]). He is quite charming and funny as Chris, who is a cross between a fraternity boy, Albert Einstein, and Groucho Marx.

"I want my MTV!"

August 1, 1981, marked the beginning of a new era in the annals of American popular culture. Early that morning—12:01 AM to be exact—the image of a rocket ship blasting off, followed by a second shot of the Apollo 11 lunar module on the moon, were transmitted to eight hundred thousand television sets around the United States. As an announcer's voice declared, "Ladies and gentlemen, rock and roll," there was a cut to a third shot of astronaut Neil Armstrong standing on the moon next to the flag he planted on the lunar surface. But instead of stars and stripes, the flag displayed the logo of the country's first music video channel, MTV.[139]

The first video to air on MTV? "Video Killed the Radio Star" by a British group, the Buggles. *The second?* Pat Benatar's "You Better Run."

By 1983, MTV could be seen in 17.5 million homes around the country. In addition to revitalizing the music industry, MTV also provided many advertisers, including movie studios, with the ideal outlet for targeting the teen market.

The channel also established music videos as both a popular form of entertainment and an effective marketing tool for promoting an artist's or group's new single or album. Some music videos promoted a film and its sound track by incorporating footage from the film into the video. At first, MTV was cautious when it came to movie-themed videos if they looked too much like commercials. For example, an executive rejected an early cut of the music video of Bob Seger's "Old Time Rock & Roll" from *Risky Business* because it played like "a trailer set to a Bob Seger song, so it was reedited to put more emphasis on the artist by inserting footage of Seger in concert."[140]

MTV also introduced a new aesthetic consisting of a stylized, slick, and fast-paced style of cutting to music. This aesthetic was soon adopted by advertisers who started to produce commercials in the same style specifically for MTV (the first was a 1982 ad for Kraft foods featuring sexually suggestive imagery of their products like Miracle Whip and Velveeta cut to Devo's "Whip It"). MTV's influence could soon be seen on television in series like *Miami Vice* and in the movies, particularly teen films, which were targeting the same audience as the music channel.

The birth and expansion of MTV ran parallel to the teen film's "golden age," so a film's sound track (and music videos) became an increasingly more important marketing tool. John Hughes's sound tracks for *The Breakfast Club*, *Pretty in Pink*, *Ferris Bueller's Day Off*, and *Some Kind of Wonderful* featured imported groups like Simple Minds ("Don't You Forget About Me," *The Breakfast Club*) from Scotland, and Orchestral Manoeuvres in the Dark ("If You Leave,"

Pretty in Pink), and the Psychedelic Furs ("Pretty in Pink") from Britain. Many of the groups featured on Hughes's sound tracks did not have record contracts with a U.S. record company, prompting MCA-Universal to make a five-album deal with MCA Records along with Hughes's own label, Hughes Music.[141]

MTV's influence is most evident in three "music video" musicals from the 1980s—*Flashdance* (1983), *Footloose* (1984), and *Dirty Dancing* (1987). All three films were box-office hits, had best-selling sound tracks (*Dirty Dancing* had two), and featured plotlines that revolved around the subject of dancing—getting the opportunity to learn (*Flashdance*), fighting for the right to (*Footloose*), and learning how to (*Dirty Dancing*). They all utilize, to varying degrees, MTV's visual style by incorporating montage sequences cut to music. For example, both *Footloose* and *Dirty Dancing* include sequences in which an audience witnesses a character's progress as she learns how to dance. In *Dancing*, teenage Frances "Baby" Houseman (Jennifer Grey) learns how to move from her hunky teacher/partner Johnny Castle (Patrick Swayze). *Footloose*'s Ren McCormack (Kevin Bacon) faces an even greater challenge teaching his pal Willard (Chris Penn) and his two left feet how to keep time with the music to Jennifer Holliday singing "Let's Hear It for the Boy."

Laurie (Jamie Lee Curtis) is reunited with Michael Myers in (1998). © Corbis

The Hollywood Teen Film Comes of Age (1989–2005)

Disaffected and Disengaged

Generation X

The Askewniverse of Kevin Smith

A Little Romance

Slash and Rehash

Girls Just Wanna Be Mean

Boys (Still) Just Wanna Get Laid

Lost in Translation

Teens on the Margins

While some critics regard the 1980s as the Hollywood teen film's "golden age," the genre as a whole did not "come of age" until the nineties. Teen movies made a strong comeback in the mid-nineties, which is a bit surprising considering the attention span of the average teenager seemed to be growing shorter and shorter at a time when movies were facing some serious competition from youth-oriented television shows (like *Beverly Hills, 90210* [1990–2000] and *Buffy the Vampire Slayer* [1997–2003]), the Internet, and other forms of electronic entertainment (Game Boy, Nintendo GameCube, XBox, et al.).

The resurrection of the Hollywood teen movie in the nineties was only one part of a massive boom in the youth culture spearheaded by the entertainment industry, which actively pursued the nation's largest generation of teenagers since the baby boomers. Between 1990 and 2000, teenagers were the fastest-growing segment of the U.S. population with the number of twelve- to nineteen-year-olds rising from 27.5 million to 32 million. By 2010, the teen population is expected to reach thirty-five million.[142]

As in the 1950s, a healthy economy in the 1990s also put more spending money in young people's pockets. According to Teenage Research Unlimited, 31 million American teenagers between the ages of twelve and nineteen spent $141 *billion* in 1997—a 16 percent increase from the previous year.[143] That figure rose to $175 billion in

2003.[144] With the help of marketing researchers, retailers at the local shopping mall, along with the thousands of merchants hocking their wares in cyberspace, continue to vie for teenagers' attention and dollars. Consequently, teenagers have become the "most polled, questioned, evaluated, scrutinized, and speculated-about" demographic group in the country.[145]

The motion-picture and television industries also catered to the growing teenage population with the help of a new generation of talented, young actors, most of whom first appeared on youth-oriented, prime-time TV series on Fox or the WB networks, such as *Beverly Hills, 90210, Buffy the Vampire Slayer, Dawson's Creek* (1998–2003), *Party of Five* (1994–2000), and, more recently, *The O.C.* (2003–) and *One Tree Hill* (2003–). TV stars like Neve Campbell, Shannon Doherty, Sarah Michelle Gellar, Seth Green, Alyson Hannigan, Jennifer Love Hewitt, Katie Holmes, Lindsay Lohan, Chad Michael Murray, James Van Der Beek, and Michelle Williams all made the transition to feature films, for some while their TV series were still airing.

Around the same time, the music industry was also overrun by a new crop of young performers, who, by the year 2000 had collectively sold over one hundred million CDs.[146] Not since the early seventies, when teenyboppers smothered their bedroom walls with posters and pix of David Cassidy, Donny Osmond, and Bobby Sherman, were teenage girls so enamored with pop singers, who arrived on the music scene in the late '90s as members of prefabricated boy bands like *NSYNC, the Backstreet Boys, and 98°. In the year 2000, during the height of the boy-band craze, Lou Pearlman, former manager of *NSYNC and the Backstreet Boys, predicted that "boy bands will continue as long as God makes little girls."[147]

When they were not listening to the harmonious sounds of Justin,

Nick, and the rest of the boys, "little girls" were keeping an eye on fashion trendsetters like singers Jessica Simpson, who was dubbed a "Red Carpet Fashion Icon" in 2005 by the Teen Choice Awards, and Britney Spears, who, in that same year, took home a Grammy for "Best Dance Recording" (for her song, "Toxic") and introduced her new fragrance, "Fantasy."

The youth culture of the 1990s was a product of a relatively small number of mega-media conglomerates. Disney/ABC, NBC-Universal, Paramount Communications/Viacom/CBS, News Corporation/Twentieth Century–Fox, and the biggest of them all, Time-Warner, are all proud owners of one major film studio, one major television network, and holdings in any or all of the following areas: commercial and pay-cable TV channels and networks, radio stations, record labels, publishing venues (books, magazines, newspapers), and Internet-service franchises. Having access to a variety of media makes it much easier for a company to get the word out on an upcoming feature film or a television series or special. For example, in addition to the usual print ads and radio and television commercials, a studio can promote a feature film by airing a special on the "making of" the film on one of its parent company's cable stations. An interview with the director can appear in one of its magazines or newspapers, while the star can promote the film on its television network's morning or late-night talk show, or on one or more of its radio stations. In addition, stills and information about the film can be featured on the company's Web site or online service.

More importantly, conglomerates have at their disposal the means to turn a single film or television program into a moneymaking franchise. For example, *Lizzie McGuire* was a popular TV series for younger teen girls (better known as "tweens") that aired on the

Disney Channel from 2001–2004. Disney, which co-produced the series, released *The Lizzie McGuire Movie* (2003), a feature-length film starring Hilary Duff and most of the series cast. Duff is also featured on the film's sound track (from Walt Disney Records) as well as the TV-series sound track (plus a "party mix" CD and a karaoke CD). Disney Press published a series of *Lizzie McGuire* books, Disney Home Entertainment released the film and episodes of the series on DVD, and Disney Interactive put out *Lizzie McGuire* Game Boy video games, which are available for purchase online or at your local Disney Store along with other *Lizzie McGuire* products.

The synergy among the various tenets within each media conglomerate certainly contributed to the revival of the Hollywood teen movie. But unlike past decades, which were generally dominated by two or three sub-genres (i.e., teen horror/sci-fi movies, juvenile-delinquent dramas, and rock musicals in the fifties; beach-party and counterculture films in the sixties), the teen movies produced by the major studios and independent companies from the late 1980s through the present day have been more diverse than their predecessors, ranging from both traditional genre films (such as romantic and sex comedies, high-school dramas, slasher movies, et al.) to modern-day adaptations of classical literature and drama and edgy indie films that touch upon current "hot-button" issues like teen suicide, violence, and sex. The eclectic roster includes:

- Films that focused on disaffected, alienated youth (*The River's Edge* [1986], *Permanent Record* [1988], *Pump Up the Volume* [1990]).
- The "Generation X" films by newbie directors like Cameron Crowe (*Say Anything* [1989], *Singles* [1992]); Richard Linklater (*Slacker* [1991], *Dazed and Confused*

[1993], *Before Sunrise* [1995], *SubUrbia* [1996]);
Kevin Smith (*Clerks* [1994], *Mallrats* [1995]); and
Ben Stiller (*Reality Bites* [1994]).

- The revival of the teen horror film and the teen sex
  comedy, which were ushered in by the success of two
  moneymaking trilogies, *Scream* (1996), a postmodern
  slasher film, and the *Porky's* of the new millennium,
  American Pie (1999).

- A new crop of teen romantic comedies and dramas
  loosely based on classical works such as Jane Austen's
  Emma (*Clueless* [1995]); Dostoyevsky's *Crime and
  Punishment* (*Crime and Punishment in Suburbia* [2000]);
  Choderlos de Laclos's *Les Liaisons Dangereuses* (*Cruel
  Intentions* [1999]); Rostand's *Cyrano de Bergerac*
  (*Whatever It Takes* [2000]); along with updated versions
  of fairy tales (*A Cinderella Story* [2004]) and
  Shakespearean tragedies and comedies (*Romeo + Juliet*
  [1996], *The Taming of the Shrew/10 Things I Hate
  About You* [1999], *Othello/O* [2001]).

- The debut work of young black filmmakers like
  Matty Rich (*Straight Out of Brooklyn* [1991]),
  Albert and Allen Hughes (*Menace II Society* [1993]),
  and John Singleton (*Boyz n the Hood* [1991]), who
  relocated the genre's setting to the inner city.

- Independent films about teenagers that tackle serious
  themes and controversial issues, including violence
  (*The River's Edge, Bully* [2001]), and sex
  (*Kids* [1995]).

Disaffected and Disengaged

In the mid-eighties, a new generation of young American writers burst onto the literary scene overnight with the publication of their first short stories and novels, which were contemporary coming-of-age stories about disaffected teenagers and twentysomethings disengaged from everything and everyone around them. In Bret Easton Ellis's *Less Than Zero* (1985), the story's first-person narrator is a rich kid named Clay who returns to Los Angeles from college for the holidays. He spends his vacation going to parties and seeing his friends, including his on-again/off-again girlfriend Blair, yet the entire time he remains, like a sleepwalker, emotionally distant. Before he heads back to school, Blair tries to get him to open up. She asks him if he ever cared about her. "I don't want to care," he says. "If I care about things, it'll just be worse; it'll just be another thing to worry about. It's less painful if I don't care."[148]

In his analysis of coming-of-age novels of the eighties and nineties, critic Kirk Curnutt questions why characters like Clay, along with the young protagonists of Jay McInerney's *Bright Lights, Big City* (1984), Michael Chabon's *The Mysteries of Pittsburgh* (1987), and in the nineties, Donna Tart's *The Secret History* (1992), "constitute a species of the walking dead" who are "emotionally and morally obtuse."[149] Unlike most young, troubled characters in adolescent-themed fiction, the "disaffected disposition" of young people in contemporary coming-of-age novels is not due to pressure from their oppressive parents or some other authority figure to conform. They are simply aimless, amoral, and in need of the very things that they lack: support, direction, and moral guidance from a parent or adult.[150]

Adapting a novel for the screen can be challenging, particularly when a story is told from the point of view of a narrator who is emotionally detached from the world. *Less Than Zero* certainly didn't fit the Hollywood mold for commercial moviemaking; the novel is essentially plotless and the main character is a passive observer. When producer Jon Avnet (*Risky Business*) read the first draft of the screenplay, a reportedly faithful adaptation by Pulitzer Prize–winning playwright Michael Cristofer, he found it "depressing and so degrading." By the time the film finally landed in theaters in November 1987, the story and characters were totally whitewashed. Clay's (Andrew McCarthy) bisexuality, along with his casual sexual encounters and drug use was gone from the story, which now could have been mistaken for a Public Service Announcement about the evils of cocaine.[151]

The film's plotline revolves around Clay and Blair's (Jami Gertz) attempt to save their self-destructive friend, Julian (Robert Downey, Jr.), a cokehead who hits bottom when he is forced to turn tricks for his sleazy drug dealer, Rip (James Spader). The ending is predictable and its moral message simplistic: drugs are bad. In a *New York Times* article about the "sanitizing" of the novel, Aljean Harmetz reported that the filmmakers admitted to softening the film's sexual content due to the AIDS crisis.[152] They also added scenes to make Clay and Blair more repentant about their drug use, including one in which she throws her cocaine down a bathroom sink (to the cheers of one audience, according to Harmetz). Producer Scott Rudin didn't deny that the final cut of the film was affected by the "tremendous conservative change in young audiences since the book was written in 1984."[153] Even with all the changes, Avnet admitted that the film still had too much of an "edge to be a mass-market success."[154] His prediction was right. The film only grossed $12.3 million at the box office.

Cocaine is also the drug of choice in both the novel and the film version of *Bright Lights, Big City* (1988). Director James Bridges, working from a screenplay by McInerney, effectively captured the coke-induced downward spiral of a yuppie named Jamie (Michael J.

Fox). His fashion-model wife (Phoebe Cates) has left him, his job as a fact-checker for a magazine is in jeopardy, his mother is dying, and his only friend is his drinking buddy and coke dealer, Tad Aligash (Kiefer Sutherland). As with *Less Than Zero*'s Julian, the audience witnesses Jamie's descent to the bottom, which picks up speed as his drug use (and his life) spin out of control over the course of a week.

In *Generation Ecch!*, a satirical analysis of Generation-X culture, Jason Cohen and Michael Krugman state that one of the central problems with the coming-of-age stories by this generation of young writers is their lack of "any sharp insight or affecting emotional glimpse into the human condition . . . [Their] portraits of solipsism, blankness and reticence . . . are themselves solipsistic, blank, and reticent."[155] The same is true for the film versions of both *Less Than Zero* and *Bright Lights, Big City*, which offer little, if any, real insight into the twentysomething generation. In her review of *Bright Lights*, critic Janet Maslin appreciated how the film doesn't moralize, but depicts Jamie's self-destructive behavior "in a nonjudgmental way, letting both the character and the audience come to their own conclusions."[156] But to draw conclusions, shouldn't the audience (and the filmmakers) have a clear picture of what's going on in Jamie's head? As *Washington Post* critic Hal Hinson observed, "Watching it, you never sense the filmmakers' attitudes toward their material, or exactly what conclusions they would like us to draw from the story."[158]

By comparison, there's plenty to ponder at the end of *River's Edge* (1986), a fictionalized account of the 1981 rape-murder of a fourteen-year-old girl, Marcy Conrad, by her sixteen-year-old boyfriend, Anthony Jacques Broussard, in a small, northern California town. The real murder received national attention when it was discovered that Broussard showed Conrad's body to his friends and two days passed before someone reported it to the police.

Twenty-two-year-old screenwriter Neal Jimenez used the incident as the basis for his cinematic investigation of what he perceived as his generation's general lack of morality and emotional detachment from the world.[159]

For most human beings it's a no-brainer: your friend admits to killing his girlfriend, who is also your friend. When he proves it by showing you her nude corpse, you immediately pick up the phone and call the police. But when Samson "John" Tollet (Daniel Roebuck) shows his friends the body of his dead girlfriend, Jamie (Danyi Deats), they don't go straight to the police, but wander around in a haze wondering what to do. A speed freak named Layne (Crispin Glover), who decides he's going to help Samson, has no problem justifying the crime: "He had his reasons," he matter-of-factly explains to Clarissa (Ione Skye). "She was shooting her mouth off about his mom." The frenetic Layne, who is as crazy as Samson, begins to revel in his self-appointed role as John's protector, but not out of loyalty. As he explains, it's what friends in the movies do for each other: "This is like some fuckin' movie. Friends since second grade . . . and then one of us gets into some potentially big trouble, and now we've got to deal with it. We got to test our loyalty against all odds. It's kind of . . . exciting. I feel like Chuck Norris, you know?" As director Tim Hunter explained in an interview, "obviously what Layne does is wrong. There's nothing more important than friendship, but Layne's a sociopath whose conceptions are only half-formed and came from the movies or media."[160]

At one point, Clarissa and her friend Maggie (Roxana Zal) come close to calling the police, but they change their minds at the last minute for reasons they don't seem to completely understand. Finally, a stoner named Matt (Keanu Reeves) goes to the police, who have trouble believing his story and grow increasingly more frustrated as he repeatedly answers their questions with "I don't know." Meanwhile, Samson has been left in the care of Layne's equally deranged friend, a sixties burnout named Fleck (Dennis Hopper), who has something in common with Samson: he killed his girlfriend many years ago, but he insists he did it out of love. The teenager touches a nerve in Fleck, who is disturbed by his fellow killer's lack of emotions. When Samson shoots Fleck's gun randomly out into the air, he gets annoyed. "It's not something I shoot off without reason," Fleck explains. "It's got sentimental value." Samson's complete lack of remorse or emotions even scares Fleck, who feels he has no choice but to kill him. "There was no hope for him. He didn't love her," he later explains. "At least I loved her. I cared for her."

So who or what is to blame for turning America's youth into a generation of zombies? Unlike the juvenile delinquent films of the fifties, the film doesn't offer any pat answers or even point fingers. The adults in the film are as screwed up as the kids. Even Clarissa's teacher, Mr. Burkewaite (Jim Metzler), a former sixties Berkeley radical, berates his students (and himself) for their lack of feeling over their classmate's death. There is indeed something terribly wrong when a teenager is more affected by a made-for-TV movie than seeing her murdered friend's dead body. It's even more disturbing that after all that has happened, Jamie's friends file past her open casket in the final scene with blank expressions on their faces.

River's Edge was a low-budget film ($1.7 million) that dealt with a subject matter that was hardly considered commercial by Hollywood standards, though the favorable critical attention the film received definitely helped it find an audience in cities across the country. There were other, more mainstream films that also touched on the alienation, the isolation, confusion, and discontent of teenagers and twentysomethings in the post-Reagan era. Although they lacked the edginess of a film like *River's Edge*, they were also intended for a much older audience than John Hughes's work and the other serious teen films that were popular in the early to mid-eighties. They also came at a time when Hollywood was making more movies for older audiences. According to the Motion Picture Association of America, movie attendance by moviegoers forty years and older rose 56 percent in the late eighties, which may account in part for the box-office success of more adult-oriented films like *Platoon* (1986), *Fatal Attraction* (1987), *The Untouchables* (1987), and *Rain Man* (1988).[161]

For example, one issue that finally found its way onto the big screen was teenage suicide. With the exception of *Ode to Billy Joe* and Robert Redford's Academy Award–winning *Ordinary People* (1980), in which a guilt-ridden, suicidal teenager comes to terms with his brother's accidental death, the subject of teen suicide was limited to television dramas, including After School Specials (*Hear Me Cry* [1984], *A Desperate Exit* [1986]) and two excellent made-for-TV films, *Silence of the Heart* (1984) and *Surviving* (1985). Airing at a time when "cluster" and "copycat" teen suicides were occurring around the country, all four dramas focused on the effects of teen suicide on those who are left behind, namely family members and friends who ask why a young person who appeared to have everything going for them would choose to take his or her life.[162]

The 1988 feature film *Permanent Record* posed a similar question. David (Alan Boyce) is a bright, talented high-school senior whose life is cut short when he falls off a cliff. His best friend Chris's (Keanu Reeves) worst fear, that David jumped, is confirmed when he receives a suicide note in the mail that reads: "I wanted everything to be perfect. It wasn't." Like David's family and friends, the audience doesn't fully understand what was going on inside David's head. While this is familiar territory, director Marisa Silver and screenwriters Jarre Fees, Alice Liddle, and Larry Ketron avoid the usual hysterics that audiences might expect from such emotionally charged subject matter. The outward signs that David is distraught to the point of suicide are not even obvious. He seems like he's under pressure, but no more than the average teenager. As is often the case in teen suicides, there is no clear-cut explanation for why David chose to end his life—which is precisely the filmmakers' point.

Unlike *Permanent Record*, there is no mystery surrounding the suicide of *Dead Poets Society*'s (1989) Neil Perry (Robert Sean Leonard), a sensitive teenager at a posh prep school, who picks up a gun and shoots himself in the head. Neil feels it's the only way to free himself from the clutches of his tyrannical father (Kurtwood Smith), who pulls his son out of school when he disobeys his orders and performs in the school's production of *A Midsummer Night's Dream*. Neil was only following the advice of his free-spirited literature teacher, Mr. Keating (Robin Williams), whose watch cry is *Carpe Diem* ("Seize the Day"). But this is 1959 and a New England boarding school is no place for nonconformists like Keating, who prefers the romantic poets over the realists, and students like Neil, who would rather be an actor than fulfill his father's dream of becoming a doctor. Neil is the story's "sacrificial lamb"—he needs to die so his classmates can prove that Keating's message did not fall on deaf ears. In the film's final moment, Neil's roommate, Todd Anderson (Ethan Hawke), pledges his allegiance to Mr. Keating, who is dismissed after being blamed for Neil's death, by standing on his desk and shouting "O Captain!, My Captain!" the title of poet Walt Whitman's homage to the late Abraham Lincoln. Todd, together with several of his classmates who were forced to sign a statement blaming their favorite teacher for Neil's death, defy the command of their evil headmaster (Norman Lloyd) to sit down. While it is certainly a touching and emotionally satisfying ending, it is a bit ironic that a film that preaches nonconformity ends with students standing on their desks verbally saluting their departing captain.

Students in a suburban Arizona high school defy authority on a larger scale in Allan Moyle's *Pump Up the Volume* (1990). The instigator in this case is Mark Hunter (Christian Slater), a loner by day who in the P.M. assumes the identity of a radio shock jock named Hard Harry, who tells it like it is via a pirate radio station in his basement. Harry quickly develops a strong following among the various groups (the jocks, the nerds, the punkers, et al.) that compose the student body of Hubert Humphrey High School. He is a rebel with a microphone, who, in a series of rants superbly delivered by Slater, expresses his generation's anger, discontent, fears, and despair over, in Harry's words, "living in a totally exhausted decade where there is nothing to look forward to and no one to look up to." According to Harry, the sixties generation already exhausted all the standard forms of teenage rebellion (sex, drugs, political activism)—so what's left? "Eat your cereal with a fork and do your homework in the dark," he tells his teenage listeners, who grow increasingly restless as they start to take Harry's mantras ("Talk Hard," "So be it," and "The Truth is a Virus") to heart, much to the dismay of the school's oppressive, intolerant administration. But things start to get serious when Harry talks to a kid on the air who makes good on his threat to kill himself and the teenagers start to get unruly. Ironically, they express their defiance in a rather subdued manner. Unlike their sixties counterparts, who would have been breaking windows, or taking over the administration building, they dance to loud music on the school grounds after dark.

Still, writer/director Moyle, who is not a member of what Harry calls the "Why bother? generation," understands the psyche of the

American teenager. Perhaps Harry, his mouthpiece, has a little too much insight into what's going on in the minds of his generation, but the bigger problem lies with the way he characterizes the opposition. Harry's primary target is the school's self-serving principal, Loretta Creswood (Annie Ross), who thinks nothing of expelling any student who doesn't live up to her academic and moral standards. Creswood is so devious and corrupt, she might as well be wearing black and twirling a mustache. Unfortunately, displacing the source of oppression onto one rotten apple weakens the film's plea to the older generation to listen to what the younger one has to say.

Generation X

We're all about to enter "the real world." That's what everybody says. But most of us have been in the real world for a long time. But I have something to tell everybody. I've glimpsed our future, and all I can say is . . . go back!

—Diane Court (Ione Skye), high-school commencement speech, *Say Anything* (1989)

And they wonder why those of us in our twenties refuse to work an eighty-hour week just so we can afford to buy their BMWs. Why we aren't interested in the counterculture they invented, as if we didn't see them disavowal their revolution for a pair of running shoes. But the question remains: What are we going to do now? How can we repair all the damage we inherited? Fellow graduates, the answer is simple: The answer is (pause) . . . the answer is . . . I don't know.

—Lelaina Price (Winona Ryder), college commencement speech *Reality Bites* (1994)

In 1990, there were an estimated forty-eight million Americans between the ages of eighteen and twenty-nine. As with the baby boomers back in the eighties, advertisers, marketing consultants, pollsters, TV network executives, sociologists, and anyone else who divided the U.S. population into demographic groups for a living, wanted to better understand this generation born between the years 1964 and 1977. They wanted to know what made them tick. What were their values? Their goals? What social issues were important to them? Where, if at all, did they stand politically?

But first they had to give them a name. A July 9, 1990, *Time* magazine article citing the lack of interest in the news among those thirty and under called them the "tuned-out" generation.[163] A *Time* cover story that appeared the following week dubbed them "twentysomethings" (a term no doubt derived from the title of the then-current ABC yuppie drama, *thirtysomething*). The same article also described them as "the unsung generation" who are "hardly recognized as a social force or even noticed much at all."[164] As author Geoffrey T. Holtz points out, most of the names used by major publications around that time were less than flattering: "the doofus generation" (*Washington Post*), "the numb generation" (*New York Times*), and "the Blank Generation" (*San Francisco Examiner*).[165]

The name that did stick was not derived from a newspaper or magazine article written by a baby boomer, but from the title of a 1991 novel by twenty-eight-year-old writer Douglas Coupland entitled *Generation X: Tales for an Accelerated Culture*. Coupland's story follows three overeducated and underemployed college graduates who try to give their lives some meaning by cutting themselves off from the world and moving to the desert.[166] The term "Generation X" first appeared in print back in 1964 as the title of a popular sociological study of British youth. It was later the name of a punk-rock band featuring singer Billy Idol.[167] In a 1995 piece for *Details* magazine, Coupland stated that the book's title did not come from Idol's band, but a 1983 book by Paul Fussell about class in American society entitled *Class*. Fussell describes an "X" category of people who, according to Coupland, wanted to "hop off the merry-go-round of status, money, and social climbing that so often frames modern existence."[168]

In the same article, Coupland recounts how his novel received no attention when it first hit the bookstore shelves in March 1991. It wasn't until the grunge music explosion in Seattle and the release of Richard Linklater's film *Slacker* (1991) that "Generation X" (along with "slacker" and "grunge") became "buzzwords" for the younger generation. Coupland explained how "trendmeisters everywhere began isolating small elements of . . . [his] characters' lives—their offhand way of handling problems or their questioning of the status quo—and blew them up to represent an entire generation."[169] He also blamed "baby boomers, who, feeling pummeled by the recession and embarrassed by their own compromised fifties values, began transferring their collective darkness onto the group threatening to take their spotlight."[170] As a result, an entire generation was labeled by boomers as whiny, apathetic, slackers. To complicate matters even more, "Generation X" was adopted by advertisers and marketers, who engaged in what Coupland called "demographic pornography" to lure young consumers, who, according to Roper Marketing and Public Opinion Research, had an estimated $125 billion in discretionary income.[171]

Just as Coupland and his book were dubbed by critics as the voice of his generation, the films of Linklater, Kevin Smith, and other young directors were also slapped with a "Generation X" label. Linklater's *Slacker* is regarded as the quintessential Generation-X film. The movie follows approximately one hundred characters who appear onscreen, mostly in pairs or in small groups of three or four, for just a few minutes. The film is essentially, in Linklater's words, "one long sequence in which each shot, each event, and character lead only to the next."[172] He claims the characters are "obsessed by their own thoughts" and the course of tension in the film is their "desire to act contrasted with their inability to do so."[173] Shot in Austin, Texas, for $3,000 with a mostly nonprofessional cast and crew, *Slacker* captured a certain segment of the twentysomething generation who are content with just hangin' out after college (usually in and around where they went to school) instead of working at a nine-to-five desk job. The nineties counterpart to members of the sixties counterculture, slackers pass the time in bookstores, clubs, and coffeehouses, where they also pass the time drinking coffee and beers and talking about everything and anything (including the sociopolitical subtext of the Smurfs).

Linklater said he never intended the film to be a "generational portrait," let alone one that painted twentysomethings as a bunch of lazy, aimless, apathetic do-nothings that lack any drive or ambition. The director sets the record straight in his 1991 essay "Slacker Culture," in which he defines a "slacker" as "anyone, regardless of age, who is striving to attain a realm of activity that runs parallel to their desires."[174] He shatters some of the specific myths surrounding the term by clarifying the slacker philosophy, in terms of time ("Slackers feel the urgent personal obligation to make sure what they're doing with it is worthwhile"), work ("It's downright dangerous to your health . . . If you aren't killed or crippled at work, you might very well be while going to work, coming to work, looking for work, or trying to work"), and politics ("[Slackers] continue to aggressively NOT participate in the symbolic 'choosing' act of empowering either of the factions of our one (business) political party that actually represents only 7% of our population").[175]

Riding on the success of *Slacker*, director Richard Linklater got his chance to direct a bigger-budgeted studio film, *Dazed and Confused* (1993), a high-school comedy loosely based on his own experiences. Set in 1976 and featuring a large ensemble cast that includes future stars like Ben Affleck, Matthew McConaughey, Parker Posey, and Renee Zellweger, the nostalgic comedy follows a variety of characters who are representative of the major social groups one expects to find in a high-school film (the brains, the jocks, the stoners, the derelicts, the incoming freshmen, and guys like Dave Wooderson (McConaughey) who graduated a few years back, yet still hangs around). But unlike other high-school films, which usually focus on the differences and rivalry between these groups, *Dazed and Confused* paints a much more democratic picture of high-school life by showing how these groups coexist and, for some students, even overlap.

For Gen-Xers, *Dazed and Confused* is an entertaining piece of nostalgia that includes a period sound track with songs from the mid-seventies by Black Sabbath, Alice Cooper, Deep Purple, and KISS. But like most nostalgia pieces, its view of the past is bittersweet. Linklater obviously has some affinity for his high-school years as he revels in his characters' adolescent antics, which are fueled by drugs, alcohol, and school tradition (a hazing ritual in which next year's seniors humiliate and intimidate incoming freshmen seems sadistic and senseless). Since Nancy Reagan started wagging her finger at America's youth in the 1980s, teen movies have been clean and sober (and for anyone who was drinking and using, there were usually consequences—and projectile vomiting). Marijuana made a comeback in Linklater's film, which doesn't demonize the kids who get stoned, like Randall "Pink" Floyd (Jason London), a football star and all-around nice guy. Pink's problem is a slip of paper he is being forced to sign if he wants to play ball next year pledging that he will not drink or do drugs. His coach makes it clear he doesn't approve of his stoner friends ("a bunch of clowns" as he calls them). As he agonizes over whether he should sign, Wooderson offers Pink some solid advice: "You know if it ain't that piece of paper, it's some other choice they're gonna make for you. You gotta do what Randall "Pink" Floyd wants to, man." And that's exactly what he does. In the end, Pink's whole attitude toward his high-school years (and for that matter, the film's and Linklater's) is one of indifference. "If I ever start referring to these as the best years of my life," Pink tells his friends, "remind me to kill myself."

One only hopes that after graduation, Pink did not end up like the teenagers in Linklater's fourth film, *SubUrbia* (1996). Based on the play by monologist Eric Bogosian, who adapted it for the screen, *SubUrbia* is unlike most teen films because the action is confined to a single setting—the outside of a suburban convenience store—where a group of bored, college-age teens spend their evenings hanging out, drinking beers, eating pizza, and talking. Jeff (Giovanni Ribisi) is a college dropout whose girlfriend Sooze (Amie Carey), an aspiring performance artist, wants to move to New York. Buff (Steve Zahn) is a total goofball on roller blades who is up for anything. Tim (Nicky Katt), who has just been discharged from the air force, is a racist with anger issues who taunts a young, immigrant storeowner (Ajay Naidu).

Jeff, who comes the closest to being the film's protagonist, is an angry white liberal male who announces early on that it's his "duty as a human being to be pissed off." In an endless stream of diatribes, he rants and raves about how everything in the world is "so fucking futile." (When Tim challenges him and asks why he's getting so upset if it's "fucking futile," Jeff answers, without missing a beat, "because I'm alienated.") As Bogosian explained in an interview, he, like Jeff, "was completely committed to doing nothing with my life. I saw this as a heroic stance, not allowing myself to be co-opted by society."[176]

What seems like is going to be another night of just hanging out takes an interesting turn when Pony (Jayce Bartok), a high-school friend who is now a rock star, returns to his old neighborhood with his publicist (Parker Posey), just to say hi. Suzy and Buff are instantly impressed, but his presence unnerves Jeff and Tim. All their anger and bitterness boil to the surface until the film's final moments when Jeff begins to realize that his alienated, futile existence is due to his own lack of commitment. As Jeff stands over the body of a young girl who has overdosed, the distressed storeowner gives Jeff (and presumably the teenage audience) a wake-up call by shouting, "You people are so stupid! What's wrong with you? You throw it all away! You throw it all away!" Although young audiences might find the film too talky, stagy, or existential, it's a powerful piece thanks to Bogosian's literate script and a talented ensemble cast.

The Askewniverse of Kevin Smith

In spite of its title, Linklater's *Slacker* inspired an aspiring writer and director from New Jersey, twenty-two-year-old Kevin Smith, to raise $27,575 (by getting advances on his credit cards, selling his comic-book collection, and borrowing money from his parents) to make his first feature film, *Clerks*. The slacker comedy is a day in the life of a convenience-store clerk, Dante Hicks (Brian O'Halloran), and his friend Randal (Jeff Anderson), who works at the video store next door. Smith shot the film in black-and-white in twenty-one consecutive evenings when the store, where Smith was still working as a clerk, was closed. His efforts certainly paid off. Smith won the "Filmmakers Trophy" at the 1994 Sundance Film Festival and received two awards at the 1994 Cannes Film Festival. The film was picked up by

BIG SCREEN/small screen

In the spring of 2000, an animated version of Kevin Smith's *Clerks* debuted on ABC. Only two episodes aired before the network pulled the plug. The series was another casualty in the long list of teen movies that didn't survive the transition from the big screen to the small. Teen movies have a particularly bad track record because the film is often old news by the time the series airs. Here is a partial list of some short-lived TV shows based on popular teen movies:

Delta House (1979): Based on the mega-hit *National Lampoon's Animal House,* this sanitized TV version was one of three *Animal House*–inspired sitcoms that debuted during the spring of 1979. *Delta House* and NBC's *Brothers and Sisters* were on double secret probation for three months before getting the ax. The CBS comedy *Co-ed Fever* barely made it through the first commercial break; it was cancelled after one episode.

Fast Times (1986): Imagine *Fast Times at Ridgemont High* without Sean Penn—and the laughs. The hilarious Ray Walston returned as Ridgemont's no-nonsense history teacher, Mr. Hand, but the rest of the cast, which included Patrick Dempsey and Courtney Thorne-Smith, were unknowns. School ended early that year. After a two-month run, Ridgemont High closed its doors for good.

Dirty Dancing (1988–1989): Patrick Cassidy and Melora Hardin stepped in for Patrick Swayze and Jennifer Grey for the small-screen version of this mega-box-office hit. Unfortunately, the viewing audience was not having the time of their lives. The series took its final bow after three months.

Ferris Bueller (1990): Bueller? Bueller? Schlatter? Poor Charlie Schlatter was given the almost impossible task of filling Matthew Broderick's shoes in this failed TV version of the hit John Hughes comedy, which also featured newcomer Jennifer Aniston as Ferris's sister, Jeannie.

Bill & Ted's Excellent Adventure (1992): Alex Winter and Keanu Reeves were totally awesome as the two righteous dudes who travel back in time. But this TV version with Evan Richards and Christopher Kennedy in the title roles was heinous.

Party Girl (1996): Christine Taylor played the title role based on the indie comedy starring Parker Posey. The party was over after four episodes.

Clueless (1996–1997): *Clueless* without Alicia Silverstone? As if.

Some teen films did enjoy respectable runs as TV series: *What's Happening!!* (1976–1979), a sitcom loosely based on *Cooley High* (1975); *Fame* (1982–1987), which aired for eight months on NBC, and then continued for four more years in first-run syndication; and the biggest BIG SCREEN/small screen success story, the new and improved television version of the 1992 horror/comedy, *Buffy the Vampire Slayer.*

Miramax and grossed $3.1 million in the United States.

As you might expect from a film set in a convenience store, *Clerks* is short on plot. Smith's comedy is more of a character piece that perfectly captures the frustrations of Gen-Xers, who, like Dante, are dissatisfied with their lives, yet are either incapable of or don't want to do anything about it. Dante and Randal are true slackers who spend most of the film sitting around talking about movies (like the *Star Wars* trilogy), sex, and their annoying customers (one of the film's advertising taglines is "Just because they serve you doesn't mean they like you"). Their banter is witty and authentic (at this point in his career Smith's writing ability surpassed his directorial skills), yet Smith doesn't let Dante, who is in a funk when he learns his ex-girlfriend is engaged, get away with all his pissing and moaning about life and the fact that he's working on his day off. Randal finally tells him to take some responsibility for his own situation. "You sound like an asshole! Jesus, nobody twisted your arm to be here," says Randal. "Us, we like to make ourselves seem so much more important than the people that come in here . . . We look down on them as if we're so advanced. Well, if we're so advanced, what are we doing here?"

As with Richard Linklater, Smith landed a deal with Universal Studios for his sophomore film, another slacker comedy called *Mallrats* (1995). Instead of a convenience store, the film is set in a shopping mall, where two guys, Brodie (Jason Lee) and T.S. (Jeremy London), who were both just dumped by their girlfriends, pass the time. Brodie and T.S. walk through the mall and talk and talk and talk (actually Brodie does most of the talking). Along the way, they meet lots of colorful characters, like the Easter Bunny, a fortune-teller, a teenager who is doing research for her sex book, a guy who spends his day staring at a poster to find the hidden image, and comic-book legend Stan Lee. In *Clerks*, Smith could get away without having a plot because his characters were confined to the inside of a convenience store (except for the hockey game they play on the roof). But in *Mallrats*, there is no excuse. The closest thing to a plotline revolves around the guys' attempts to win back their respective girlfriends, by appearing on a dating show, *Truth or Date*, that's taping in the mall.

In Kevin Smith's "View Askewniverse," both the suburban mall and the corner convenience store are havens for overgrown adolescent males, a place where they can get away with extreme antisocial behavior.[177] Brodie is a true-blue slacker who is more interested in comic books and playing his Sega game than spending time with his girlfriend, Rene (Shannen Doherty). He is a highly intelligent, very opinionated guy; some of his observations are actually quite insightful. But he knows very little about women and, like a child, he is easily agitated and has a tendency to start screaming and shouting at anything or anyone that's in his way. By comparison, T.S. is much calmer and more of a romantic. He's bummed because he was ready to propose to his fiancée, Brandi (Claire Forlani), during a trip to Disney World. So with help from Jay (Jason Mewes) and Silent Bob (Smith), who appeared in *Clerks*, Brodie and T.S. hatch a scheme. Mewes and Smith are supposed to be the film's comic relief, but their stunts fall flat because these guys are not skilled enough performers and Smith is not an experienced enough director to pull off physical comedy. On the whole, the final sequence involving the dating show lands with a thud.

Smith's sense of humor is often crude (in *Clerks*, Dante's girlfriend accidentally screws a dead guy), particularly the misogynistic ramblings of potty-mouthed Jay. Yet, his third film, *Chasing Amy*, which is the final part of Smith's New Jersey trilogy, showed definite signs that he was maturing as a filmmaker and was beginning to work out some of his issues around sex and women. The film's lead character, Holden McNeil (Ben Affleck), who Smith admits was modeled after himself, has trouble accepting his girlfriend Amy's (Joey Lauren Adams) sexual history. "And rather than enter therapy," Smith wrote, "I decided to exercise my demons on screen. *Chasing Amy* was conceived as a sort of penance/valentine for the women who made me grow up, more or less—a thank-you homage that marked a major milestone in my life, both personally and professionally."[178]

A Little Romance

In addition to worrying about the world they inherited and their future, Gen-Xers also had issues around relationships, commitment, and the "M" word. Twentysomethings were certainly in no rush to get married. In fact, they waited longer than any previous generation to walk down the aisle. In 1992, the median age for getting married was 26.5 for men and 24.24 for women. Back in 1975, the ages for both sexes were significantly lower: 23.5 for men and 21.2 for women.[179] In a 1990 piece for *Time* magazine, aptly titled "Proceeding with Caution," David M. Gross and Sophfronia Scott concluded that most young people are afraid of relationships and skeptical about marriage. They would rather wait and find a mate they can have for life. Some are even hesitant about dating, because, in the words of one twentysomething, "not getting hurt is a big priority for me."[180]

The ambivalence Gen-Xers feel about love and relationships is evident in Richard Linklater's romantic comedy-drama, *Before Sunrise* (1995). In the opening scene, two total strangers Celine (Julie Delpy), a French student, and Jesse (Ethan Hawke), an American, meet on a train. She is heading back to Paris to go to school, while he is flying home from Vienna the next day. He convinces her to spend the day with him in Vienna while he waits for his plane to leave. They spend the rest of the film walking about the city, discussing everything from sex to reincarnation to what pisses them off. They also share their insights about relationships. He claims that people start to grow apart and hate each other when each partner begins to anticipate the other's reactions and get tired of his/her mannerisms. She is more of a romantic. "I think I could fall in love when I know everything about someone," she admits. "The way he's gonna part his hair. Which shirt she's gonna wear that day. Knowing the exact story he's gonna tell in any situation. I'm sure that's when I'd know I'm really in love."

While it takes time to learn everything there is to know about another person, Linklater and co-writer Kim Krizan succeed in compacting the major stages of most relationships (meeting, being in love, and parting) into a single day. Delpy and Hawke are engaging as the couple, and they got a chance to reunite onscreen nine years later in a sequel, *Before Sunset* (2004), which earned an Oscar nomination for its screenplay, with a story by Krizan and Linklater, who then collaborated with actors Delpy and Hawke on the script.

Although Cameron Crowe is perhaps too old to qualify as a Gen-Xer (he was born in 1957), the writer/director whose *Fast Times* captured high-school life in the pre-conservative 1980s, started his filmmaking career at the end of the decade with a pair of comedies about relationships among high-school graduates (*Say Anything . . .* [1989]) and twentysomethings who are at that point in their lives when it's time to really start acting like a grown-up (*Singles* [1992]). *Say Anything . . .* was heralded as one of the best teen romantic comedies because the two lead characters, Lloyd Dobler (John Cusack) and Diane Court (Ione Skye), both recent high-school grads, are actually intelligent human beings.

There is nothing extraordinary about Lloyd. As his friend Corey (Lili Taylor) tells him, "You're a really nice guy," which is why she and friend D.C. (Amy Brooks) are worried when he asks out Diane, who is a "brain . . . trapped in the body of a game-show hostess." Diane, who is valedictorian of her class, has her future planned out. But Lloyd has no idea what he wants to do with his life, and is skeptical that the other kids in his graduating class don't really know either (he tells his career counselor, who corners him at a party, that he's looking for a "dare-to-be-great situation"). But what Lloyd does know is that he doesn't want to follow the path of the baby boomers. "I don't want to sell anything, buy anything, or process anything as a career," he tells Diane's less-than-impressed father (John Mahoney). "I don't want to sell anything bought or processed, or buy anything sold or processed, or process anything sold, bought, or processed, or repair anything sold, bought, or processed. You know, as a career, I don't want to do that."

Lloyd and Diane grow closer and even get intimate, much to the disapproval of her father, who has problems of his own when an IRS investigation leads to his arrest for stealing money from the residents of the nursing home he owns and operates. The IRS plotline feels too much like a movie "device" next to the Crowe's mature and refreshingly honest portrayal of two young people in love, which manages to avoid all the phony contrivances that usually provide the source of tension between young couples (rich vs. poor, his friends vs. her friends, etc.) and by sticking with his characters' most basic human emotions. In all of its simplicity, *Say Anything* . . . raised the bar for the teen romantic comedy.

Unfortunately, there's something missing from Crowe's next film, *Singles* (1992), which takes a look at the lives of folks in their twenties living in Seattle. Crowe's story shifts between an assortment of characters: Linda (Kyra Sedgwick), who is afraid her bad luck with men is going to continue after she meets nice guy Steve (Campbell Scott), a city engineer. Steve's neighbor, Janet (Bridget Fonda) has it bad for a flaky, smooth-talking musician named Cliff (Matt Dillon), whom she later realizes is the wrong guy for her. Then there's Debbie (Sheila Kelley) who tries video dating, and Bailey (Jim True), who collects phone numbers from girls he doesn't have the courage to call. Crowe's characters spend far too much time reflecting on their lives, and because their problems are not terribly compelling, the end result feels like a well-written episode of *Melrose Place*. What's so great about *Say Anything* . . . is that Crowe doesn't allow his characters to overanalyze their relationships, even when Diane breaks it off with

Lloyd because she's leaving for England anyway and her father needs her. Fortunately, she soon realizes that she needs Lloyd even more.

A fear of commitment also plagues the characters in *Reality Bites* (1994), a coming-of-age romantic comedy directed by Ben Stiller. The film follows four recent college grads (actually, one never finished) as they enter the so-called "real world," where they discover there is not a whole lot waiting for them in terms of relationships and careers. Lelaina (Winona Ryder), an aspiring videographer, is the most ambitious. She sabotages her job on a local morning show to work on her own stuff. Opportunity presents itself in the guise of a TV programming executive, Michael Grates (Stiller), who works for In Your Face TV, which Lelaina describes as "MTV, but with an edge." A love triangle of sorts develops between Michael, Lelaina, and her college chum, Troy (Ethan Hawke), who is the character in the film who comes closest to being a slacker. He is highly intelligent, plays in a band, and has a reputation as, to quote Lelaina, "a master at the art of time suckage."

There is plenty of angst to go around. When Lelaina finally sleeps with Troy, the smarmy, self-assured musician panics and eventually disappears. She is consoled by her relationship-phobic roommate, Vickie (Janeane Garofalo), who keeps a running log of the men she sleeps with, none of with whom she gets romantically involved.

At one point Vickie has to deal with one of the realities of being sexually active in the nineties when she has to take an HIV test. In one of the film's most memorable exchanges, Vickie is freaked out about getting tested. "And it's not like it's not even happening to me," she admits. "It's like I'm watching it on some crappy show like *Melrose Place* or some shit, right, and I'm the new character. I'm the HIV/AIDS character and I live in the building and I teach everybody that 'It's okay to be near me, it's okay to talk to me.' And then I die.

And there's everybody at my funeral wearing halter tops or chokers or some shit like that." Lelaina tells her everything is going to be all right, takes a pause, and says "*Melrose Place* is a really good show."

Vickie's idea of seeing her life as an episode of *Melrose Place* is just one example of how twenty-three-year-old screenwriter Helen Childress reveals the depths to which her generation is media-saturated (a drinking game in which participants name episodes of the sitcom *Good Times* is another). But this point is made clear when Lelaina gives Michael a sample of her documentary, which consists of raw footage she shot of her friends interacting and talking about their lives. As she explains to Michael, it's a film about "people trying to find their own identity without having any real role models." But when Michael gets through with it, it has been re-cut in a slick, sensationalistic style similar to that of MTV's *The Real World*. Lelaina, an idealist who says she "wants to make a difference in people's lives," gets a major reality check. Childress and Stiller are careful not to make Michael into a total villain, though it's not surprising when it's revealed during the credits that he basically used Lelaina's concept and turned it into a cheesy (and poorly acted) soap opera.

To suggest that *Reality Bites* reflects what an entire generation is thinking and feeling about their lives would be absurd. This was certainly not the intention of the filmmakers, who went out of their away to avoid labeling it a Generation-X film. As he stated in an interview published after the movie's opening in February 1994, Stiller was especially aware that "Generation X stuff will scare them off."[181] And it did. The film opened to good reviews, but grossed only $20.9 million at the box office.

Slash and Rehash

As if the world that was waiting for them wasn't scary enough, teens were once again forced to confront their fears when the slasher film made a surprise return in the mid-nineties. Although the genre had reached its peak in the early to mid-eighties, *Halloween*'s Michael Myers, *Friday the 13th*'s Jason Voorhees, and *Elm Street*'s Freddy Krueger, never fell off the radar completely. They continued their reign of terror throughout the nineties, but as their popularity started to wane at the box office, the studios behind these franchises found it increasingly more difficult to keep audiences interested. Even the genre's most diehard fans, who are also its toughest critics, were growing restless. The Internet, particularly online forums, newsgroups, and e-film critic Web sites provided anyone with a computer and something to say a chance to vent about the dumb premises of films like *Halloween: The Curse of Michael Myers* (1995), in which Michael is controlled by evil druids (c'mon!), and the futuristic *Jason X* (2001), in which Jason runs amok on a spaceship in the year 2455 (oh, please!).

There was one attempt to get back to the basics. Twenty years after *Halloween*, former scream-queen Jamie Lee Curtis reprised her role as Laurie Strode in the aptly titled *Halloween H20* (1998). Laurie, who now goes by the name Keri Tate, is the headmistress at a private school. She's also a nervous, overprotective mother of a teenage son, John (Josh Hartnett), especially around Halloween time. Michael's bloody rampages in parts four through six, which involved members of the Strode family, are never acknowledged (that's actually a plus), which made it easier for the filmmakers to go back to square one. Only this time forty-year-old Laurie is fighting back in what culminates with a long-awaited brother-vs.-sister showdown.

Halloween H2O grossed a respectable $55 million, so Dimension Films, the division of Miramax responsible for *Scream*, couldn't stop there. In *Halloween: Resurrection* (2002), we discover Laurie did not succeed in decapitating Michael at the end of *H2O*. Apparently he pulled the old switcheroo with an ambulance driver whose vocal cords were so damaged, Laurie couldn't understand his cries for help. It's a cheap trick that negated what was an otherwise satisfying conclusion to the Laurie/Michael plotline. Laurie finally meets her maker in the opening sequence of *Halloween: Resurrection*, which revolves around six students who spend the night in the Myers's house for a reality-TV series (a premise better executed in another horror film released the same year, *My Little Eye* [2002]). *Resurrection* has little to do with *Halloween*—it's just another example of a studio trying to keep a franchise alive.

Meanwhile, over on Elm Street, there's trouble brewing when Freddy Krueger, in an effort to revive his career as the neighborhood's *numero uno fearmeister*, digs up Jason Voorhees and sets him loose. Freddy's reputation has suffered ever since the local police and doctors have been whisking teenagers whose dreams he invaded to an institution outside of town, where they are given dream inhibitors to prevent Freddy from making a return engagement. Once Jason starts terrorizing the neighborhood, Freddy grows stronger and is ready to get back into action, only this time he's facing some "stiff" competition from Jason.

The opening sequence of *Freddy vs. Jason* is straight out of *The Slasher Moviemaker's Handbook* (if such a book existed): a teenage couple have sex and afterwards she takes the obligatory shower, while he opens a can of beer, which he doesn't get to finish because Jason arrives just in time to teach him that premarital sex and alcohol don't mix. The blood fest commences, leading to the moment the audience is waiting for: a bloody battle between Jason and Freddy. Everything about *Freddy vs. Jason* is excessive, yet, in the end, it's not a terribly scary film. Jason is at his best when he sneaks up on people. Seeing him walking through a cornfield with a machete in his hand swiping at teenagers left and right just doesn't cut it—it's more silly than horrific. The same with Freddy, who talks way, way too much in this film to the point where he's more annoying than menacing.

Michael Myers, Freddy, and Jason would have probably remained in development hell if it weren't for the success of the *Scream* trilogy. Kevin Williamson, creator of TV's *Dawson's Creek*, penned a clever and funny script about a high-school student named Sidney (Neve Campbell), who is terrorized by a killer with a penchant for scary movies. In terms of scares per seconds, the most intense sequence in the trilogy is the opening of the first film, in which the killer terrorizes an innocent teenager (Drew Barrymore) over the phone and brutally murders her when she fails to answer one of his questions correctly about slasher films (she mistakenly identifies Jason as the killer in *Friday the 13th* instead of his mother). The sequence, which ends with Casey's brutal murder, establishes the trilogy's self-reflexive tone. *Scream* is considered a postmodern slasher film because it does more than merely make an occasional reference to other films—the genre is discussed, dissected, and even analyzed by the characters. One character in particular, Randy (Jamie Kennedy), recites the rules that govern slasher films (no sex and drugs and never say "I'll be right back" or you're a goner), which Williamson adheres to closely.

In *Scream 2* (1997), the events from the first film have been turned into a best-selling book by reporter Gale Weathers (Courtney Cox) called *The Woodsboro Murders*. The sequel opens in a movie theater where a screening of the film version, entitled *Stab* (featuring Heather Graham in the Barrymore role), is interrupted by a double murder. *Scream 3* (2000) is set in Hollywood, where yet another killer strikes again on the set of *Stab 3* and starts knocking off cast members.

At one point in *Scream 3*, Randy's sister Martha (Heather Matarazzo) shows up with a tape her late brother made that explains the "Super Trilogy Rules" for the third and most likely the final chapter:

1. the killer is superhuman.
2. anyone, including the main character, can die
   (that means Sidney).
3. the past is not at rest: any sins committed in the past
   are about to break and destroy you.

In the end, Sidney retains her position as the Final Girl and the film fills in all the blanks about Sidney's late mother, whose crimes (infidelity, abandoning her bastard son, etc.) are the impetus, either directly or indirectly, for the murders in all three films.

Scream, which grossed over $100 million, had its share of imitators, which, in their attempt to duplicate its success at the box office, followed what I call the "Super Rip-off Rules":

1. Hire an ensemble cast featuring a mixture of established
   and up-and-coming twentysomething actors. You must
   include at least one cast member from either *Dawson's Creek*
   (Jonathan Jackson, Katie Holmes, Kerr Smith, and Michelle
   Williams) or *Buffy the Vampire Slayer* (Julie Benz, Marc
   Blucas, David Boreanaz, Eliza Dushku, Sarah Michelle
   Gellar, and Seth Green).
2. Get a gimmick.
3. Pepper your script with pop culture references,
   particularly to old horror movies.

In the first *Scream*, the killers follow the rules of the slasher genre that were established by *Halloween* and *Friday the 13th*. Unfortunately, most of the gimmicks used in the post-*Scream* films seemed forced. As their titles suggest, *Urban Legend* (1998) and its sequel, *Urban Legends: Final Cut* use the subject of urban legends as their source of horror. The opening of the first film is genuinely scary (always check the backseat of your car before getting in!), but the whole urban legend gimmick starts to wear thin. The gimmick takes a backseat in the sequel, which is yet another horror movie about people making a horror movie. At least this time it's a female filmmaker, actually a college student who is competing for the coveted "Hitchcock Prize" at her school. Unfortunately, she is having trouble completing her film when a killer starts knocking off her cast and crew.

Several recent horror movies have stolen—I mean borrowed—their plots from classic horror films and sci-fi thrillers like *Invasion of the Body Snatchers* (1956) and *The Stepford Wives* (the 1975 original, not the crappy 2004 remake) with mixed results. In *Disturbing Behavior* (1998), a mad scientist uses troubled teens for his mind control experiments in order to transform them à la *Stepford Wives* into an *über*-race of well-groomed, moralistic, overachievers. They are also judgmental, exclusionary, violent toward nonmembers, and have a tendency to go psycho when they are sexually aroused. James Marsden stars as the new kid in town who teams up with fellow nonconformist, played by Katie Holmes, to find out why their school has been taken over by a race of students who are a cross between aliens and Young Americans for Freedom. Unfortunately, the film's climax is not particularly satisfying. With a running time of eighty-four minutes, *Disturbing Behavior* certainly had the time to delve a little deeper into some of the issues it raises about conformity and the enormous amount of pressure teenagers are under to succeed from adults and authority figures.

The Faculty (1998) is just as schlocky, but in a more entertaining and satisfying way. A cross between The Breakfast Club and Alien (1979), the film is slickly directed by Robert Rodriguez and written by Scream's Kevin Williamson (from a story by Bruce Kimmel and David Wechter). The Faculty also has the look and feel of a 1950s B horror movie, like Invaders from Mars (1953) and the original Body Snatchers. In true Williamson fashion, Body Snatchers is even discussed by a group of students, who begin to notice that the faculty at their high school, in the words of Casey Conner (Elijah Wood), are acting like "they've all turned into fucking pod people." (When another student doesn't get the reference to "pod people," he has to explain, "Invasion of the Body Snatchers. Small town gets taken over by aliens.") Casey's observation is right on the money: an alien force has taken over the faculty and it's up to the 1990s version of The Breakfast Club, five teenagers who are all going through an identity crisis, to destroy the creature: a jock (Shawn Hatosy) who wants to quit the team; a science whiz who peddles inhalants and fake IDs (Josh Hartnett); the outsider (Clea DuVall) who dresses in black and has a major attitude; the loner (Elijah Wood) who is always getting bullied; and the southern belle (Laura Harris), who is new in school and trying to make friends. Like most of Williamson's work, The Faculty is chock full of pop-culture references and humor, which is delivered by the first-rate teen cast and an inter-esting mix of adult performers, which includes Piper Laurie, Bebe Neuwirth, Christopher McDonald, Robert Patrick, and comedian Jon Stewart. The Faculty is entertaining because it doesn't take itself too seriously, which is what sinks some of the other Scream clones, like I Know What You Did Last Summer (1997), in which a bunch of teenagers are terrorized by a fisherman with a hook hand who they acci-dentally ran over and killed the previous summer, and its unnecessary sequel, I Still Know What You Did Last Summer (1998).

In addition to *Scream*, there were a couple of bright spots. *The Craft* (1996), directed by Andrew Fleming, is a well-crafted horror flick about a troubled teenager (Robin Tunney), who joins up with a coven of high-school witches at her new school. With the help of some terrific special effects, the film's highlight is a "witch-off" between good witch Tunney and a bad witch, convincingly played by Fairuza Balk. A favorite with fans, the scene won the MTV Movie Award in 1997 for "Best Fight" sequence.

The Craft featured four teenage witches, yet, in spite of its title, there is not a single witch in *The Blair Witch Project* (1999). But that's not the only thing that's deceiving about this low-budget horror film, which broke box-office records thanks to an innovative marketing campaign. The fake documentary was sold to the public via the Internet and TV commercials as actual found footage shot by Heather Donohue, Michael C. Williams, and Joshua Leonard, who supposedly disappeared in the woods of Maryland while researching a documentary about a two-hundred-year-old local legend, known as the Blair Witch.

Everything about *The Blair Witch Project* seemed real. Commercials that aired on the Sci-Fi Channel featured family members of the missing film crew. A book was found containing pages from their journal. There was even a traveling exhibit of Blair Witch lore. Most important of all was the Blair Witch Web site (www.blairwitch.com), which included background information on the Blair Witch mythology, photographs of the evidence found by police, and video interviews with the authorities and a clip from a the local newscast about the missing filmmakers. Some folks figured out that it was a hoax, but it didn't seem to matter. The film, which cost $35,000 to make, grossed an estimated $240 million worldwide. The sequel, a stinker called *Book of Shadows: Blair Witch 2* (2000), cost $15 million (around 428 times more than the original) and grossed a paltry $26.4 million.

Since *Blair Witch*, most teen horror movies continue to rehash (and usually not in a good way) stuff that's been done before, like the unnecessary 2003 remake of the classic *The Texas Chainsaw Massacre*, or the rash of "backwoods" slasher films in which teens are terrorized by a flesh-eating virus (*Cabin Fever* [2003]), inbred rednecks named Three-Finger, Saw-Tooth, and One-Eye (*Wrong Turn* [2003]), and the Jersey Devil (no doubt a distant cousin of the Blair Witch) who inhabits New Jersey's Pine Barrens in *Satan's Playground* [2005].

The terror just never seems to end.

Girls Just Wanna Be Mean

Since the silent-film era, the roles assumed by male and female characters have mirrored the traditional gender roles constructed and reinforced by patriarchy. As feminist critic Laura Mulvey points out in her groundbreaking essay, "Visual Pleasure and Narrative Cinema," it's the male characters who are typically "active" and in control of the narrative. Their gaze is directed at the female, who, in classical Hollywood cinema, is passive and the object of the male's desire.[182] Consequently, there is something subversive about a film in which the female character takes control, like the Final Girl in a slasher movie, yet even horror films with strong female protagonists get to have it both ways. The audience gets to "enjoy" the Final Girl being stalked, terrorized, etc., for most of the film, and then she is allowed to use her smarts (which the other characters lack) to turn the tables on her attacker. In *Scream*, Sidney literally takes control of the narrative. When Randy warns her in the film's climax to be careful because "this is the moment when the supposedly dead killer comes back to life for one last scare," she fires her gun at the killer when, right on cue, he comes charging after her. "Not in *my* movie," Sidney declares.

But having the upper hand also gave teenage girls a chance to be naughty. Bad girls, ranging from just plain meanies to full-blown psychotics, were running rampant on the big screen in the nineties. The typical bad girl is a rich kid or an upper-class wannabe. She might work alone or be one of the in-crowd. The clique is usually ruled by the meanest girl in town. Most bad girls are sexually active. They also like to drink and may enjoy the occasional bump of coke. The plots of bad girl movies usually center around the new girl in town, who is either the nice girl who falls in with a bad crowd, or is a bad girl herself, who arrives with a dark past and a whole lot of emotional baggage, which gives her cause to snap.

Some bad girls, particularly the really crazy ones, bear a close resemblance to two of Hollywood's most memorable female psychos: *Fatal Attraction*'s (1987) Alex Forrest (Glenn Close) and *Basic Instinct*'s (1992) Catherine Tramell (Sharon Stone) (both of whom, incidentally, terrorized a character played by Michael Douglas). Like Alex, teenage girls who are scorned by the object of their desires (whether they hooked up with him or not) are usually adept at getting someone's attention. In *Devil in the Flesh* (1997), Debbie Strand (Rose McGowan) is the new naughty girl in town who sets her eye on her handsome teacher (Alex McArthur). He's married and not interested, which is the cue to let the body count begin. Evil also arrives in the guise of the new girl-in-town (look out for those new girls!) in *Swimfan* (2002). Madison Bell (Erika Christensen, a talented actress who deserves better) is the meanie who has a liaison in the school swimming pool with Ben Cronin (Jesse Bradford). He already has a sweet girlfriend, Amy (Shiri Appleby), but that doesn't stop Madison from pursuing Ben and then making his life a living hell when he scorns her advances. He loses his job, his place on the swim team (he tests positive for drugs), and his best friend (who is found floating dead in the pool). Amy fortunately survives both of her "run-ins" with crazy Madison, whose present and past "crimes" (her old boyfriend is on a respirator) don't go unpunished.

A pre-*Clueless* Alicia Silverstone had a chance to play a similar role in *The Crush*. Fourteen-year-old Darian Forrester is jailbait, but that doesn't stop a handsome writer (Carey Elwes) from looking. He does, and so do we. *Washington Post* critic Hal Hinson, who calls the movie "an invitation to child abuse," objected to director Alan Shapiro "panning his camera up one side of Silverstone's body and down the other as if it were perfectly all right for us to visually caress the things of a 14-year-old. Or if it weren't, the movie was giving us its special permission. Just this once."[183]

The film credited for launching the "Lolita cycle" is the delightfully cheesy *Poison Ivy* (1992). Drew Barrymore plays Ivy, the new girl at a posh private school who befriends Sylvie (TV *Roseanne*'s Sara Gilbert), who describes herself as a "politically, environmentally correct, feminist, poetry-reading type." Sylvie is also a loner with an unhappy home life. Her mom (Cheryl Ladd) is a pill popper with suicidal tendencies and her dad (Tom Skerritt) is a recovering alcoholic. Ivy bonds with Sylvie and before you know it, she moves in with the family. It's only a matter of time before Mom plunges to her death over the balcony and Ivy is seducing Dad.

Poison Ivy suggests that there is a lesbian attraction between the two teenage girls. The film opens with slow-motion shots of Ivy, wearing a short dress and a leather jacket, on a swing. She's being watched by Sylvie, who is sketching Ivy's tattoo. "I guess she's sort of beautiful. I don't know—those lips," Gilbert observes (in voice-over). "You know lips are supposed to be a perfect reflection of another part of a woman's anatomy. Not that I'm a lesbian. Well, maybe I am. No, definitely not." Sylvie and Ivy spend much of their time together cuddling in bed, which is more indicative of Ivy's Oedipal delusions of taking Ivy's mother's place. Sylvie's lesbian desires never fully surface and can be easily passed of as an adolescent crush, though even after putting her through hell, Sylvie admits in the end, "I miss her."

In several trashy teen thrillers of the late nineties, there are more overt displays of lesbianism, though its primary purpose is to either add to the decadent lifestyle of the young characters and/or a means for a bad girl to manipulate her rival. Critic Sarah Warn points out that the "Evil Bisexual Girl" has become a staple in the teen thriller. For example, Suzie (Neve Campbell) and Kelly (Denise Richards), the title characters in *Wild Things* (1998), make out when they are not stabbing each other in the back.[184] Part of manipulative Kathryn's (Sarah Michelle Gellar) plan in *Cruel Intentions* involves teaching virgin Cecile Caldwell (Selma Blair) how to kiss (in the middle of Central Park). The clique in *New Best Friend* (2002) includes a bisexual named Sydney (Dominique Swain), who seduced the group's new member, Alicia (Mia Kirshner). And the reigning bitch (Susan Ward) of a group of socialites in *The In Crowd* (2000) swings both ways.

The reigning queen of mean girl films is the devilish, yet uneven comedy, *Heathers* (1989). Two-thirds satire, one-third black comedy, *Heathers* exposes the underlying viciousness and cruelty that fuels the high-school popularity machine. Every school has one—a social clique who are revered and feared by the student body. The most popular clique at Westerburg High is composed of the commander in chief Heather Chandler (Kim Walker) and her lackeys, Heather McNamara (Lisanne Falk) and Heather Duke (Shannon Doherty). The fourth member is Veronica Sawyer (Winona Ryder), who has what the other three appear to be lacking—a conscience. She doesn't appreciate the other girls' cruel antics, like publicly humiliating an overweight girl nicknamed Martha "Dumptruck" Dunnstock (Carrie Lynn) by slipping her a fake love note. Veronica is also aware that she's blown off her long-time friends, like Betty Finn (Renée Estevez), which is why she reaches her breaking point when Heather #1 cuts her off for embarrassing her at a frat party.

What starts off as satirical suddenly turns pitch black when Veronica decides to fulfill every high-schooler's fantasy and seek revenge on Heather #1. She gets some help from the new kid in school, J.D. (Christian Slater), who, as his name suggests, is trouble. J.D. already got suspended for shooting blanks in the cafeteria at two homophobic football players, Kurt (Lance Fenton) and Ram (Patrick Labyorteaux), who start harassing him. What J.D. and Veronica didn't count on was Heather #1 downing the milk they spiked with detergent and falling onto a glass coffee table. The wicked witch was dead, so they had no choice but to make it look like a suicide, complete with a note that read, "People just thought because you're beautiful and popular, life is easy and fun. No one understood I had feelings too. I die knowing no one knew the real me."

After accidentally offing Heather #1, Veronica goes after Kurt and Ram when they start spreading rumors that they had a "nice little swordfight" in her mouth. She only intended to humiliate them, but when J.D. uses real bullets in the gun (confirming that he is a psycho), they are forced to stage another—in this case double—suicide. The jocks are found half-naked with a suicide note declaring their "forbidden love."

At this point director Mike Lehmann and screenwriter Daniel Waters shift the focus of their satire to the subject of teen suicide. Veronica's worst nightmare comes true when Heather #1 is suddenly treated as a martyr. Everyone who hates her is sharing their fond memories with the press, and the yearbook staff is suddenly devoting an entire spread to her legacy (complete with the suicide note). There's even a hit record on the airwaves: "Teenage Suicide: Don't Do It." After the second "double suicide," a New Age-ish teacher, Pauline Fleming (Penelope Milford) wrangles up all the students in the cafeteria and has them join hands just in time for the television cameras. When the footage is later shown on TV, Veronica is disgusted how "these little programs eat up suicide with a spoon. They make it seem like the cool thing to do." Veronica is correct, because Heather McNamara arrives and shares the big news that Martha Dumptruck tried to "buy the farm" by walking into traffic but didn't succeed.

Apparently the film's producers were concerned about the film's cynical treatment of such a serious subject, which was still fresh in the public's mind due to a series of cluster suicides that occurred between 1985 and 1987. But the filmmakers were adamant that their film was not about suicide. In a *Los Angeles Times* article published around the time of its release, producer Denise Di Novi insisted the film is about "the tyranny of social groups."[185] Director Lehmann stated in the same article that *Heathers* is not about suicide. "It's a movie about cruelty," he explained. "This is a movie about moral issues. It doesn't gloss over them."[186] Writer Waters argued that the film actually "takes the glamour out of suicide."[187] The *Los Angeles Times* also asked two mental health professionals to watch the film; they gave it two thumbs-up. Dr. Michael Strober, an associate professor and co-director of the Child and Adolescent Mood Disorders Program at UCLA's Neuropsychiatric Institute and Hospital, believed the film delivers a "very subtle" message about the "way some teens fall upon self-destructive behavior as a means of dealing with their emotional troubles. You hope that teens watch this movie and think about what it is."[188] Dr. Michael

Peck said that the film "doesn't pose a danger because teens aren't likely to feel any emotional bond to the characters, most of whom are ridiculed by the filmmakers."[189]

As in most satires and black comedies, the characters and situations in *Heathers* are so far removed from reality, it's doubtful whether young audience members would actually make the connection between these teens and their own behavior. At the same time, the suggestion that a young audience has no emotional bond with the characters is questionable because Veronica, whose role in the "suicides" is limited to that of accomplice, does emerge as the film's moral center. She is empowered at the end ("There's a new sheriff in town," she tells Veronica) and makes it clear that things will change when she asks Martha if she wants to spend prom night watching videos with her.

While a mixture of the macabre, nihilism, and high-school comedy, *Heathers* was in many ways the perfect film to close out the end of the Reagan era. But it was also ahead of its time and a difficult film to market, so at the time of its theatrical release, it never found an audience and grossed only $1.1 million. Today *Heathers* is considered a cult classic. It was also clearly the inspiration for *Jawbreaker* (1999), which should have been called "*Heathers* Lite," It's about three popular high-school girls, Marcie, Courtney, and Julie (Julie Benz, Rebecca Gayheart, Rose McGowan), who kidnap the fourth, the school's prom queen, as a birthday surprise and accidentally kill her when she suffocates on a jawbreaker. When a geeky girl named Fern Mayo (Judy Greer) learns the truth, they give her a major makeover, complete with a name change ("Vylette") to keep her quiet. With a detective on their trail and "Vylette" the school's new "it girl," Marcie, Courtney, and Julie's friendship is put to the test. Unfortunately, writer/director Darren Stein miscalculated the entertainment value in watching high-school girls being mean to one another. (*Girls?* Benz, Gayheart, and McGowan were in their mid-twenties—at least Ryder was eighteen.) In her review for salon.com, Mary Elizabeth Williams calls these women "cartoons" and "not particularly fresh or relevant cartoons." "It's unsurprising that in such a shallow, bitter world as this one," she continues, "the cruelest retribution the girls dream up for each other isn't criminal prosecution or even the pangs of conscience, but the loss of popularity."[190]

Neither *Heathers* nor *Jawbreaker* offer much of a critique, let alone insight, into why girls are so mean to each other. *Heathers* comes the closest by suggesting that it's simply human nature. When Veronica flat out asks Heather Duke why she can't just be a friend instead of "such a mega-bitch," Heather replies, "Because I can be! Do you really think if Betty Finn's [Veronica's uncool friend] godmother made her cool, she'd still act nice and hang out with her dweebette friends? No way!" Depending on how you look at it, popularity gives you a license to be mean, or is one of its perks.

The subject of mean girls has attracted the attention of educators and psychologists over the past few years, beginning with a study conducted by Kaj Björkqvist, a Finnish professor of developmental psychology. Professor Björkqvist and his research team studied aggressive behavior among eleven- and twelve-year-old girls. The study concluded that girls can be just as aggressive as boys, though instead of physical fighting their superior social intelligence enables them to wage complicated battles with other girls aimed at damaging relationships or reputations . . ." This phenomenon, called "relationship aggression," is the subject of several comedies (and one drama) featuring mean girls who are capable of doing anything—lie, cheat, manipulate, even commit murder.

The R-rated *Heathers* and *Jawbreaker* paved the way for *Mean*

Laughing With You and At You

Although teen movies addressed some serious issues in the '90s, they also developed a sense of humor about teenagers and the teen genre itself. For the first time, teens were the direct target of parodies, spoofs, and political satire.

High School High (1996): This parody of *Blackboard Jungle, Lean on Me* (1989), *Dangerous Minds* (1995), and other troubled-high-school-teen movies was written by David Zucker, who was part of the Zucker/Abrahams/Zucker team that gave us *Airplane!* (1980) and *The Naked Gun* (1988). Unfortunately, the film doesn't deliver because while it tries to play it straight (like a good parody should), it also tries to get laughs out of Jon Lovitz, who is more annoying than funny. Still, there are some humorous moments, such as the parody of the "chickie run" in *Rebel Without a Cause*, but they are few and far between.

Election (1999): A wicked, top-of-the line comedy about a high-school election that pits an overachiever named Tracy Flick (Reese Witherspoon) against nice, but dim football player, Paul Metzler (Chris Klein), who doesn't have a clue why he is even in the race. When a principled teacher (Matthew Broderick) allows his feelings toward Tracy to get the best of him, his entire life begins to fall apart. Director Alexander Payne, who co-wrote the screenplay (with Jim Taylor), based on Tom Perrotta's book, tells his story from multiple perspectives, so the line between right and wrong, which is so fixed in most teen movies, keeps moving around. If only more teen movies were this smart.

Drop Dead Gorgeous (1999): Teenage beauty contests, in this case the Miss Teen Princess America contest, are the subject of this mockumentary written by Lona Williams, a former beauty-pageant contestant. In this year's pageant, the front-runner, Becky Leeman (Denise Richards), daughter of the pageant's chair and a former Miss TPA herself, Gladys (Kirstie Alley), competes against a sweetheart named Amber (Kirsten Dunst), who lives in a trailer park with her alcoholic mother (Ellen Barkin). Richards, Alley, Dunst, Barkin, along with Allison Janney as Barkin's friend, are all a hoot, although the jokes are hit and miss (some highlights are the Lutheran Sisterhood Gun Club and a dramatic reading from *Soylent Green*). Make it a double feature and watch the made-for-TV movie *The Positively True Adventures of the Alleged Texas Cheerleader-Murdering Mom* (1993), with Holly Hunter giving an Oscar-caliber performance in the title role.

Psycho Beach Party (2000): A clever parody of *Gidget* and the beach-party genre starring its author, Charles Busch, in drag as the no-nonsense Captain Monica Stark, who is on the trail of a killer who's been reducing a coastal town's population. Lauren Ambrose, best known as the depressed daughter on *Six Feet Under*, shows off her comedic talents as a tomboy surfer with a personality disorder.

Not Another Teen Movie (2001): The five writers of this parody of teen movies certainly did their homework. The script, which is chock-full of jokes targeting teen movies in general as well as send-ups of specific films, covers a lot of territory. Unfortunately, the cast of mostly unknown actors simply lacks the comic talent (and timing) to pull it off. Granted, it is difficult to send up material that is light and comedic to begin with (as opposed to horror movies and Westerns). Still, there are just too many jokes that fall flat, though there are a few funny cameos that are worth the rental price.

Girls (2004), a smart and very funny comedy that charted the same territory, but with one important difference: *Mean Girls*, which was rated PG-13, is about and directed at a female teenage audience. The film is based on the best seller, *Queen Bees and Wannabes: Helping Your Daughter Survive Cliques, Gossip, Boyfriends, and Other Realities of Adolescence* by Rosalind Wiseman. The book, which is written as a guide for parents, examines the "secret world of girls' friendships" and the impact cliques and popularity have on their lives. The screenplay by *Saturday Night Live* head writer Tina Fey zeros in on the underlying question: "Why are teenage girls so mean to each other?" As Wiseman explains,

> girls are often their own and other girls' worst enemies, and for some, the rivalry defines their adolescence. I have watched time after time as a sweet, intelligent girl plots another girl's humiliating downfall. It's hard to admit when the evildoer is your own child or one of her close friends.[191]

Mean Girls envisions the world of teenagers as a jungle and as the new girl, sweet Cady Heron (Lindsay Lohan), soon discovers, it's all about survival of the meanest. She is enlisted by two outsiders, Janis Ian (Lizzy Caplan) and her gay pal Damian (Dan Franzese), to infiltrate the most popular clique in school, known as the Plastics, which consists of queen bee Regina George (Rachel McAdams), and her drones, Karen Smith (Amanda Seyfried), the dumb one, and Gretchen Wieners (Lacey Chabert), who knows everything about everyone. Janis calls it a "fun little experiment," but actually it's part of her own personal vendetta to destroy Regina for spreading a rumor back when she was thirteen that she was a lesbian. Cady agrees to the plan, but once she becomes more involved with the Plastics and continues to sabotage Regina, she turns into a major queen bee herself.

Tina Fey, who plays a concerned teacher, Ms. Norbury, stands in for Rosalind Wiseman when she gathers the school's female population together and says, "You have got to stop calling each other sluts and whores. It just makes it okay for guys to call you sluts and whores." She then has the girls write out apologies to people they hurt and read them (and then, as a demonstration of their trust, each girl falls backward into the arms of the classmates).

Mean Girls has a Hollywood ending which for some is a bit too sappy. The girls have changed their attitude and behavior and actually appear to be coexisting. "Finally," Cady, the film's narrator says, "Girl World was at peace." In terms of the teen genre, *Mean Girls* broke new ground by showing that teen movies can be entertaining and send an important message to their young audiences. The film grossed $86 million, which also proved that a teen movie with a female-driven narrative can make money without gross-out jokes about bodily functions and fluids.

Boys (Still) Just Wanna Get Laid

Seventeen years after *Porky's* was a surprise hit in the spring of 1982, another teen sex comedy scored at the box office. *American Pie* (1999) grossed over $100 million and resurrected a genre that had been gathering dust on video shelves since the mid-eighties. The plot is hardly original: four high-school male virgins—Jim (Jason Biggs), Finch (Eddie Kaye Thomas), Kevin (Thomas Ian Nicholas), and Oz (Chris Klein)—make a pact to lose their virginity by the night of the prom. This is not a competition. In fact, they agree to help and support each other. "Separately we're all flawed and vulnerable," Kevin quips, "but together we are the masters of our sexual destiny."

Jim, who is mega horny, is the most desperate of the bunch. His anxiety surrounding the opposite sex is compounded by a series of sexually humiliating moments that continue throughout the film's sequel (*American Pie II* [2001]) and the conclusion of the trilogy, *American Wedding* (2003).[192] In the first film, Jim experiences every teenage boy's worst nightmare when his parents walk into his bedroom while he is, to borrow a euphemism later used by Jim's dad (the hilarious Eugene Levy), "stroking the salami." Later, when he finally gets the chance to lose his virginity to a nubile foreign-exchange student (Shannon Elizabeth) (the kind only seen in teen movies), he ejaculates prematurely. To make matters worse, the whole incident is broadcast over the Internet. Then, of course, there is the incident with the apple pie. At one point, Jim asks his friends what "third base" feels like. "Like warm apple pie," says Oz. So when Jim comes home one day and an apple pie is staring at him with a note from his mom telling him to enjoy it, he puts two of his fingers in the middle and gets an idea. Cut to Jim's dad arriving home and walking into the kitchen, where he finds his son lying on the kitchen table humping the pie. His dad later suggests that they tell his mother that they finished the whole pie.

Jim's sexual mishaps don't end after he loses his virginity at the end of the first film to Michelle (Alyson Hannigan), who he will later marry in the third installment (a bit retrograde—how many kids these days marry their first partner?). *American Pie II* opens with Jim's parents paying a visit to his dorm room and finding him in bed with a girl (her parents walk in right behind them). Then he accidentally uses glue instead of lube and gets stuck (literally) in the middle of pleasuring himself.

Jim, Finch, Kevin, and Oz may have only one thing on their minds, but they are still basically decent guys—perhaps too decent for a genre that has earned a reputation over the years based on its crude, lewd, and sexist sense of humor. The void in the *American Pie* trilogy is filled by a guy named Stifler (Seann William Scott), or as he likes to refer to himself, "the Stifmeister." Stifler is all the guys in *Porky's* rolled into one. He is the guy who throws the parties, is up for anything, and says anything he is thinking no matter how crude or inappropriate (if it is, he doesn't care).

The humor in *Porky's* is consistently crude. Some of the comic bits in *American Pie* are not only crude, they're downright gross. But gross humor was all the rage in 1999 thanks to the box-office success of two Farrelly Brothers comedies, *Dumb and Dumber* (1994), and *There's Something About Mary* (1998), which are both chock full of jokes about bodily fluids and functions, including visual gags involving flatulence, masturbation, and fellatio. The *American Pie* films continued what the Farrellys started with gags designed to make you gag, like Stifler drinking out of a cup of beer in which Kevin just ejaculated (ha, ha); and, in the sequel, Stifler thinking a girl is pouring champagne over his head but is actually getting peed upon from a guy on a balcony. The filmmakers and cast justified the gross humor in *American Pie* and the film's R rating because, as producer Craig Perry points out, "High school is an R-rated experience. The funniest things you remember from high school were R-rated too. Why not see something real?"[193] Director Paul Weitz claimed that "it's acceptably gross if it's an understandable situation for that character to be in— and it's good-natured enough."[194] Actor Eddie Kaye Thomas, who plays Finch, agreed. In one scene, Stifler torments germ-phobic Finch, who refuses to use the public bathroom, by putting a laxative in his drink, thereby forcing him to relieve himself in the nearest girls' restroom. "If you're entertaining people, nothing's too gross," Thomas said. "People will say we've crossed lines. But we never went over the boundaries of high-school reality. When you get false and not real, that's when you cross the line."[195]

Thomas's assessment of *American Pie* is quite accurate. Their hijinks might not be to everyone's taste, but the filmmakers at least tried to "keep it real." Unfortunately, this is not the case for most gross-out teen movies, which may not be malicious or violent but which contain scenes—getting one's arm stuck in a cow's rectum (*Say It Isn't So* [2001]); eating a pastry filled with dog semen (*Van Wilder* [2002]); or in the *Citizen Kane* of gross-out comedies, *Freddy Got Fingered* (2002), getting sprayed by elephant semen or cutting a baby's bloody umbilical cord with one's teeth—that could hardly be labeled "good-natured." Even John Waters had his limits.

So did the critics, who took delight in fingering the sudden deluge of gross-out comedies that ushered in the new millennium, with *Freddy* and its star Tom Green at the top of the list. *Variety* called the comedy about an unemployed cartoonist who is forced to move back into his parents' house as he tries to get his life together "the most brutally awful comedy ever to emerge from a major studio." Stephen Hunter of the *Washington Post* considers *Freddy* to be a testament to the utter creative bankruptcy of the Hollywood film industry."[196] Roger Ebert gave it zero stars and called it a "vomitorium consisting of ninety-three minutes of Tom Green doing things that a geek in a carnival sideshow would turn down."[197]

The basic problem with both the teenage sex and gross-out comedies is they are films made by, about, and for males. The filmmakers are mostly college-educated guys in their late twenties and thirties who must all be in a perpetual state of adolescence. Like their young male characters, they still think fart jokes are funny. They are also either unwilling, uninterested, or incapable of creating a three-dimensional female character. Or they subscribe to the age-old *Pygmalion* myth and give a girl a makeover (as in *She's All That* [1999]). She might be the sexy, yet unattainable girl like Amanda (Jennifer Love

Hewitt) in *Can't Hardly Wait* (1998), who Roger Ebert calls, along with the film's male lead, Preston (Ethan Embry), "a couple of clueless rubber stamps." Then there are the female fantasy figures, like Nadia (Shannon Elizabeth), the horny exchange student in *American Pie*, or Danielle (Elisha Cuthbert), a young porn star who fulfills Matthew's (Emile Hirsch) (and every teenage boy's) fantasy when she becomes *The Girl Next Door* (2004).

The story behind *Coming Soon* (1999) illustrates just how deep the double standard concerning female sexuality is embedded in our culture. Colette Burson directed and co-wrote (with Kate Robin) a teenage sex comedy about a trio of teenagers who attend a posh Manhattan prep school. Like most teenage girls, their minds are consumed with boys and college. Jenny (Gaby Hoffmann), the one with the smart mouth, is the most experienced of the three when it comes to men. Nell Kellner (Tricia Vessey) is indifferent about them for reasons that soon become clear. Stream (Bonnie Root) is dating a handsome, insensitive, rich asshole (James Roday), who uses her to get off and has no interest in her needs. While relaxing alone in a Jacuzzi one day, Stream sits too close to one of the jets and discovers what she's been missing. She loses the asshole and begins seeing a smart and funny guy named Henry Rockefeller (Ryan Reynolds), who goes by the last name of Lipschitz.

Coming Soon is a fairly entertaining sex comedy with some funny lines, and a likable cast, which also includes Mia Farrow (hilarious as Stream's New Age-ish mom), Ryan O'Neal, and the late Spalding Gray. By teen sex comedy standards it's also fairly tame, considering there's no nudity. So why, when the film was shown to the Motion Picture Association of America Ratings Board was the film slapped with an NC-17? Such a rating is the kiss of death for a movie geared for a teenage/twentysomething audience because it's difficult to sell tickets when TV stations won't air your spots and newspapers won't run your ads. According to Burson, the board thought the orgasm in the Jacuzzi was too lurid and told her she needed to cut the scene in which Stream gives her boyfriend a blowjob off-screen because by showing her head leaving the frame and then coming back into it implied duration. (Of course, as Burson explained in an interview with salon.com, "That was the whole point! It's a classic inside joke for women!")[198] After some editing, *Coming Soon* was eventually released with an R rating in May 2000, though it only played in one theater in New York City before coming out on DVD. It remains an important testament to how far teen sex comedies have to go to satisfy the other half of their audience.

Lost in Translation

In the 1990s, filmmakers added some cache to the teen genre by turning to the classical novels and plays for source material. The works of William Shakespeare, along with other texts equally unlikely to appeal to most teenagers, have served as the basis for some of the decade's most popular and innovative films. Teenagers did not have to necessarily be familiar with the original book to understand the modern version, but in most instances, a little extra "required reading" on their part definitely added something to their viewing experience.

In the opening of *Emma*, Jane Austen describes twenty-one-year-old Emma Woodhouse as "handsome, clever, and rich, with a comfortable home and happy disposition . . . in a world with very little to distress or vex her." In writer/director Amy Heckerling's (*Fast Times at Ridgemont High*) version, Emma is a Beverly Hills high-school student named Cher Horowitz, who is rich, shallow, and self-absorbed. But unlike most rich teenagers in movies (like the "richies" in John Hughes's *Pretty in Pink* and *Some Kind of Wonderful*), Cher is neither a bitch nor a snob. She's also not very smart, unless it's a reference to popular culture—then she has a chance (she thinks Ren and Stimpy are "way existential" and Tony Curtis starred in *Some Like It Hot* and *Sporadicus*). What Cher lacks in brains, she makes up with her colorful fashion sense (Silverstone dons a total of fifty-six outfits). Like Austen's heroine, Cher also likes to meddle in people's affairs and play matchmaker. She gives the new girl in school, a fashion victim named Tai (Brittany Murphy), a total makeover, and when she gets a low grade from two of her teachers (Wallace Shawn and Twink Caplan) she convinces each of them that the other is a secret admirer because happy teachers give higher grades. Cher and her girl-friends, who converse in a modern-day version of Valley girl–speak (a "Betty" is an attractive female, a "Baldwin" is a cute guy [as in one of the Baldwin brothers]) may not be the sharpest tools in the shed, yet Heckerling doesn't choose style over substance and succeeds in making them equally likable and laughable. Jane Austen would have definitely approved.

Shakespeare would have been less than pleased with the way his plays were "loosely" adapted for the screen in the nineties. In 1968, Franco Zeffirelli directed a lavish version of *Romeo and Juliet* starring newcomers seventeen-year-old Leonard Whiting and sixteen-year-old Olivia Hussey. Twenty-eight years later, the tragic tale was once again brought to the big screen in director Baz Luhrmann's modernized, MTV-style, 1996 version starring Leonardo DiCaprio and Claire Danes as the young lovers. Zeffirelli and Luhrmann and their respective film versions of *Romeo and Juliet* actually have some points in common. Both directors have directed operas for the stage, so there is an element of theatricality in their work with special attention given to visual detail (Zeffirelli started his film career as a production designer). They also remained faithful to Shakespeare's text in terms of casting

Required Reading (and Viewing)

Shakespeare, French literature, and drama provided the source material for several teen films released in the early 1990s. They all took some liberties with the original texts; in most instances, they only retained the central plotline along with some of the characters' names.

My Own Private Idaho (1991)/Shakespeare's *Henry IV, Part 1* (1597): For this "teen movie" for adults, writer/director Gus Van Sant borrowed part of the story line for this art film about street hustlers from Shakespeare's play, in which Prince Hal, the King's rebellious son, cavorts with commoners and lowlifes. Van Sant's Hal is the mayor's rich, rebellious son, Scott (Keanu Reeves), who befriends a fellow hustler, a gay narcoleptic named Mike (River Phoenix). The scenes between Mike, who has fallen in love with Scott, are quite moving, yet the film's haunting visuals and surreal, somber mood are disrupted when the characters, including the film's Falstaff (William Richert), start speaking in verse.

10 Things I Hate About You (1999)/Shakespeare's *The Taming of the Shrew* (1594): Shakespeare's comedy about two sisters—Bianca, the youngest, who can't get married before the shrewish Katarina—is difficult to update. The plot is convoluted and its sexual politics problematic. The script is simply not clever enough to pull either off, though the romantic comedy does benefit from some good performances, particularly by Julia Stiles, who manages to turn the snide and cynical Kat into a likable and sympathetic character.

Cruel Intentions (1999)/Choderlos de Laclos's *Dangerous Liaisons* (1782): De Laclos's novel has been adapted for the stage, the screen, and as a TV miniseries. Now it's a teen movie with *Buffy the Vampire*

Slayer's Sarah Michelle Gellar playing the wicked Kathryn, who cooks up a scheme with her stepbrother Sebastian Valmont (Ryan Phillippe) that's designed to ruin the reputations of her ex-beau's new girlfriend (Selma Blair) and a self-proclaimed virgin (Reese Witherspoon). Gellar makes a good bad girl (she played a similar role on *All My Children* when she actually was a teenager) and it's fun to watch her get it in the end. *Cruel Intentions II* (2000), which is a direct-to-video prequel, was originally shot as a series pilot, *Manchester Prep*. A third film was released on video in 2004.

Whatever It Takes (2000)/Edmond Rostand's *Cyrano de Bergerac* (1897): Unless they've seen that "old Steve Martin movie" in which he's got a big nose, most teenagers probably aren't familiar with Rostand's play about Cyrano, who helps his friend Christian woo the lovely Roxanne, the woman Cyrano loves. In the teen version, two guys, Ryan (Shane West) and Chris (James Franco) agree to help each other to get the girl of his dreams, which requires them to switch personalities. Chris, the jock, becomes the geek, Ryan becomes a jerk, and the audience becomes bored.

O (2001)/Shakespeare's *Othello* (1603): Shakespeare's story of love, jealousy, and betrayal is effectively transposed to a high-school setting in this faithful adaptation that was delayed two years due to the Columbine massacre. In this version, Othello is Odin (Mekhi Phifer), an African-American basketball star in an all-white school. His Desdemona is the dean's daughter, Desi (Julia Stiles). Iago is Odin's teammate, Hugo (Josh Hartnett), a steroid user who grows increasingly jealous of his father/coach's (Martin Sheen) affection for Odin. Like Shakespeare's play, *O* is heavy-handed, extremely violent, and ultimately tragic.

young actors to play the lovers and having his characters speaking in verse. Unfortunately, Luhrmann's overall concept overshadows the otherwise simple story of doomed lovers from rival families, the Capulets and the Montagues. With the look and feel of a music video, *Romeo + Juliet* assaults its audience with its excessive, in-your-face visual style and MTV cutting, which, with its beach setting substituting for the city of Verona, looks like an episode of *Miami Vice*.

The opening confrontation between the Capulet and Montague "boys" is staged as a gun battle between two rival gangs at a gas station. With a pastiche of music blaring on the sound track that includes everything from rap to opera, the actors shout their lines at the camera and start shooting it out. Luhrmann thankfully slows things down for the scenes between DiCaprio and Danes, who make a good pair, even if they seem as if they are in another movie. In all, it feels Luhrmann is trying to do too much all at once and, as a result, the pieces simply don't gel.

As long as there have been teen movies, there have been movies about troubled teens. In the fifties, Hollywood warned American audiences about the "epidemic" known as juvenile delinquency through low-budget, exploitation films and major studio productions that claimed to have ripped their stories from the headlines. Most movie juvies, who fell in with the wrong crowd due to peer pressure and an unstable home life, ended up dead or in the slammer. The lucky ones received some harsh words and a second chance from a sympathetic judge.

Teens on the Margins

Although the majority of teen films produced between the late 1980s and the present day have been primarily horror films and romantic/sex comedies, there were signs of progress within the genre as well. By the early nineties, teen movies would no longer be inhabited by predominantly white, middle-class, heterosexual teenagers. Films began to tell stories from the point of view of teens who for the last three decades were relegated to the genre's margins, namely young people from different racial, ethnic, and economic backgrounds as well as gay, lesbian, and transgender teenagers. With a few exceptions, the majority of these films were not produced by major studios. Most of them are independent films that played at festivals around the world before landing a North American distributor.

In 1991, a record total of twenty-one black films were released in the United States. In addition to films from well-established Hollywood actor/directors like Spike Lee (*Jungle Fever*), Robert Townsend (*The Five Heartbeats*), and Mario Van Peebles (*New Jack City*), there were several independent films directed by newcomers like Julie Dash, Matty Rich, and John Singleton. Dash's *Daughters of the Dust* and Rich's *Straight Out of Brooklyn* premiered at the 1991 Sundance Film Festival, where *Daughters* was honored for Arthur Jafa's cinematography and Rich received a "Special Recognition Award" for his direction. For his first feature, *Boyz n the Hood* (1991), twenty-four-year-old Singleton became the youngest director to receive an Academy Award nomination for Best Director as well as a nomination for Best Screenplay Written Directly for the Screen. Dash, Rich, and Singleton, along with cinematographer Ernest Dickerson (*Juice* [1992]) and writer/directors Albert and Allen Hughes (*Menace II Society* [1993]), were considered the next generation of young black filmmakers, all of whom made a name for themselves at the very start of their careers.

With the exception of Dash's *Daughters*, their first films all follow the plight of young, black men who live in either South Central Los Angeles or parts of New York City that are overrun by guns, drugs, gangs, and violence. On the brink of adulthood, these characters arrive at an important crossroad in their lives where they are forced to make a decision regarding their future. They must choose between being a criminal and "doing the right thing," which means making a better life for yourself by getting an education, making an honest living, etc. The presence or the lack of a father figure in their lives is usually a contributing factor to which path the teenager will follow. While there are certainly differences in regards to their plotlines, characters, and visual style, these films all call for the end of the vicious cycle of crime and violence plaguing the black community that has taken the lives of thousands of young black men.

Boyz n the Hood makes this point with the opening title card, which reads: "One out of every twenty-one black American males will be murdered in their lifetime. Most will die at the hand of another black male." So how can this cycle be broken? *Boyz* suggests that a young black male needs a loving, attentive father like Jason "Furious" Styles (Laurence Fishburne), who is determined that his teenage son Tré (Cuba Gooding, Jr.) will not become a statistic. Furious has three basic rules Tré must follow in order to be a proud, responsible, black man: 1) always look a person in the eye because he will respect you more; 2) never be afraid to ask for anything; 3) and never respect anyone who doesn't respect you back.

Unfortunately, Tré's best friends, Ricky (Morris Chestnut), and his half-brother, Doughboy (Ice Cube), are not so lucky. Singleton implies that the brothers are unable to escape the violence on the streets because they do not have a father or father figure to serve as a role model. Furious's influence on his son becomes apparent when Tré is forced to make an important decision. After witnessing the cold-blooded execution of Ricky by a rival neighborhood gang, Tré goes with Doughboy when he rides off to avenge his brother's death.

But when they find the gang members who murdered Ricky, Tré decides not to pull the trigger. He makes a conscious decision not to be part of the cycle of violence or, as Doughboy calls it, "this shit that goes on and on." The epilogue tells us Doughboy was murdered two weeks later, while Tré went to college in the fall.

A teenager's attempt to use violence to break the cycle of poverty that has entrapped his family leads to tragedy in *Straight Out of Brooklyn*. Dennis Brown (Larry Gilliard, Jr.) thinks the only way to get his parents and sisters out of the confines of the Red Hook section of Brooklyn is to make some major cash quickly. His girlfriend Shirley (Reana E. Drummond) tells him to be patient and take the honest route out of Brooklyn by earning a college degree, and getting a job. Dennis wants things to change now, so he and his two friends, Kevin (Mark Malone) and Larry (director Rich), rob a guy who collects money for a neighborhood drug dealer. But Dennis and his friends are strictly amateurs. Their victim has no trouble identifying them because they don't cover their faces and so the dealer is out looking for them the next morning.

Straight Out of Brooklyn is more a family melodrama than a teenage crime film because Rich devotes equal (if not more) time to Dennis's home life, particularly his father, Ray (George T. Odom), a gas-station attendant who blames white people for his misfortunes. Ray is a beaten-down man, but he's not entirely sympathetic because he is also an abusive alcoholic who hits his wife Shirley, who won't get help and even defends her husband by claiming that he doesn't mean to hit her—he's just angry. Her bruises and welts get her fired from her job, and eventually land her in the hospital. In the film's dramatic conclusion, which is like a scene out of a Greek tragedy, Shirley flatlines at exactly the same moment that Ray is being gunned down outside of the apartment building by the drug dealer who is out for revenge.

The film's low-budget production values add some grittiness to the more melodramatic moments involving Dennis's father, who Rich is careful not to make a total villain. When Ray drinks, he is out of control, but when he is sober, he can be a caring and loving father. In one father-and-son moment, Ray reflects on his childhood, his parents, and his dream to be a doctor. But father and son are also linked by their capacity for violence. Ray's abusive behavior results in his wife's death, while Dennis's violent act ends with his father's brutal murder. Rich makes his point very clear with the closing title, which calls, like *Boyz*, for an end to the cycle of violence: "First things learned are the hardest to forget. Traditions pass from one generation to the next. We need to change."

First things learned are indeed the hardest for some of the troubled youth in *Menace II Society* and *Juice*. These teenagers were not necessarily born evil. Their need or desire to rob and murder is usually linked to their upbringing and/or their environment. For example, in the opening sequence of *Menace II Society*, Cain's (Tyrin Turner) life takes a turn for the worse when his friend O-Dog (Larenz Tate) loses it in a Korean grocery store and shoots both the grocer and his wife. After the opening credits, there's a flashback to Cain's childhood, where he witnesses his father killing someone over an argument during a card game and his mother overdosing. "I heard a lot and I saw a lot," he says. "I caught on to the criminal life real quick. Instead of keeping me out of trouble, they turn me on to it." Although he gets love and support from his grandparents and the mother of his son, his life just continues on a downward spiral as if it is his destiny to wind up either dead or in jail.

Some guys have the strength and the smarts to pull themselves out before it's too late. The filmmakers establish in the opening of *Juice* that Q (Omar Epps) is determined to keep his three friends—

Bishop (Tupac Shakur), Steel (Jermaine Hopkins), and Raheem (Khalil Kain)—out of trouble. His own dream of becoming a "mix-master" (a turntablist) is put on hold when he reluctantly joins his friends out of loyalty when they rob a grocery store. Like O-Dog, Bishop gets carried away and shoots the owner. Q starts finding himself deeper and deeper in trouble, until the final showdown with Bishop. The title is slang for power, which Q earns by being the last man standing. The final freeze-frame of Q's face makes it clear that he's not interested.

These coming-of-age tales were sold to the public and received by critics as realistic depictions of black urban life. The advertising tagline for *Menace II Society* reads: "This is the truth. This is what's real." Trailers for *Straight Out of Brooklyn* emphasized its "realness" by stating that the film comes from director Matty Rich's own life, including a sound bite from Rich himself, who draws a comparison between *Straight Out of Brooklyn* and the upper-middle-class black family depicted on the highly rated sitcom *The Cosby Show*. "This is not the Huxtables. This is the struggle." In his review, *Washington Post* critic Hal Hinson praised Rich's film for having a "raw, plucked-from-life authenticity of a documentary; it gives us a bare-knuckled account of the black experience . . ."[199]

The line separating fiction and reality also became blurry in the minds of the media when the openings of *New Jack City*, a crime drama about two cops trying to take down a drug lord, and *Boyz n the Hood* were overshadowed by violence that occurred in and around theaters in New York, Los Angeles, Chicago, and Detroit. Gunfire was exchanged at one Brooklyn theater that was screening *New Jack City*, leaving one dead and one wounded. Another incident occurred outside of the Mann's Theatre in the Westwood section of Los Angeles on opening night. When approximately 1,200 to 1,500 people could

Troubled Teens

Jim Carroll (Leonardo DiCaprio) in *The Basketball Diaries* (1995): DiCaprio gives an electrifying performance in this adaptation of poet Jim Carroll's book, which chronicled his transformation from a high-school basketball player at a parochial school to a heroin addict living on the streets. The film carries a strong anti-drug message by showing how casual drug use can take you down hard and fast.

Dawn Wiener (Heather Matarazzo) in *Welcome to the Dollhouse* (1995): Director Todd Solondz apparently didn't have fond memories of junior high if his life was anything like that of seventh-grader Dawn Wiener, who is an easy target for her cruel classmates (when she asks one, "Why do you hate me?" the classmate responds, "Because you're ugly") as well as her parents and teachers. Solondz succeeds in injecting some dark humor into this insightful tale and not making her character, who is so desperate for attention, particularly likable. To find out what happens to Dawn Wiener, watch Solondz's underrated *Palindromes* (2004).

Max Fischer (Jason Schwartzman) in *Rushmore* (1999): Max is an odd kid in an odd movie about an underachieving overachiever. He's smart and well-spoken and his school record boasts a long list of extracurricular activities, but when it comes to grades, he's a total failure. Instead of channeling his energy in the right direction, he ultimately becomes his own worst enemy and jeopardizes his relationships with his pint-size protégé (Mason Gamble); a British schoolteacher (Olivia Williams), who takes a shine to him; and a millionaire named Herman Blume (Bill Murray at his quirky best), who identifies with Max's status as an outsider.

Eric (Eric Deulen) and Alex (Alex Frost) in *Elephant* (2003): The 1999 tragic shootings at Columbine High School, which left fourteen students and one teacher dead, stunned the nation and sparked a debate on gun-control laws and the effects of media violence on young people. *Elephant* begins with what looks like an ordinary day in any American high school: students, played by nonprofessional actors, are in class, wandering the hall-ways, eating lunch in the cafeteria. Then Eric and Alex arrive to school dressed as commandos and casually open fire. What follows is difficult to watch. Director Gus Van Sant lets his audience draw their own conclusions about what caused the high-school students to snap, though he does make some suggestions: prior to the shooting, Eric plays a violent video game and is later seen watching a documentary about Hitler.

Tracy (Evan Rachel Wood) and Evie (Nikki Reed) in *Thirteen* (2003): In both the movies and on TV, most thirteen-year-old girls spend their time talk-ing to their girlfriends on the phone about boys, going to slumber parties, and getting teased by their brothers. The lives of thirteen-year-olds have cer-tainly changed if *Thirteen* is an indicator of the kind of peer pressure today's kids face. Tracy is an insecure teen who hides the fact that she cuts herself from her mom (Holly Hunter), a recovering alcoholic. She believes she has found her soulmate, a "cool," yet very troubled girl named Evie, who teaches her how to shoplift, drink, and snort prescription drugs. Mom eventually catches on, and Tracy's world comes crashing down. Director Catherine Hardwicke, who co-wrote the script with Reed, generally shoots the film on video with a handheld camera. The pseudo-documentary style is at times distracting and the narrative is uneven, but neither detracts from the first-rate performances by Wood, Reed, and Hunter.

not get into the sold-out screenings, a riot broke out on the streets of Westwood Village.[200]

There were twenty-five incidents around the country when *Boyz n the Hood* landed in theaters four months later. A man was shot while leaving a drive-in in a Chicago suburb and five people were wounded when gunfire broke out in an eighteen-screen Cineplex Odeon in Universal City.[201] The media was quick to link the violence in and around the theaters to the violence depicted up on the screen, which *New York Times* critic Janet Maslin believed was ironic and unfortunate because in the process, the antiviolence message of a film like *Juice* "tends to be distorted and oversimplified."[202] The cycle of black crime films reached its conclusion in 1995 with Spike Lee's adaptation of Richard Price's 1992 novel, *Clockers*. Set in the Brooklyn projects, *Clockers* contains what Lee described as all of the elements of a "black shoot-'em-up hip-hop drug gangsta-rap film."[203] The film follows a pair of detectives (Harvey Keitel, John Turturro) investigating a murder that is linked to a drug lord (Delroy Lindo) and his nineteen-year-old protégé (Mekhi Phifer). Lee hoped the film would be a success and "the nail in the coffin" of the urban-gangster genre. Although the film was by no means a hit at the box office, it did mark the end of a phase.[204]

The portrayal of black male teenagers was not limited in the nineties to urban crime dramas. *House Party* (1990), starring rap duo Kid 'n' Play (Christopher "Kid" Reid and Peter "Play" Martin) is a "high concept" comedy about a suburban teenager (Reid) who disobeys his father and sneaks out of the house to attend a party being thrown by Play while his folks are out of town. The film is short on plot, the characters border on the cartoonish, and the jokes are hardly original, but none of that seems to matter because what *House Party* is really all about is teenagers having a good time. Writer/director Reginald Hudlin manages to keep the tone light and the story moving. The one sour note is the homophobic humor, particularly when Kid is threatened in jail with homosexual rape. (The rap Kid uses to talk his way out of it includes the line "me a homo, that's a no-no.") *House Party* cost around $2.5 million and grossed a whopping $25 million, so a sequel (actually three) was inevitable. *House Party II* (1991) follows the characters to college, where Kid 'n' Play's attempt to party is once again interrupted by a series of comical characters, misunderstandings, etc. The saga continued in 1992 with *House Party 3*, in which Play throws a bachelor party for Kid.

While the youth crime films and the *House Party* trilogy may have increased the visibility of young black males in American cinema, it did little for the image of young black women. The male characters were always at the center of the narrative, while the females were underdeveloped and limited to the role of girlfriend, whose main function was to support her man. The misogynistic attitudes of the male characters toward women, who are more commonly referred to as "bitches" and "hos," are rarely challenged or critiqued in these films. One notable exception occurs in John Singleton's second film, *Poetic Justice* (1993), a romantic drama told from the point of view of a young poet named Justice (Janet Jackson), who quarrels but eventually falls in love with a postal carrier, Lucky (Tupac Shakur). When Lucky accuses the outspoken Justice of being "one of them angry bitches, huh? A feminist," she turns around and sets him straight. "Fuck you, I ain't no bitch," she fumes. "I am a black woman. I deserve respect. If I am a bitch, your momma's a bitch!"

Young, tough-minded, black, Hispanic, and white women started to having their say in the mid-nineties in a series of award-winning independent features. *Mi vida loca/My Crazy Life* (1993) is, in many ways, the female version of the urban crime family. Set in the Echo

Park section of Los Angeles, the drama uses multiple narrators to tell the story of two teenage homegirls, Sad Girl (Angel Aviles) and Mousie (Seidy Lopez), who become enemies when the same guy, Ernesto (Jacob Vargas) fathers their children. Their lives change when Ernesto is gunned down over a dispute about a car by a guy from nearby River Valley. Like the male characters in *Boyz n the Hood* and *Juice*, the bond between these women is strong, yet they are powerless because they have no man to take care of them and they lack the money, skills, and education to make better lives for themselves. In the spirit of the film's title, Anders's narrative is unwieldy. It constantly shifts focus between the various girls, the most interesting being an ex-con named Giggles (Marlo Marron), who returns with plans to make a better life for herself and her young daughter. She tells her homegirls that she wants to get a job in computers. "Computers? That's fucked up, eh?" says one girl to another. Her reaction signifies just how much the lives of these young women are predetermined at such a young age to the point where their world is so limited, they aren't even able to entertain the idea that they are capable of making a better life for themselves.

The death of a close friend actually serves as a wake-up call for three young women in the critically acclaimed *Girls Town* (1996). Patti (Lily Taylor), Angela (Bruklin Harris), and Emma (Anna Grace) are devastated when their friend Nikki (Aunjanue Ellis) commits suicide. The tragedy makes them realize that despite their close bond, they don't necessarily tell each other everything. In hopes of finding some answers, Emma swipes Nikki's diary, which reveals that she had been raped. Angela is angry—she can't believe Nikki didn't confide in them. Emma understands—she was date-raped by a boy from school and had kept it a secret until now.

Once Emma's secret is revealed, the three teenagers decide to start taking matters into their own hands. They spray-paint "rapist" on the car belonging to Emma's attacker, which is where the rape took place. Emma hunts down the guy who raped Nikki, and together the women physically assault the guy on the sidewalk in broad daylight. After a confrontation with Angela's abusive ex-boyfriend (and the father of her child), they break into his apartment and steal his TV, stereo, and CDs, which they cash in for money to take care of her kid. The film is careful not to turn the women into vigilantes. Both the destruction of the car and the apartment robbery were not premeditated. Instead, they just seized the opportunity when it presented itself. The film's failure to deal with the consequences of their actions (everyone in school seems to know they destroyed the car, yet the guy never confronts them?) is the way in which *Girls Town* tries to keep it real. "This ain't no *90210*," says Patty, right before the final credits roll. She's right because none of the conflicts in the film are neatly tied up in the end (as an in-joke, Emma's current boyfriend, who she blows off during the film, is named Dylan (Guillermo Diaz), just Luke Perry's character on *Beverly Hills, 90210*). Although the women in *Mi vida loca* are involved with gangs and guns, *Girls Town* has more of an edge to it because the dialogue is delivered in an improvisational style reminiscent of John Cassavetes's work. In fact, Taylor, Harris, and Grace share writing credit with Denise Casano and director Jim McKay.

McKay's next film, *Our Song* (2000), is a more traditional coming-of-age story of two girls who live in the Crown Heights section of Brooklyn. Lanisha (Kerry Washington), Jocelyn (Anna Simpson), and Maria (Melissa Hernandez) are all members of the Jackie Robinson Steppers Marching Band. Like most teenage girls, they giggle, talk about boys and clothes, go to the movies, and look out for one another. The film deals with the issues many teenagers face when they start moving closer to adulthood and their lives start to branch out beyond their close circle of friends. For this trio, their lives take an unexpected turn when their high school closes down for asbestos removal and they are forced to make some decisions about their future. Lanisha is determined to continue with her education, while Jocelyn prefers a weekly paycheck and hanging out with the friends she makes at work. Maria has it the toughest: she's pregnant and the father displays the same indifference toward her as he does toward his son. Although it's a much tighter film than *Girls Town*, *Our Song* still maintains an air of spontaneity, thanks to the naturalistic performances of the three young actresses. McKay also avoids the pitfalls of most Hollywood movies, which are never content with showing even the most dramatic events as being part of characters' everyday lives. When they hear about something tragic (a teenage mother jumps off a roof with her baby) or near-tragic things happen (Lanisha's asthma attack), the film treats them like things that are simply part of life. In his positive review of the film, critic Roger Ebert points out that the film "deals with the daily reality of many girls under 17," so it has been rated R, which, ironically, will prevent those who could learn from "the movie's insights" from ever seeing it.

Real Kids, Real Problems

There's no doubt that many of the issues teenagers grappled with back in the fifties, like peer pressure, popularity, relationships, and sex, are the same issues facing teenagers today. But today's teens are also living in a more complex world, where they are forced to grow up faster, and deal with adult problems and make adult decisions at a younger age.

Back in the fifties, an issue like juvenile delinquency was tailor-made for Hollywood because government and law-enforcement agencies, along with the media, established juvenile crime as a serious social problem with a clear set of conditions and causes. But the problems teens now face out in the real world, particularly those related to sex, drugs, and violence, are not so clear-cut, nor are they so easily resolved. As a general rule, the major Hollywood studios are not interested in releasing films with limited commercial appeal, let alone a film about teenagers containing potentially controversial subject matter. Consequently, most of these films end up in the hands of smaller distribution companies and are often screened in only a few cities before getting a DVD release.

Certainly the most controversial films about teens produced over the past decade have been made by Larry Clark, a photographer best known for his provocative photo essays *Tulsa* (1971) and *Teenage Lust* (1983), which contain explicit images of teenagers having sex, shooting up, and posing with firearms. Clark utilizes the same in-your-face aesthetic in three films that capture the underside of American teenage life: *Kids* (1995), *Bully* (2001), and *Ken Park* (2002). As with his photography, Clark approaches teenagers like an anthropologist. His films capture teens in their natural habitat doing what they presumably *really* do when adults aren't around, which apparently involves lots of sex and drugs. Consequently, some mainstream critics have objected to the explicit sexual content in Clark's films and even accused the director of exploiting his young actors. "Some of his detractors have called Mr. Clark a pornographer," wrote *New York Times* critic A. O. Scott in his review of *Bully*, "but this is an insult to honest smut-peddlers, who treat their subjects with more respect than he does." [205]

Clark's first film, *Kids*, chronicles a summer day in the life of a pair of sex-obsessed teens, Telly (Leo Fitzpatrick) and Casper (Justin Pierce), as they wander the streets of New York. The film opens with Telly convincing a young virgin, to go all the way. There is nothing erotic about the encounter, or even Telly's play-by-play account to Casper ("That bitch was bleeding when I first put it in," he exclaims). The frank and graphic exchanges between these junior hedonists not only reveal their around-the-clock obsession with sex, but their total disregard for their sexual partners. As Telly explains at the close of the film, "When you go to sleep at night, you dream of pussy. When you wake up it's the same thing. It's there in your face. You can't escape it. Sometimes when you're young the only place to go is inside. That's just it—fucking is what I love. Take that away from me and I really got nothing."

While Telly is heading toward his next conquest, another virgin named Darcy (Yakira Peguero), one of his previous partners, Jennie (Chloë Sevigny)—who has just been told she's HIV-positive—tries to track him down. The situation has great dramatic potential, yet Clark resists resolving the conflict in a Hollywood fashion. Jennie arrives just as Telly is deflowering Darcy, but she doesn't stop them—she just stands there watching, as if in a trance. The reason why is not entirely clear. On the following morning, Jennie, who has passed out after a night of partying, is raped by Casper, who may have exposed himself to the virus.

On the surface, Clark's raw treatment of teen sexuality, which he captures in a pseudo-documentary style through his use of nonprofessional actors, handheld cameras, and location shooting, makes Hollywood teen comedies like *Porky's* and *American Pie* (which *Kids* predates by four years) seem like Disney movies.[206] But one element they all share is their predominantly male point of view (*Kids*'s script was written by nineteen-year-old Harmony Korine). Like a public service announcement, the film's warnings about HIV and the dangers of unprotected sex are crystal clear. In the process, the risk of spreading and contracting AIDS becomes a plot point, which undermines what little critique the film offers of the male characters' misogynistic attitude toward women. Are the filmmakers okay with the way these guys talk about and manipulate them for sex? Jennie doesn't stop Telly as he is infecting Darcy, so there's no confrontation. Consequently, the audience is set up to care more about the fact that Casper is putting himself at risk when he rapes Jennie, rather than the fact that he is committing a violent act.

Clark's subsequent films, *Bully* and *Ken Park*, have similar problems. Like *River's Edge*, *Bully* is based on the true story of a group of Florida teenagers who murder a bully who has made all of their lives miserable. Bobby Kent (Nick Stahl) is one of the most vile and viscous teenagers in American cinema. He humiliates and physically abuses his best friend, a surfer named Marty Puccio (Brad Renfro), who, out of some sense of twisted loyalty, finds himself doing whatever Bobby wants, including dancing onstage at a local gay strip club on amateur night. Although it is never fully explored, there is an underlying homoerotic dimension to Bobby's passive-aggressive behavior toward Marty. Bobby watches Marty having sex with his girlfriend, and, at one point, interrupts them by hitting Marty from behind. He also likes to watch gay porn while he brutally rapes and nearly kills her.

Once Bobby and his friends agree that they must kill the monster, a plot is set in motion. Ironically, the murder as well as the aftermath (the young killers were eventually, caught, tried, and imprisoned) only comprises the final third of the film. In the first two-thirds, Clark focuses on Bobby and Marty's relationship and the sexual escapades of his young characters. While this is necessary to establish that these kids are out of control, despite their clueless parents' futile and, in some instances, misguided efforts to discipline them, his camera does, in fact, linger far too long on the naked bodies of his young, female actors. The issue here is not really one of exploitation (these young actors know what they are doing), but one of repetition. Clark has a tendency to approach cinema in the same manner as a photo essay. He is more interested in capturing the carefree, decadent lifestyle of his characters than telling a story.

Bully was released in the United States without a rating (though it would have certainly qualified for an NC-17). *Ken Park*, which not only contains male and female frontal nudity, but contains explicit scenes of heterosexual sex and male masturbation (including male ejaculation), never even made it into American theaters. The film focuses on several teenage characters and their respective relationships with adults, yet instead of demonizing the teens, it's the adults who are characterized as predators in some form or another. Shawn (James Bullard) is seduced by his girlfriend's mother. Peaches (Tiffany Limos) is caught having kinky sex by her crazy, tyrannical, Bible-thumping father. Tate (James Ransone) is pushed to the breaking point by his irritating grandparents, who he eventually kills. Claude (Stephen Jasso) is verbally as well as sexually abused by his stepfather.

Clark offers a solution to the tortured lives of his young characters. The film concludes with three of the characters—Shawn, Peaches, and Claude—engaging in what appears to be a nonstop ménage à trois. But unlike the sexual activity in *Kids* and *Bully*, intimate moments between these three characters is tender and pleasurable—a welcome relief from the previous scenes of abuse and mind control. It suggests that perhaps there is a kinder, gentler Clark on the horizon.

To Be Continued

In tracing the evolution of American film gen-res, historian Thomas Schatz proposes that film genres are both "static" and "dynamic" systems.[207] A genre has certain components that are fixed (what would a Western be without horses, guns, and wide, open plains?) and others that change over time. As a genre, the teen film may not be as well-defined as the Western, yet there are stock characters (the rebel, the jock, the brain, the mean girl) and settings (high school, the after-school hangout, etc.) as well as universal themes and issues (rebellion, love, and sex) that teen movies have tackled over the past five decades.

At the same time, Hollywood has also, with limited success, tried to keep in step with the times. Teens today grow up faster, so in addition to dealing with the problems that have plagued generation after generation of teenagers, they are confronted with a whole new set of issues and pressures. In a Gallup Youth Survey, which has been conducted every five years since 1977, teenagers were asked the question,

"What do you feel is the biggest problem facing people your age?" The number one answer in 1977 and 2003 was the same: drug abuse. But back in 1977, only 5 percent of the students indicated peer pressure, which ranked number two (17 percent) in 2003. Today's teens are also more concerned about their future career and making money. Ranking third and fourth, respectively, on their list of problems were education (13 percent) and career/employment/economy/money/future (10 percent), two issues about which teens back in 1977 had expressed little concern.[208]

As a genre, the teen film is unique because unlike the Western and the other major genres (the gangster film, the detective film, the musical, et al.), teen movies touch on a period in the life of every audience member. Everyone will be, is, or was a teenager (as opposed to a cowboy, a mobster, a private eye, or a song-and-dance man). Every American teenager did not grow up in a white, middle-class suburbia, which is where most teen films take place, yet that doesn't necessarily mean that a teenager in the audience from a different social, economic, or cultural background can't relate on some level to what's going on up there on the screen.

There is certainly a need for more diversity in American teen movies, which seems less likely to happen since Hollywood has discovered yet another untapped demographic group—the tweens. As their name suggests, tweens are "in between" being a kid and a teenager. Although their age range can vary, the term generally refers to boys and girls between the ages of eight and twelve. According to the 2000 Census, there are 20.9 million tweens in the United States. They account for about 40 percent of all children and 7 percent of the total population. In terms of dollars and cents, tweens control an estimated $10 billion in spending. But when it comes to selling them merchandise, marketers like Ogilvy Public Relations divide tweens into two groups; older tweens (ten and over) tend to have more buying power and influence than single-digit tweens, whose buying decisions are still being made by Mom.[209] According to *Broadcasting & Cable* magazine, cable channels like the Cartoon Network, the Disney Channel, and Nickelodeon, along with its spin-off cable channel, Noggin—which features a mixture of programming for preteens, tweens, and teens (depending on the hour of the day)—continue to "slug it out to score with the 9–14 demographic."[210]

The major studios have also pursued the tween market with a series of films that are geared mostly to the young female audience. The queens of tweens are twins Mary-Kate and Ashley Olsen, who started their careers at the ripe old age of fifteen months as a regular on the situation comedy *Full House* (1987–1995). Seventeen years later, the twins, who turned eighteen in 2004, now share the title of president of their own $1 billion media empire, Dualstar Entertainment, which has amassed a sizable fortune through the sale of their straight-to-video films, books, clothes, cosmetics, and other stuff.

The Olsen twins are now sharing the limelight with other tween stars, like Amanda Bynes (*What a Girl Wants* [2003]), Hilary Duff (*The Lizzie McGuire Movie* [2003], *A Cinderella Story* [2004]), Anne Hathaway (*The Princess Diaries* [2001], *Princess Diaries 2: Royal Engagement* [2004], *Ella Enchanted* [2004]), and Lindsay Lohan (*Freaky Friday* [2003], *Confessions of a Teenage Drama Queen* [2004]), proving there is money to be made by appealing to tween girls. While not all tween films turn a profit during their initial release, the ones that did scored big. The receipts for the two *Princess Diaries* films totaled $195 million (and that's not counting video and DVD sales). The remake of *Freaky Friday* grossed $110 million at the box office. Most of these films are rated PG due to "mild language" or "mild thematic elements," which in the mind of an older tween separates it from a G-rated film, which is considered "kids' stuff."

The first *Princess Diaries* film, which is based on the novel by Meg Cabot, established the formula. Girls want someone they can identify with, so the female protagonists in these films are not perfect, nor are they the prettiest, smartest, or most popular girl in school. In fact, Lizzie McGuire (Duff) is a little dizzy, *Princess Diaries*'s Mia Thermopolis (Hathaway) is socially awkward and a bit of a klutz, and *Freaky Friday*'s Anna Coleman (Lohan) has a major attitude and talks back to her mother. As actress Mandy Moore (*The Princess Diaries*, *How to Deal*) explains, all of these films explore "similar themes because as a teenager, that's what you're going through, trying to find a sense of self, discovering love for the first time and all these crazy feelings that come along with it."[211] These films aim to capture the mixed emotions that often accompany the experience of coming into your own as a person, the experience of being a teenager, etc. On the whole they succeed, thanks mostly to the appeal of the talented crop of lead performances, but they are not without their limitations. The world of the tween film is a very, very white world. In addition, far too many of these films, many of which have been adapted by popular youth fiction, are modern-day versions of the Cinderella story. While they don't necessarily carry the same message as the fairy-tale ending (these young women are more three-dimensional, and happiness is not necessarily equated with getting a man), it would be refreshing to see a film about an ordinary teenager, who, in the final reel, is still ordinary, yet happy.

For generation after generation of teenagers, the Hollywood teen film has always been, and continues to be, a work in progress.

ENDNOTES

[1] Grace Palladino, *Teenagers: An American History* (New York: Basic Books, 1996): 195.

[2] John Kenneth Galbraith, *The Affluent Society* (Boston: Houghton Mifflin, 1958).

[3] Television sets, which only the wealthy could afford in the late 1940s, were no longer considered a luxury item in the 1950s. In fact, the number of households with a TV skyrocketed from less than 6 percent in 1948 to 42 percent in 1952. See James S. Olson, *Historical Dictionary of the 1950s* (Westport, CT: Greenwood Press, 2000): 285.

[4] Palladino, 105. For an excellent overview of the rise of the teenage market, see Palladino, 96–115.

[5] James J. Nagle, "News of the Advertising and Marketing Field," *New York Times,* 19 April 1953: F8.

[6] Palladino, 98.

[7] Olson, 18.

[8] Thomas Doherty, *Teenagers and Teenpics: The Juvenilization of American Movies in the 1950s*, Second Edition (Philadelphia: Temple University Press, 2002): 35.

[9] Shailer Upton Lawton and Jules Archer, *Sexual Conduct of the Teen-ager* (New York: Berkley Publishing, 1951): 5.

[10] Elizabeth Laine, *Motion Pictures and Radio: Modern Techniques for Education* (New York: McGraw-Hill, 1938): 49, 50.

[11] Ken Smith, *Mental Hygiene: Classroom Films (1945–1970)* (New York: Blast Books, 1999): 28. Smith offers a thorough history of social-guidance films and entertaining summaries of over 260 films.

[12] Ken Smith, "Mental Hygiene: Manners and Morals in Quirky Classroom Films," *Rowan* magazine 5.3 (Summer 2000): 1.

[13] Smith, *Mental Hygiene: Classroom Films (1945–1970)*: 30.

[14] Ellis Weitzman, "Growing Up Socially," *How to Be a Successful Teen-ager*, ed. William C. Menninger (New York: Sterling Publishing Co., Inc., 1954): 119.

[15] David Riesman, *The Lonely Crowd* (New Haven: Yale University Press, 1950).

[16] Mark Voger, "Call Me Sam (Arkoff, that is)" (interview with Samuel Z. Arkoff) *Filmfax 73* (April/May 1991): 76.

[17] Richard Gehman, "The Hollywood Horrors," *Cosmopolitan*, November 1958: 10.

[18] Irving Rubine, "Boys Meet Ghouls, Make Movies," *New York Times*, 16 March 1955: X7. Arkoff reportedly did receive a letter from Senator Paul Douglas of Illinois, who accused him of making a "scandalous and immoral" movie. See Mark Thomas McGee, *Faster and Furiouser: The Revised and Fattened Fable of American International Pictures* (Jefferson, NC: McFarland and Company, Inc.): 89.

[19] Cyndy Hendershot, "Monster at the Soda Shop: Teenagers and Fifties Horror Films," *Images: A Journal of Film and Popular Culture*, n.d.: 4. www.imagesjournal.com/issue 10/features/monster/default-nf.html.

[20] In *How to Be A Successful Teenager*, the authors stress the importance of a girl's parents meeting her date: "When the man of the evening comes to pick you up, it's the natural thing to invite him in and have him talk to your parents while you're getting your coat or putting on the finishing touches." Lester A. Kirkendall and Ruth Farnham Osborne, "Dating Days," Menninger, 225.

[21] Cohen and Kandel wrote *Teenage Werewolf* under the pseudonym Ralph Thornton and *Teenage Frankenstein* under Kenneth Langtry. Kandel used Thornton again on his screenplay for *Blood of Dracula*.

[22] "Setting the Record Straight, Robert J. Gurney, Jr. Remembers Working on Invasion of the Saucer-Men," *Filmfax*, 93–94 (October/November 2002): 124.

[23] Ibid, 129.

[24] Benjamin Fine, *1,000,000 Delinquents* (New York: The World Publishing Company, 1955): 26. The U.S. Bureau of Census reported the total number of delinquency cases handled in juvenile court in 1952 at 332,000. Fine may have arrived at 400,000 by adding the 98,000 cases involving child dependency and neglect. The 45 percent increase in juvenile cases between 1945 and 1953 is exaggerated. The U.S. Bureau of Census reported a total of 344,000 delinquency cases involving ten- to seventeen-year-olds in 1945 versus 374,000 in 1953, an increase of 9 percent. *Historical Statistics of the United States Colonial Times to 1970, Bicentennial Edition*, Vol. II (Washington, D.C.: Bureau of the Census, 1975): 419.

[25] Fine, 26, 27–28.

[26] Fredric Wertham, *Seduction of the Innocent* (Port Washington, NY: Kennikat Press, 1953); Albert K. Cohen, *Delinquent Boys: The Culture of the Gang* (Glencoe, IL: Free Press, 1955); and Dale Kramer and Madeline Karr, *Teen-Age Gangs* (New York: Holt, 1953).

[27] "FBI Head Spurs Delinquency Fight," *New York Times*, 3 April 1958: 33.

[28] Gilbert, 69.

[29] Ibid, 71.

[30] Ibid.

[31] "Doctor Urges Comic Book Ban," *New York Times*, 4 September 1948: 16.

[32] U.S. Congress, Senate Subcommittee to Investigate Juvenile Delinquency. Interim Report, *Comic Books and Juvenile Delinquency: A Part of the Investigation of Juvenile Delinquency in the United States*, 83rd cong., 1st sess., 195, n.d.

[33] According to the Code, producers of comic books were not permitted to use the words "horror" or "terror" in a comic's title; profanity, the depiction of nudity, and use of the word "crime" alone on a cover were equally verboten. The entire Code is available at www.comics.dm.net/codetext.html.

[34] Thomas M. Pryor, "Hollywood Test: Movies Defend, Assailed in Kefauver Probe of Films' Effects on Youth," *New York Times*, 26 June 1955: X5.

[35] Ibid.

[36] Ibid.

[37] The 1937 screen version of Sidney Kingsley's play *Dead End* (1937) dealt with the effects of poverty and neglect on boys growing up on New York's East Side. The film marked the start of a twenty-year cycle of B-films about a group of lower-class kids (known as the Dead End Kids (1937–1939); the Dead End Kids & Little Tough Guys (1938–1943); the East Side Kids (1940–1945); and the Bowery Boys (1946–1958)) that eventually turned into a series of comedy-dramas in which the boys face off against career criminals and the occasional Nazi.

[38] "Blackboard Jungle Banned," *New York Times*, 29 March 1955: 33; "Loew's Fights Atlanta Ban," *New York Times*, 4 June 1955: 34.

[39] To read more about the controversy surrounding *Blackboard Jungle*, see Gilbert, 184–185.

[40] Thomas M. Pryor, "U.S. Film Dropped at Fete in Venice," Lowe Says Ambassador Luce Urged Committee to Erase *Blackboard Jungle,*" *New York Times,* 27 August 1955: 9.

[41] Leonard Budes, "2 Reports Clear School in Bronx," *New York Times,* 17 July 1955: 39.

[42] When *Rebel* was filmed in March–May 1955, Sal Mineo and Natalie Wood were both sixteen, seven years younger than Dean.

[43] In addition to the way Plato gazes at Jim, the closest Stern and Ray could come to suggesting Plato might be something other than heterosexual is hanging a still photo of movie star Alan Ladd in his locker. An early draft of the script reportedly contained a kiss between Jim and Plato, which would have never made it past the Production Code Administration. One of the early memos from the censors to Warner Brothers stated, "It is of course vital that there be no inference of a questionable or homosexual relationship between Plato and Jim." Randall Riese, *The Unabridged James Dean: His Life and Legacy from A to Z* (Chicago: Contemporary Books, 1991): 427.

[44] A one-hour version of *Crime in the Streets* was performed live on March 8, 1955, on *The Elgin Hour,* an biweekly anthology sponsored by the Elgin Watch Company. John Cassavetes originated the role of Frankie Dane, which he later repeated in the film version. Ben Wagner was played by Robert Preston. Dino aired on January 2, 1956, on *Studio One.* Sal Mineo played the title role and his "head doctor" was portrayed by Ralph Meeker.

[45] Peter Blecha, *Taboo Tunes: A History of Banned Bands and Censored Songs* (San Francisco: Back Beat Books, 2004): 25.

[46] "Rock 'n' Roll Fight Hospitalizes Youth," *New York Times,* 15 April 1957: 23; "Rioters Rock 'n' Roll in Oslo," *New York Times,* 24 September 1956: 3.

[47] "Belgian Town Bans U.S. Film," *New York Times,*
17 December 1956: 34.

[48] "British Rattled by Rock 'n' Roll," *New York Times,*
12 September 1956: 40.

[49] Lester A. Kirkendall, *Premarital Intercourse and Interpersonal
Relationships: A Research Study of Interpersonal Relationships
Based on Case Histories of 668 Premarital-Intercourse Experiences
Reported by 200 College-Level Males* (New York: Julian Press,
1951): 3.

[50] Ira L. Reiss, *Premarital Sexual Standards in America*
(Glencoe, IL: The Free Press, 1960): 91–92 . For an illuminat-
ing discussion of Reiss in relation to sexual-hygiene films,
see Eric Schaefer, *"Bold! Daring! Shocking! True!": A History
of Exploitation Films, 1919–1959* (Durham: Duke University
Press, 1991): 204–205. Reiss has made his book available
online at www2.hu-berlin.de/sexology/Reiss1/index.html.

[51] Reiss, 110–111.

[52] The Alan Guttmacher Institute, *Sex and America's Teenagers*
(New York: Alan Guttmacher Institute): 25.

[53] Ibid, 20.

[54] Frank Miller, *Censored Hollywood: Sex, Sin, and Violence on
Screen* (Atlanta: Turner Publishing, Inc., 1994): 296.

[55] As quoted in Gerald Gardner, *The Censorship Papers*
(New York: Dodd, Mead, and Company, 1987): 191.

[56] Bosley Crowther, "The Screen: *Blue Denim,*" *New York Times,*
31 July 1959: 12.

[57] Evelyn Millis Duvall, *Facts of Life and Love for Teen-Agers*
(Toronto: Popular Library, 1957): 280.

58 Terry DuFoe, Tiffany DuFoe, and Becky DuFoe with Meredith Asher, "That Bewitched, Lucy Lovin', Beach Party Movie Guy!: An interview with William Asher," *Filmfax 102* (April/June 2004): 89.

59 Howard Thompson, "Screen: 'Beach Party'," *New York Times*, 26 September 1963: 40.

60 Howard Thompson, "Off the Deep End," *New York Times*, 3 June 1965: 24; Howard Thompson, "'Wild Bikini' Appearing in Neighborhoods," *New York Times*, 12 January 1967: 48.

61 "The Inheritor," *Time*, 6 January 1967: 18.

62 Ibid.

63 According to the U.S. Census Bureau, 46 percent of the U.S. population in both 1966 and 1970 were twenty-four years of age or younger. The total number of U.S. citizens twenty-four years or younger in 1970 was 94.3 million. *Historical Statistics of the United States*, Vol. 1: 10.

64 "The Inheritor," *Time:* 18.

65 "The Inheritor," *Time:* 23.

66 "On Not Losing One's Cool about the Young," *Time*, 24 December 1965: 16.

67 "Z as in Zzzz, or Zowie," *Time*, 5 May 1967: 61.

68 Alan Betrock, *The 'I Was a Teenage Juvenile Delinquent Rock 'n' Roll Horror Beach Party Movie' Book: A Complete Guide to the Teen Exploitation Film* (New York: St. Martin's Press, 1986): 132.

69 "Riot on Sunset Strip Ignites Hot Controversy," *American International Pictures Newsletter: 4. Riot on Sunset Strip* file, Margaret Herrick Library, Academy of Motion Pictures Arts & Sciences, Los Angeles, CA.

70 Ibid.

[71] Dale Munroe, "Problem Exploited, But Never Explored," *Hollywood Citizen-News*, 7 April 1967.

[72] Jesse Monteagudo, "Remember When and Who: Tommy Kirk," *Gay Today* (13 February 2005). gaytoday.badpuppy.com/garchive/people/013100pe.htm. Although he was "blacklisted" from the industry and considered "box-office poison," Kirk did appear in several films in his post-Disney days at A.I.P., including *Pajama Party* (1964) (opposite another Disney survivor, Annette Funicello); *Dr. Goldfoot and the Bikini Machine* (1965); *The Wild, Weird World of Dr. Goldfoot* (1965); and *The Ghost in the Invisible Bikini* (1966).

[73] McGee, p. 260.

[74] Richard Schickel, "Overpraised Quickie on a Vital Theme," *Life*, 26 July 1968: 10.

[75] "Wild in the Streets," *Film Bulletin*, 4 March, 1968: 1.

[76] Aniko Bodroghkozy, "Reel Revolutionaries: An Examination of Hollywood's Cycle of 1960s Youth Rebellion Films," *Cinema Journal* 41.3 (Spring 2002): 41–43.

[77] Ibid.

[78] "The Hippies," *Time*, 7 July 1967: 18.

[79] Allen Cohen, "A Prophecy of a Declaration of Independence," n.d. www.redhousebooks.com/galleries/haight/prophecy.htm.

[80] Albi Mason, "The Haight Happening," *Keep On Truckin' Re-Visited, Vol. 1, No. 6* (January 1998). www.vipgrafx.com/hippy/archives/january_98.txt.

[81] Hunter S. Thompson, "The 'Hashbury' is the Capital of the Hippies," *New York Times*, 14 May 1967: 120.

[82] Harry M. Benshoff, "The Short-Lived Life of the Hollywood LSD Film," *The Velvet Light Trap 15* (Spring 2001): 29–44.

[83] Svetlana Boym, *The Future of Nostalgia* (New York: Basic Books, 2001): 3–4.

[84] Gerald Clarke, "The Meaning of Nostalgia," *Time,* 3 May 1971: 77.

[85] Judy Klemesrud, "'Graffiti' is the Story of His Life," *New York Times,* 7 October 1973: 13.

[86] Dale Pollock, *Skywalking: The Life and Films of George Lucas* (New York: Harmony Books, 1973): 29.

[87] Jack Slater, "'Cooley High': More Than Just a Black 'Graffiti'," *New York Times,* 10 August 1975: 95.

[88] Fred Davis, *Yearning for Yesterday: A Sociology of Nostalgia* (New York: The Free Press, 1979): 222.

[89] Pollock, 201.

[90] Earl C. Gottschalk, Jr., "The Spectaculars," *The Wall Street Journal,* 15 August 1974: 1, 21.

[91] David A. Cook, *Lost Illusions* (Los Angeles: University of California Press, 2000): 26.

[92] Gottschalk, 1.

[93] Joseph D. Phillips, "Film Conglomerate Blockbusters: International Appeal and Product Homogenization," *The American Movie Industry: The Business of Motion Pictures*, ed. Gorham Kindem (Carbondale, IL: Southern Illinois University Press, 1982): 330–331.

[94] Jonathan Bernstein, *Pretty in Pink: The Golden Age of Teenage Movies* (New York: St. Martin's Griffin, 1988).

[95] Pollock, 186.

[96] Timothy Shary, *Generation Multiplex* (Austin: University of Texas Press, 2002): 6.

[97] Lawrence Cohn, "Filmers Resort to Old Scare Tactics," *Variety,* 8 June 1988: 1; see also, Prince, 352–53.

[98] "Exploding the Myth About Teenagers," *U.S. News & World Report,* February 10, 1986: 80.

[99] Ibid.

[100] Ibid.

[101] "Quackery Targets Teens," *FDA Consumer* 22.1 (February 1988): 24+.

[102] Stephen Koepp, "Teenage Orphans of the Job Boom," *Time,* May 13, 1985: 46–47.

[103] "The Latest Worry for Parents of Teens," *Fortune,* February 2, 1987.

[104] "Exploding the Myths about Teenagers," 80.

[105] "What World Teenagers are Saying," *U.S. News & World Report,* June 30, 1986: 68.

[106] "Teen Drug Abuse—The News is Bad," *U.S. News & World Report,* November 18, 1985: 16.

[107] "Reported Drug Use and Alcohol Use Within Last 12 Months among High School Seniors, by Type of Drug, 1980–1992," *Statistical Handbook on Adolescents in America*: 254.

[108] R. Weiss, "Teen Suicide Clusters: More than Mimcry," *Science News,* November 25, 1989: 342.

[109] "Bergenfield's Tragic Foursome," *U.S. News & World Report,* March 23, 1987: 11.

[110] Ibid.

[111] John Leo, "Could Suicide Be Contagious? A Trio of Deaths Provokes Questions and Fears in Omaha," *Time,* February 24, 1986: 59.

[112] Susanna McBee, "A Call to Tame the Gene of Teen Sex," *U.S. News & World Report,* December 22, 1986: 8.

[113] Rollin, 291.

[114] Chadwick and Heaton, 280.